The Shark Almanac

The Shark Almanac

Thomas B. Allen

The Lyons Press

Printed in the United States of America

10 9 8 7 6 5 4 3 2 1

Design by V&M Graphics, Inc.

Library of Congress Cataloging-in-Publication Data
Allen, Thomas B.
    The shark almanac / Thomas B. Allen.
      p.   cm.
    Includes index.
    ISBN 1-55821-582-4
      1. Sharks.   I. Title.
    QL638.9.A438   1999
    597.3—dc21   98-38524
                                         CIP

CONTENTS

INTRODUCTION

Two
Blue Sharks

The first shark I ever saw outside an aquarium was a blue shark, a beautiful creature that gleamed just below the surface in the sunlit water off Montauk, Long Island. As part of my research for a book, *Shadows in the Sea*, I had gone to Montauk in the summer of 1962, to sail on a charter boat that fished for sharks. Someone on the boat had hooked that beautiful blue shark and, knowing I was on my first (and only) hunt, gave me the honor of landing it. It was a little under six feet long. It did not put up much of a fight in the water, but it struggled when it was gaffed and hauled into the boat.

I wanted the jaws, and while others kept fishing, I hacked away, slicing through a thick, sandpaper hide, severing arteries, sawing through cartilage. All the while, the blue shark quivered and moved its large black eyes. I finally cut the head from the glistening body and set to work slicing the jaws from the head. I remember a steaming hot day, sweat pouring down my face, blood on my hands and shirt, and the jaws still moving as I cut around them. The jaws never stopped flexing. Next to me on the deck, the tail kept twitching and the rest of the body shivered under the sun. I felt no sympathy, but I thought, *This shark will not die*. And I wondered at its strength and power.

When I was done, I threw the remains of the head overboard. With another man I picked up the headless body and slid it over the rail. The body, trailing blood, began to sink. Then the tail started moving rhythmically, as it had when the shark had approached the hook two hours or so before, and the body swam away from the boat, still sinking, but still moving forward. We stood watching it, fascinated, yet somehow repelled by such an obscene display of endless life.

The jaw had an awful stench. When I got ashore, I buried it so that ants could finish my work. But the next day, when I dug it up and wrapped it for the journey home, the flesh still hung to it and it still stunk. After a long soaking in formaldehyde, the stench slowly vanished, the cartilage hardened, and the row upon row of teeth retained their pale white color. I hung the jaw in my office, a reminder of a day when I caught a shark.

In the spring of 1997, while on an assignment for *National Geographic* magazine, I was on board a ship off Kaikoura, New Zealand, where a deep-sea canyon shelters sharks, sperm whales, giant squid, and dolphin. An amateur scientist looking for abyssal creatures had put a line down 1,200 feet. At some unknown depth a blue shark had snapped at the bait, and as the scientist winched the line up and it came out of the sea, the blue shark hung from it, moving feebly.

It flopped onto the deck, a male about nine feet long, iridescent blue and weakly pulsing with life. We had not intended to catch this shark. We tried to get it back into the water, but on a pitching deck, its struggles and gnashing teeth made it impossible for any of us to get it overboard. As it began to die, one of the passengers asked for the jaws. I left him there, hacking away as I had done so long before.

I felt sympathy for that blue shark, because now I knew about sharks, now I knew that sharks like my beautiful butchered blue shark of long ago were not my enemy, were not the villains of *Jaws*, were not deserving of the adjectives we had given them—murderous, savage, vicious, ravenous, brutal. I had used those words in *Shadows in the Sea*, the book I was writing in 1962. You will not find those words in this book. I do draw from *Shadows in the Sea* for some timeless shark lore and data on attacks and shark fishing. But I write today from a new perspective. The shark of *Jaws* is gone, along with the gory adjectives. The shark we know today is a shark endangered.

The populations of some species have declined as much as 80 percent from the 1980s to the 1990s. The year 1997, the year of my second blue shark, seemed destined to be the year when the shark emerged from centuries of abuse. In that year, a marine biologist predicted that some shark species might become extinct within the next decade; the Convention on International Trade in Endangered Species (CITES) said that dozens of shark species were in danger because of unregulated international trade in shark fins, meat, oil, and cartilage. CITES also tried unsuccessfully to get some international protection for shark species that biologists believe to be on the way to extinction.

Between 1980 and 1990, CITES said, the *reported* annual volume of shark product exports had more than doubled. China was importing more than a billion pounds of shark fins a year for shark fin soup, the newly approved delicacy that the People's Republic once had denounced as too elite for communist taste.

"Shark" is a word long rooted in fear, a fish whose name probably comes from *Schurke*, the German word for "villain." A petty thief or swindler was called a shark as far back as Elizabethan times. Today we still have loan, pool, card, and business sharks. But now the shark itself is gaining respect as a magnificent creature and achieving a status much higher than the humans called sharks.

Rifles, traps, barbed wire, and urbanization have rid us of once-feared terrestrial predators, the large cats and bears. Occasionally a crocodile or an alligator may stray from its shrinking realm and cross the path of a terrified human being. But sharks still threaten us, still lurk in the sea, still include among their kind species that can kill us. Sharks are the last animals to fear.

And so the fear is real, as real as the sharks whose jaws are big enough to devour us. But we also are beginning to understand them. There are two kinds of shark myths—those of folklore (see chapter 6) and those of ignorance. The following, chosen and answered by researchers at the Mote Marine Laboratory, are myths that ignorance spawned:

- *Sharks are harmful to people:* Of the more than 390 shark species, about 80 percent cannot hurt people or rarely encounter them.

- *Sharks eat continuously:* Sharks eat periodically, depending on their metabolism and the availability of food. Juvenile lemon sharks, for example, eat less than two percent of their body weight per day.

- *Sharks prefer human blood:* Most sharks don't appear to be especially interested in the blood of mammals, as opposed to fish blood.

- *Sharks are not discriminating eaters and scavenge the sea:* Most sharks prefer to eat certain types of invertebrates, fish, and other animals. Some sharks eat mainly fish. Others eat other sharks or marine mammals or plankton.

- *Great white sharks are common, abundant sharks found off most beaches visited by humans:* Great whites are relatively uncommon large predators that prefer cooler waters. In some parts of their range, great whites are close to being endangered.

- *Sharks have peanut-size brains and cannot learn:* Sharks' relatively large and complex brains are comparable in size to those of supposedly more advanced animals like mammals and birds. Sharks also can be trained.

- *Shark meat is poisonous:* The meat from the majority of sharks is edible and delicious when properly handled and prepared, although there have been some reports of people being poisoned by presumably spoiled shark meat.

- *Sharks must swim continually:* Some sharks can respire by pumping water over their gills or through opening and closing their mouths while at rest on the bottom.

- *Sharks have poor vision:* Sharks' eyes, which are equipped to distinguish colors, employ a lens up to seven times as powerful as the human eye.

- *Sharks are easy to kill:* Sharks cling tenaciously to life. The myth stems from the fact that stress of capture weakens a shark, and so some sharks are easily killed in hook-and-line or net fishing.

- *Sharks are not found in fresh water:* Specialized organs enable the cub shark (*Carcharhinus leucas*, also known as the bull shark) to cope with dramatic changes in salinity, from the fresh waters of some rivers to the highly saline waters of the ocean.

- *A shark is a shark is a shark:* There is no "typical" shark. The more than 390 species all differ in habitat, lifestyle, and body form.

- *Sharks are trash fish:* Sharks are a critical part of marine ecosystems.

We know that sharks have remained essentially unchanged for hundreds of millions of years. During their long evolutionary history, they have developed adaptations so subtle and so specialized that we barely can perceive them. We have, however, learned enough about them to know that most grow and mature slowly, producing far fewer young than other fishes. Shark populations, and ultimately shark species, can be wiped out more easily than any other kind of fish.

Realizing this, realizing that we can lose the shark, we owe to ourselves and to our future a debt of knowledge. This book is an attempt to contribute to that debt.

—Thomas B. Allen
Bethesda, Maryland

CHAPTER 1

The Enduring Shark

B efore there were dinosaurs, before there were trees, there were
sharks. They have been swimming in the seas of Earth for at least 400
million years, survivors of a long evolutionary process that left them
little changed. Shark fossils look like rock sculptures of modern sharks.
The earliest sharks became extinct, but their descendants endured, producing a long line of changeless sharks—the cat sharks, cow sharks, and
bullheads of today.

As the early shark thrived and evolved, at least four global mass
extinctions wiped out 80 percent of the large animals on Earth. Before and
after the dinosaurs, the shark lived on. Sharks were the first vertebrates
with fully functioning jaws, and it would be their jaws that would bring
them such notoriety when humans arrived, eventually went to sea, and
there discovered the ocean's ultimate animal.

The first hint of the existence of ancient sharks came in the seven-
teenth century, when fossil shark teeth were first found. Naturalists classified
the finds as fossilized birds' tongues or vipers' teeth. It was inconceivable
that they could have come from a shark.

The shark fossil record is relatively scant. Most shark fossils are only
teeth. Hundreds of fossilized shark teeth have been found on the plains of
central Kansas; in Wyoming, Idaho, New Mexico; in New Jersey, South

Carolina, New York, and Maryland. In Alabama cotton fields, shark teeth have been unearthed amid the fossilized bones of the zeuglodon, a prehistoric whale that grew to seventy feet and may have been a prey of sharks.

In 1853 a geologist with the Pacific Railroad Survey found several shark teeth on a parched California hill more than 100 miles from the sea. Since that day, thousands of shark teeth have been found in that hill and in the cluster of hills around it. The area, about seven miles northeast of Bakersfield, California, is called Sharktooth Hill.

Some 20 million years ago, the Temblor Sea, as paleontologists call it, covered the area. Around what is now Sharktooth Hill the sea was no more than 200 feet deep, and the thousands of fossils found there today show that it teemed with marine life. There were whales, porpoises, dolphins, sea cows, seals, and sea lions. Aloft and on the surface, where they were frequently snatched by predators, were seabirds not unlike today's gannets, petrels, albatrosses, and geese. And prowling about this rich hunting ground were giant stingrays weighing several hundred pounds, and twenty-five or more species of sharks.

Because the shark's skeleton is cartilaginous and not as susceptible to fossilization as bone, skeletal fossils are rare. Fossils of a sharklike creature that lived at the beginning of the Devonian period (see Table, pages 6–7) were found in limestone deposits along the Rocky River, near Cleveland, Ohio.

Time	*Life-Forms*
Precambrian 2.5 billion–540 million years ago (mya)	blue-green algae, flagellates, amoebas, sponges, worms
PALEOZOIC ERA	
Cambrian period 540–505 mya	trilobites and other marine animals with shells and skeletons; *Pikaea* (creature with stiffening notochord)
Ordovician period 505–438 mya	squidlike cephalopods, mollusks, worms; *Arandaspis:* armored jawless fishes, the first vertebrates
Silurian period 438–408 mya	first "spiny sharks," arthropods, crinoids, corals
Devonian period 408–360 mya	*Cladoselache* and *Hybodus*, primitive shark; first amphibians

Time	Life-Forms
Carboniferous period 360–286 mya	sharklike *Stethacanthus* and *Helicoprion;* flying insects, reptiles; ferns, fernlike trees
Permian period 286–245 mya	reptiles, dimetrodon, a mammal-like reptile; conifers
MESOZOIC ERA	
Triassic period 245–208 mya	small dinosaurs, first mammals, turtles, ammonites, clams, snails
Jurassic period 208–144 mya	sharks rising to dominance in sea, dinosaurs on land; *Archaeopteryx,* an early bird
Cretaceous period 144–66.4 mya	dinosaurs rise and fall, then disappear; snakes, lizards appear; modern fishes and trees
CENOZOIC ERA *TERTIARY PERIOD*	
Paleocene/Eocene epoch 66.4–36.6 mya	primates, alligators, kangaroos, modern birds, early horses, pigs, whales, rodents
Oligocene epoch 36.6–23.7 mya	apes, bats, modern horses, rhinoceroses, elephants; cats, dogs evolving
Miocene epoch 23.7–5.3 mya	sabertooth tiger, hyena, bear, seal, raccoon
Pliocene epoch 5.3–1.6 mya	mammals increase in size and numbers
Pleistocene epoch 1.6 millon–10,000 years ago	human beings; extinction of mastodon, mammoth, sabertooths; all modern sharks exist

This earliest shark has been classified as *Cladoselache,* branch-toothed shark, for its daggerlike three-pointed teeth, which are amazingly similar to the teeth found in some species of modern sharks. The fossil record, so detailed that muscles and kidneys can be discerned, shows a creature about five feet long with the general outline of a shark. Fossil fish were in its stomach.

Cladoselache, which probably grew to a length of six and a half feet, appeared about 360 million years ago. Its pectoral fins were wider than those of most modern sharks and its mouth was more at the end of its snout than underslung, as in modern sharks. Its caudal fin was like that of the modern mako and the structure of the fin's upper lobe—an extension of the vertebral column—is the same as the structure found in all sharks. Specimens are one and a half to six feet long. The fossil record ends by the dawn of the Permian period.

Cladoselache and another primitive shark with similar characteristics, *Stethacanthus* (formerly *Ctenacanthus*), are believed to be close to the source of the shark's earliest ancestors. *Stethacanthus*, which spans the Carboniferous and Permian periods, had what looks like a brush jutting from its back. The "brush" was lined with tiny toothlike scales called denticles, as was a patch of skin on its head. The odd structures may have aided the shark in gripping large fish, or it may have looked like a mouth and frightened off predators. *Stethacanthus* was about three and a half feet long.

Another sharklike fish, *Helicoprion*, emerges from the Carboniferous period. We know this fish only from fossil teeth found in many places throughout the world. The teeth, arranged in whorls or spirals, seem to be a precursor to the rotating rows of teeth in the jaws of modern sharks. According to one interpretation of the strange fossils, a whorl formed as new teeth rotated for use, replacing old teeth, which then entered a chamber in the jaw.

Some scientists believe that *Helicoprion* is so odd that it should get its own lineage outside the shark dynasty. There is no such doubt about *Hybodus*, which appeared about 320 million years ago. No trace of it is found after about 65 million years ago. From *Hybodus* comes the modern shark.

Hybodus, which grew to about seven and a half feet, had sharp spines jutting from behind each of its two dorsal fins, which enhanced its resemblance to several species of modern sharks. It also had a remarkable arrangement of teeth—sharp teeth in the front for seizing prey, flat teeth in the back of the jaw for crushing the shells of mollusks. Thus, they could alternate between two kinds of prey: fast-swimming fish and sedentary bottom dwellers. This ability to vary feeding habits in the event of a shortage of one kind of food undoubtedly aided the hybodonts' survival. For, by the Triassic period (245 to 208 million years ago), the hybodonts apparently were rare and the only cartilaginous fish in the sea. Their principal competitors were probably carnivorous, fish-shaped reptiles, some of them almost thirty feet long. Roaming the open seas, the sharp-toothed reptiles sought the same prey as the *Hybodus*.

The hybodonts, which had both freshwater and oceanic habitats, eventually vanished, possibly because they were competing with more successful fishes. Driven from fresh water, they eventually disappeared completely, becoming extinct around the same time as the dinosaurs, for reasons unknown. But before the hybodont line expired, other new shark forms were developing. From one of these new lines descended the Port Jackson shark (*Heterodontus portusjacksoni*), which has changed little since Triassic times. Its form—a blunt, bull-like head and a sway-backed body—looks like that of its ancestor.

Scientists once thought that cartilaginous fish were primitive precursors to bony fish. Recent research, however, has shown that sharks were less primitive. Their cartilage was a radically new development—a structural material lighter and more flexible than brittle bone, an advantage that helped to make sharks the apex predators in many marine ecosystems. Sharks are creatures of the sea, not fresh water, which is the origin of bony fishes.

By the Jurassic period, when pterosaurs flew and the great dinosaurs roamed, sharks began to flourish, forming many families, including variants we now call the skates and rays. And, by the close of the Miocene epoch (23.7 to 5.3 million years ago), sharks were among the most abundant creatures in the sea. Every shark family existed, from the ancestor of the common dogfish to what may have been the colossal forebears of the modern great white shark—a monstrous shark known as *Carcharodon megalodon* (Latin for "rough-toothed, huge-toothed").

For many years, scientists believed that *Carcharodon megalodon* grew to lengths of 120 feet or more. Estimates were based on measurements of its enormous teeth. Some found at Sharktooth Hill, for example, weighed twelve ounces and were nearly six inches long; three- and four-inch teeth were common. They are triangularly shaped, similar in shape to those found in today's great white sharks, whose teeth are about one and a half inches long. Some thirty species of sharks and their kin of 12 to 15 million years ago have been found in and around Sharktooth Hill. Other large, triangular fossil shark teeth also have been found in many geologic sites and in several present-day coastal areas, such as Staten Island, New York; Venice, Florida; the Calvert Cliffs on the western shore of Chesapeake Bay; and also in the West Indies and New Zealand.

Scientists at the American Museum of Natural History built a model of the jaws of *Carcharodon megalodon*, basing the size on the largest discovered teeth. The jaws would fit a shark at least 80 feet long. And that was thought to be only a medium-size member of the species. The museum circulated a frequently published photo showing four men standing and two men kneeling inside the giant jaws.

But the scientists had erred. They had used only large teeth, all about the same size, in constructing the jaw and made it about one third too large. In 1985, scientists of the Smithsonian's National Museum of Natural History, working with a full set of the varied size of teeth that would be found in *Carcharodon megalodon*, created a new jaw. This one would fit a shark about

43 feet long. Ten years later, Dr. Michael Gottfried, curator of the Calvert Marine Museum, and Dr. Leonard Compagno, a renowned shark expert, developed new calculations that put the maximum size of *Carcharodon megalodon* at about fifty-two feet in length and fifty-two tons in weight.

Although *Carcharodon megalodon* is extinct, it seems not to be very extinct. Early in this century, four-inch *Carcharodon* teeth were dredged from the bed of the Pacific Ocean. And in 1964 a fishing boat off the Maine coast pulled up a fossil tooth four inches long and four and a half inches wide at its base. The fact that all of these teeth were dredged up indicated that they had been deposited recently. Older teeth would probably have been covered by so much silt that the dredging gear could not have snagged them.

The label of extinction does not always stick. Sharks long thought to have been extinct still appear. At the end of the nineteenth century, an unknown shark was caught off the coast of Japan. It was about four feet long, had a long snout shaped like a paper knife, and a snaggle-tooth jaw. The shark's teeth, which were sharp, with thornlike cusps, resembled fossils found in Europe, North and South America, Asia, Africa, and New Zealand. The shark that bore these teeth, believed to have been extinct for about 100 million years, was known as *Scapanorhynchus*. And that name was given to the newly discovered shark. Its common name, inspired by its strange shape and face, is goblin shark.

Japanese waters in the nineteenth century also yielded another seemingly extinct shark, *Chlamydoselachus anguineus*, the frilled shark, which had six gill slits, an eel-like appearance, and resembled shark fossils more than it looked like any modern shark.

In 1976 another ancient shark was discovered when a U.S. Navy research ship pulled from the depths a type of shark previously unknown to science, a 1,653-pound plankton eater. Its wide, gaping mouth gave it its common name, megamouth. It was assigned its own family, the Megachasmidae and given the scientific name *Megachasma pelagio*. Since then, other megamouths have been found, and scientists have a new group of sharks to study. (See insert.)

"Modern" sharks have five gill slits (except for *Pliotrema*, one of the saw sharks). But members of the Hexanchidae family (see page 45) have six or seven gill slits and so resemble their fossilized ancestors that they are virtually perfect copies of sharks that swam in Jurassic seas.

From fossil to living creature, sharks have an unbroken line. They are very old and very competent. "The sharks have succeeded," wrote Edwin H. Colbert in *Evolution of the Vertebrates*, "because, with the exception of some of the bottom-living skates, they have been very aggressive fishes, quite capable of taking care of themselves in spite of earth changes, changes in food supply, and competitors. It looks as if sharks will continue to inhabit the seas for a long time."

CHAPTER 2

The Fish Called Shark

Sharks can live in lakes and rivers, and they do live in all oceans, some in the shallows, others in the deep, beyond the reach of the sun. Most live in temperate and tropical seas, though the Greenland shark thrives in Arctic waters and the huge basking shark ventures into seas around Antarctica. Sharks range in size from the dwarf shark, which can fit in the palm of a hand, to the great whale and basking sharks, giants fifty or more feet long. Some members of the great shark family—the skates and rays—look like sharks with flattened bodies and long tails. All these family members are fish, but they differ from most fish in many ways.

Even though their backbones are made of cartilage, sharks are in the phylum of the bony backbone—the Chordata, encompassing all vertebrates: fishes, amphibians, reptiles, birds, and mammals. Only about 800 species of cartilaginous fish are known, compared to more than 40,000 known species of bony fishes.

Cartilage, a light but tough tissue, forms the skeleton, giving the shark a strong, flexible support. Cartilage is found in other animals, but usually only in embryos and young. The human nose is made of cartilage, and there is cartilage in human ears and in caps on the ends of bones.

Sharks are in the class Chondrichthyes. Species in this class have cartilage instead of bone, jaws, paired fins, and paired nostrils. The

Chondrichthyes consist of two groups, the subclass Elasmobranchii, which includes sharks, skates, and rays, and the subclass Plagiostomi, which includes ratfishes and the curious chimaeroids, sometimes called ghost sharks. These cousins of the sharks are big-eyed, deep-sea creatures that have an upper jaw fused to the cranium (unlike the sharks, whose upper jaw hangs down from the skull). Chimaeroids are believed to have evolved from a sharklike ancestor. Their scientific name derives from the Greek mythological monster *Chimaera*, which breathed fire, had the head of a goat, the body of a lion, and the tail of a dragon. One chimaeroid genus (*Callorynchus*) has a trunklike proboscis, or snout, and is variously known as the elephant shark or, with a touch of taxonomic whimsy, the southern beauty.

The shark's subclass Elasmobranchii is divided into two superorders, the Selachii (or selachians), which are the true sharks, and the Batoidei (or batoids), which include skates, rays, guitarfish, and sawfish. The entire family, including all the species of sharks, skates, rays, and the links like the elephant shark, are sometimes called the selachians (after the Greek word for shark).

There are about 40,000 known species of fish: the cyclostomes, eel-like creatures such as lampreys and hagfish, which have no jaws and no bones; the teleosts, which have bony skeletons; and the selachians. More than 95 percent of the world's fishes are teleosts. There are about 390 species of sharks. Skates and rays, recognizable by their flattened bodies and long tails, number about 500 species, and undoubtedly many more remain to be discovered and classified.

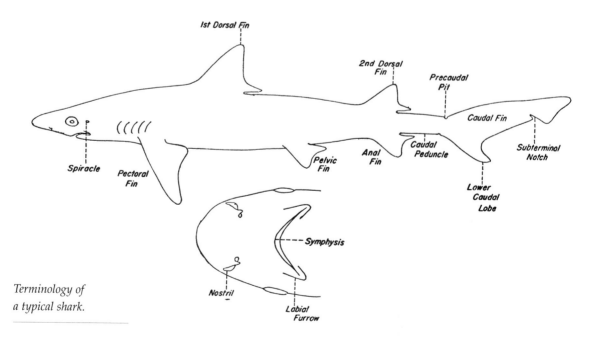

Terminology of a typical shark.

Although the body shapes of sharks vary considerably, some general features are common to most species. Typically, sharks have fusiform bodies, rounded and tapering at both ends. In color, most are countershaded— a form of camouflage in which either the top or bottom of an animal is lighter or darker than the other side. In the sea, most often the top is darker than the bottom. Thus, from the viewpoint of an animal above, the countershaded animal will blend in with the ocean depths; from the viewpoint of an animal below, the countershaded animal will blend in with surface reflections. White sharks, also known as great white sharks, are, like most pelagic sharks, countershaded.

A shark has five kinds of fins, supported by cartilaginous rods:

- A pair of pectoral fins that lift a shark as it swims.

- A pair of pelvic fins that help to stabilize the shark.

- One or two dorsal fins that also aid in stabilization.

- An anal fin on those species that need the extra stabilization.

- A caudal fin of varying size and structure that propels the shark.

Unlike most fish, sharks have a skeleton of cartilage rather than bone and they lack the swim bladders that give bony fish their buoyancy. Instead, sharks have large livers that make up as much as 75 percent of their body weight, giving them a state close to neutral buoyancy. Instead of typical fish scales, a shark's body is covered with a completely difference kind of scale called a **denticle**.

Scales That Are Teeth

The possession of denticles is one of the many characteristics shared by sharks, skates, rays, and the links between them. These scales, called dermal denticles, are tiny teeth. Each is covered by dentine and has a central pulp canal containing a nerve and blood vessels. In some species, these denticles are visible to the naked eye; in other species, they are microscopic. Denticles give the tough hides of most sharks a sandpaperlike roughness that can scratch or even tear a swimmer's flesh. This abrasive hide, called shagreen, can smooth down the hardest woods and, in fact, was once used for that purpose by cabinetmakers.

Denticles are anchored in the skin of the shark much as collar buttons are held in a shirt. The subsurface base of the denticle is larger than the opening through which the visible portion projects. In some species, such as the nurse shark, the denticles are so large and so closely spaced that they form a shield that can ward off a harpoon.

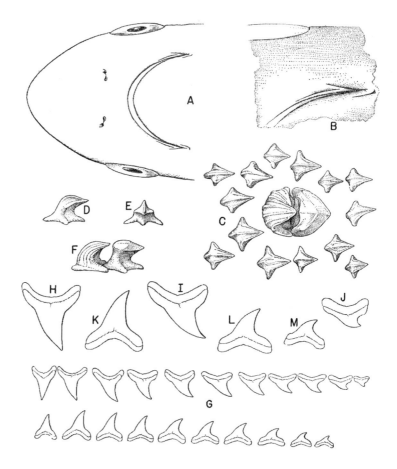

Aspects of a thresher shark. A—view of head from below; B—labial furrows in corner of mouth; C—large and small dermal denticles; D and E—side and front views of small denticle; F—large denticle; G—upper and lower teeth; H, I, and J—close-ups of individual upper teeth; K, L, and M—lower teeth.

Denticles come in many shapes—blunt, scalloped, spade-shaped, thornlike, geometric, and even heart-shaped. By a growth process called **hypertrophy**, certain denticles develop independently of others and become comparatively gigantic structures.

By one form of hypertrophy, denticles modify into the fin spine, a thornlike quill that emerges in such species of sharks as the spiny or piked dogfish and the Port Jackson shark. Other modifications include the saw tooth found in the sawfish and the stinger of the stingrays.

The denticles and skin of the shark have been studied intensely by American and Russian researchers. They have been working since the 1960s—usually in deep secrecy—to learn whether some of the shark's techniques for fast swimming can be adapted to submarines and torpedoes.

Research has shown that sharks cut down on drag by secreting a slime through pores strategically located amid the denticles. The denticles themselves are so designed that they aid in reduction of drag in what engineers call the "boundary layer" between the moving body and the sea.

Ridges on the denticles, like the keel ridge that runs longitudinally along the shark's body, help in drag reduction and in the smoothing of boundary layer turbulence. In an attempt to copy the shark's speed physiology, a kind of slime, in the form of strips of sticky polymer, has been applied to racing ships.

In the embryonic dogfish, there is virtually no distinction between the denticles near the mouth and those elsewhere on the body. As the embryo develops, the denticles around the jaws become bigger and complete their growth as teeth.

The Shark Has Many Teeth

The teeth of sharks, skates, and rays are lined up in several orderly rows, as many as a thousand or more. They vary from the stiletto-shaped teeth of the sand shark to the blunt teeth arranged like pavement stones in the mouths of most skates and rays. Other sharks have triangular-shaped teeth, and these in turn vary, some having finely serrated edges and others flanking the triangle with cusps. In some rays, there is even a variation by sex in the teeth, the female having flat teeth and the male sharp ones.

Some sharks may call into action as many as five rows of teeth, which erect or depress when needed. And behind these teeth on active duty are row upon row of reserves lying in deep grooves inside the jaw. Sharks of some species may shed 30,000 teeth during their lifetime.

When a tooth is worn or lost, another moves up to replace it. The teeth are on a kind of somatic escalator, with the developing teeth reposing in the jaw until they are needed. The ability of these escalators to continually bring forward identical teeth has been demonstrated in the examination of abnormal teeth found in some captured sharks. In one shark, for instance, an oddly split tooth was found to be duplicated by all the teeth on its escalator track. Each one of them, including the reserve teeth covered by gum tissue, was split down the middle, exactly as the first-row tooth was. Further investigation showed that a stingray's stinger had become imbedded in the shark's jaw, evidently while the shark digested the stingray. The stinger apparently had pierced a tooth bud deep in the jaw, dividing the bud into approximately equal halves. As each succeeding tooth (or, more correctly, half tooth) moved forward, it carried this deformity with it.

In some of the larger sharks, such as the tiger shark, the flashing teeth are backed by a huge, powerful jaw. The skull of a horse was found in a tiger shark not quite eleven feet long. The tiger was able to swallow the horse's skull because of the peculiar construction of the tiger's jaws and the muscles that power it. The upper and lower jaws have joints at each corner of the mouth. The joint is manipulated by strong, elastic muscles

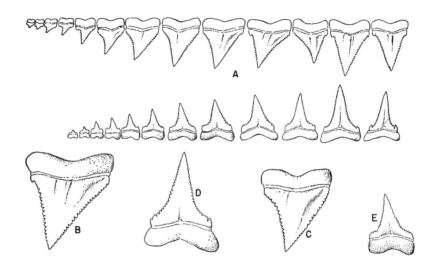

*A—teeth in upper and
lower portions of jaw;
B and C—upper teeth;
D and E—lower teeth.*

that enable the shark to distend its mouth. Each jaw, upper and lower, is hinged in the center, so that the lower jaw can gape into a deep $\vee$ and the upper jaw can erect into a $\wedge$. With this mechanism, the jaws of a large shark could easily pass over the head and shoulders of a swimmer. Closing, the jaws can bite the swimmer in half.

Shark gills differ from the gills of teleost fishes. Sharks have five to seven pairs of gill slits, located above and behind each eye. As a shark swims, water passes through the slits and over gill filaments richly supplied with blood vessels. The respiratory organs are supported by pairs of gill arches in the throat.

When the shark opens its mouth to inhale water, the gill slits close. The water passes over the gill filaments, carbon dioxide is released from the blood, and oxygen dissolved in the water is absorbed.

Most species must swim continuously so that enough water can pass over the gills and provide sufficient oxygen. Bottom-dwelling sharks usually have **spiracles**, a respiratory opening on the back of the head above and behind each eye. This enables them to breathe more easily while lying on the bottom. Spiracles, found in most other species, may aid in aerating the blood destined for the eyes and the brain.

It once was thought that sharks had to roll on their sides to bite. Researchers who have observed sharks in action, however, report that sharks attack their prey in whichever way is most convenient, and they can protrude their jaws to bite prey in front of their snouts. They have also been seen rolling back their eyes just at point of attack, apparently to protect their eyes from the fleshy flak that sprays the sea when a shark snaps down on prey.

Sharks have been clocked at bursts of speed of about 25 miles per hour. Usually, however, a shark typically cruises at about 5 or 6 miles per hour.

A Long, Healthy Life

Sharks rarely have infections, do not grow cancerous tumors, and do not suffer any circulatory diseases. They recover rapidly from severe injuries. These facts have inspired much medical research into the physiology of the shark—and much quackery about the alleged cure-all properties of shark products (see chapter 7).

Sharks have relatively long lives and mature slowly. The thresher shark, for example, lives forty-five to fifty years; the dusky shark has about the same life span. The spiny dogfish, a small shark, lives thirty or more years.

Unlike most other fishes, sharks reproduce slowly and have few off-spring. Some species reproduce only every other year. Salmon and tuna—typical teleosts—lay millions of eggs, while sharks typically have litters of a dozen or so.

Rates of reproduction are low among sharks. Most species produce fewer than twenty young per litter, compared to fish that may produce thousands of young each season. The gestation period may be as long as two years. These low rates of reproduction, long gestation periods, and the overharvesting of sharks all mean that their survival is increasingly threatened. Until recent years, low reproduction rates have not affected the continuity of the species. But as commercial fishermen increased pressure on shark populations, they have been swift to decline and slow to recover. This fact is well documented in the collapse of commercial fisheries for sharks. By some estimates, nearly 90 percent of these fisheries have failed in the twentieth century.

Norwegian fishermen, for example, started hunting porbeagle sharks in the 1950s. By the mid-1960s the porbeagle populations were down and the fishery collapsed. By the end of the mid-1990s, the populations had still not recovered. The porbeagle usually produces only two to four young a year.

Similar crashes of shark populations are occurring with increasing frequency. The National Oceanic and Atmospheric Administration (NOAA) reported in 1995 that from the 1970s to the mid-1980s the abundance of many shark species along the southeast coast of the United States may have declined by 50 to 75 percent (see chapter 8). Particularly vulnerable are mating and nursery areas, which offer young sharks abundant food and some protection from the predators that seek them the most—adult sharks. For most species sought by commercial fishermen, nurseries are in shallow waters close to shore. Such sites put the young sharks in the path of human pollution, development, and both commercial and sport

Whitetip reef sharks gather in shallow water to mate in the Galapagos Islands, Ecuador. (Photo by Norbert Wu)

fishing. Shrimp trawlers and near-shore long-liners often scoop up sharks and discard them. Inshore nurseries are not covered by federal management regulations, so state laws prevail.

"Florida and Texas," says a federal report on shark nurseries, "are two states that have actively protected inshore nursery areas through regulations; others, such as North Carolina, have important nursery areas that should be regulated. Florida regulations should serve as a model for other states, limiting catches to one shark per person per day and two sharks per boat and prohibiting 'finning,' the inhumane and wasteful practice of removing fins after capture without retaining the carcass for consumption."

Most shark species in the western North Atlantic migrate, moving northward along the U.S. East Coast as water temperatures increase in the spring and summer, then moving southward in the fall as temperatures drop. Commercial fishermen track the migrations, targeting certain species and even certain sizes.

Shark Reproduction

Many teleost species breed externally, the female depositing eggs and the male spewing sperm in the water to fertilize the eggs. Fertilization among selachians is invariably internal and is still not fully understood in many species, even though knowledge about shark sexual behavior goes back to Aristotle, who saw sharks embrace and wrote with amazing insight about their breeding and the prenatal development of their young. The males perform intercourse with **claspers** (mixopterygia). Each male has two claspers, located between the two pelvic fins. The claspers trail close to the fins and are often mistaken for part of the fins themselves. When copulation is to begin, the fins are erected at right angles to the body.

The shark's use of two claspers is not fully understood, but apparently only one is used at a time. The seminal fluid passes along a groove in the clasper. The female has two body openings (which, in maiden sharks, are sealed by hymenlike membranes, a fact discovered by Aristotle). Whether singly or simultaneously, both orifices of the female appear to be used during mating. In some species, this may last for about twenty minutes.

At least some females have the ability to store spermatozoa in their oviducal gland, presumably allowing the fertilization of several litters by one insemination. Research by Dr. H. L. Pratt, Jr., showed that several species of large Atlantic sharks—thresher sharks, hammerheads, porbeagles, dusky sharks, and blue sharks—were able to retain sperm. Male sharks also store spermatozoa in sperm packets called spermatophores or spermozeugma. The packets disintegrate before reaching the oviducal gland.

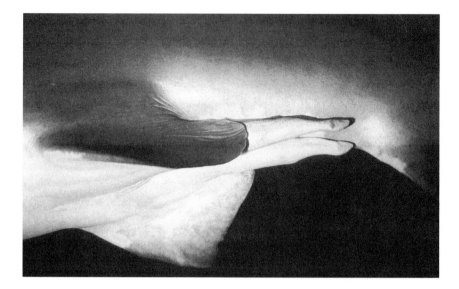

A male shark has two claspers trailing behind the last two fins on his body. (Photo by Bob Cranston)

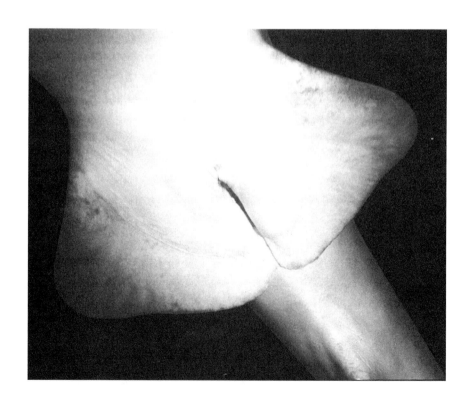

A female shark has an opening called a **cloaca**, *between the last two fins on her body. (Photo by Bob Cranston)*

Two whitetip reef sharks
mating. (Photo by
Jay Ireland &
Georgianne E. Bradley)

Male and female sharks of the same species seem to be specially formed for each other sexually. Male claspers vary considerably in size and shape. Males of some species have claspers equipped with hooklike structures apparently used to aid in grasping the female. Females of these species are protected by thick layers of skin on their back and flanks.

Sharks can fast for long periods, living on the oil in their livers. Males fast during courtship and mating, and females fast when giving birth in nurseries.

All selachian young develop within the mother. The types of gestation vary among species.

Oviparity In this primitive type of reproduction, the young are in large eggs, nourishing themselves through development on the yolk. The mother lays an egg case and development continues in the egg case for months. Sharks using this method include cat sharks (Scyliorhinidae) and Port Jackson or horned (Heterodontidae) sharks. In oviparous sharks, the fertilized eggs pass down the two oviducts to the shell gland, where a capsule or envelope is formed around the eggs. It contains a semifluid substance (similar to the white of a chicken egg) that surrounds the eggs.

The egg capsules are formed of a substance resembling **keratin**, the same ingredient that imparts hardness to animals' claws, hoofs, and horns. In sharks, the outer surface of the capsule is usually smooth or finely ribbed. The four corners of the capsule are drawn out to form long tendrils that coil themselves around rocks or other objects on the sea bottom. Not only do these tendrils act as anchors for the egg capsule, but they also seem to aid in the delivery of the capsule from the mother. The tendrils project

A swell shark embryo develops in an egg case. (Photo by Bob Cranston)

A swell shark hatches from its egg case on a California reef. (Photo by Bob Cranston)

from the mother and coil around some object. The mother tugs against the pull of the tendrils, easing the passage of the capsule.

Ovoviviparity The most common form of shark reproduction. Embryos in the female's uterus are nourished by yolk stored in a yolk sac. There is no placental connection to the mother. Young are born at the completion of gestation. In some species, the fetuses feed on each other. In each of the female sand tiger's two uteruses, the first shark fetus to consume the yolk, for example, eats the rest of the embryos and unfertilized ova. One young is born from each uterus. Uterine cannibalism, known as **oophagy,** also occurs among the mako shark and species in the order Lamniformes. Other ovoviviparous sharks include nurse sharks, spiny dogfishes, six- and seven-gill sharks, and angel sharks.

Viviparity The most advanced reproduction process. Embryos at the beginning live on stored yolk. Later, what is known as a "pseudoplacental connection" forms, linking the yolk sac and the wall of the uterus. The arrangement is analogous to the placenta in mammals. The young are relatively large at birth. Members of the large Carcharhinidae family— requiem sharks, ground sharks—are viviparous, as are hammerheads.

Most shark species give birth only about every two years. Other species, including hammerheads and sharpnose sharks, give birth to litters every year. The gestation period of the spiny dogfish is eighteen to twenty-four months, the longest known of any vertebrate; these dogfish produce a litter, usually of ten or fewer pups, every two years. Some of the largest litters in sharkdom—thirty to forty, and sometimes fifty—are produced by the extraordinarily fertile tiger shark. Gestation can take as long as eighteen months for the gigantic basking shark, as short as nine months for the blue shark, which on average produces a litter of forty pups.

Hammerhead sharks and spiny dogfish, which bear spikelike quills in front of the dorsal fins, are born alive and fully formed without injury to the mother. The head of the newborn hammerhead is pliable and the hammer lobes fold back during birth. The spiny dogfish's quills, or spines, as they are usually called, are covered with small knobs of cartilage when the shark is born. The knobs are sloughed off right after birth, so that the dogfish is able to use its weapons.

Whatever the method of gestation, after birth or after hatching, the young are on their own. For sharks, there is no parental care.

The Brain of Smell

The biggest parts of the shark's brain are the olfactory lobes and the centers of the sense of smell. Because of the enormous size of these lobes, the shark's brain has been called a "brain of smell," able to detect the scent of prey one quarter of a mile away. Sharks have been observed following bathers who had merely scratched their legs while wading in the shallows. The sharks had detected these minute traces of blood. As zoologist A. D. Hasler has remarked, "We are concerned here with a sense of such refined acuity that it defies comparable attainment by the most sensitive instruments of modern chemical analysis."

Odor travels through the water to the olfactory pits, or nostrils, on the underside of the shark's snout. The pits, rarely used for breathing, are lined with a sensitive membrane that is usually folded into a series of ridges coated with scent-sensitive tissue. As the shark or ray swims, a current of water constantly passes over this olfactory tissue. Since the swimming is more or less uninterrupted, so is the flow of smell messages being transmitted to the scent-oriented brain.

Sharks have been seen zigzagging through the water in an apparently aimless pattern. What is happening is this: Each nostril is divided by a skin flap that separates water into an inflowing current and an outflowing current. As the shark moves its head from side to side, water enters the nostril and passes through an area that contains a large number of tiny sensory organs known as **lamellae**, which are covered with millions of olfactory cells. Since the water travels over so many of these lamellae, it in turn passes over most of the olfactory cells, giving the sharks a primary sensitivity to odors in the water. The cells in turn are directly connected to the olfactory bulb in the brain—the brain of smell.

Dr. George Parker of Harvard once demonstrated that sharks homed in on a scent by veering to the right if the right nostril detected a stronger scent and vice versa. He plugged the left nostril and the shark swam clockwise, seemingly relying on the messages transmitted by its right nostril; it swam counterclockwise when the right nostril was plugged.

Recent studies of the brain of the white shark—the shark of *Jaws*—show that its olfactory bulb is larger and better developed than the bulb of any other shark. The visual centers in its brain are only moderately developed. Researchers also discovered that the white shark has a vascular system that warms the blood going to the eyes and brain; this apparently enables the white shark to live—and hunt—in waters whose temperatures widely vary. The research was conducted by Dr. Leo Demski, a professor of biology at New College of the University of South Florida, in collaboration with R. Glenn Northcutt of the Scripps Institution of Oceanography.

What Sharks See

Sharks have good eyesight and can see colors. Their eyes vary in size from the enormous one bulging from the heads of some deep-sea species to the relatively tiny eye of the huge whale shark. Many nocturnal sharks have rudimentary eyes, and electric rays of at least one genus (*Typhlonarke*) are blind. Some South African sharks, caught mostly at night, are called *Skaamoong*, or "Shy Eye," because, when one is taken from the water, it folds its tail over its head, as if to shield its eyes from light.

Behind the retina of the eyes of at least some sharks are light-reflecting tissues similar to those in a cat's eye. These natural mirrors intensify the feeble underwater light. If the shark is in water made dazzling by bright sun, a kind of curtain of nonreflecting cells drops over the mirrorlike tissue. The iris muscle of the eye will continue to expand or contract in shadow or light, even when it is removed from the head. Experiments have indicated that the muscle responds directly to light falling on it and does not act through a nervous impulse from the brain.

For many years, the theory has persisted that sharks do not have sharp eyesight. But tests conducted by Dr. Perry W. Gilbert, pioneering chairman of the Shark Research Panel, indicate that sharks depend considerably on their eyes in hunting prey. Gilbert anesthetized tiger sharks and lemon sharks, put opaque plastic caps over their eyes, and turned them loose in outdoor pens. He reported that a blinded shark is often helpless.

Gilbert believed that a shark's eyes become important as it nears the food that its olfactory senses have detected. At about 100 feet from the prey, Gilbert reported, the sense of vision seems to take over from other senses. The distance depends on the clarity of the water.

When Gilbert and his associates obliterated both senses simultaneously by putting shields over the eyes and plugging the nostrils, the sharks swam about helplessly, and usually injured themselves by crashing into the pen barriers. They died in three to five days.

Though there seems to be some evidence that sharks can—and do—distinguish between light and dark objects, there still is not full understanding of their ability to discern colors. The retinas of the eyes of most species do not seem to have color-perceiving cones. But some sharks do respond to light and bright colors, and experimenters noticed a preference for a certain shade, dubbing the standard lifejacket color "yum-yum yellow."

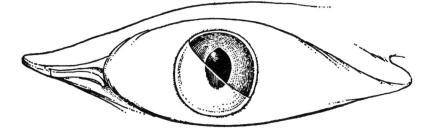

The eye of a scalloped hammerhead shows the nictitating membrane.

25

Sharks' eyes are protected by a nictitating membrane that moves up instead of down, as eyelids do. The membrane protects the shark's eye, particularly from thrashing prey as the shark feeds. Some bottom-dwelling species, such as rays, have a fold of skin that acts as an awning to protect the eye from light coming from above.

Although the ears of the shark appear externally as only small holes in the head, they are internally similar to the inner, balance-aiding structure found in the typical ears of other vertebrates. Suspended in a cartilaginous braincase are the elements of the inner ear: three semicircular canals at right angles to one another. When a shark moves, shifting liquid in the canals sends to the shark's brain information about movement along three planes and detection of three phenomena: sound, gravity, and acceleration.

The Shark's Extra Senses

Sharks can detect the vibrations of other animals, picking up the motion via a sense called the **lateral line**, a network of fluid-filled channels that run the length of the shark's body and fan out on its head and jaw. Reaching up vertically from the channels are other channels that end as large pores of the skin, open to the water. Within the channels are tiny tendrils, receptors that respond not only to vibrations but also to pressure changes and water movements. Sharks can react to vibrations, such as those produced by a writhing or splashing fish, at distances of a mile or more.

The importance to the shark of the lateral line has been dramatized by experiments in which sharks, rendered deaf and blind, still responded to wave motions, such as those produced when a stone is thrown into the water. When the nerves linking the lateral line to the brain were severed, the shark showed no response to movements in the water.

Subtle movements in the water far from a shark send out feeble vibrations that travel through the sea at about 5,000 feet a second. It may be that the lateral line picks up such vibrations, and, through some process, the shark, using the lateral line like a sense of distant touch, may "read" vibrations as, say, waves lapping a shore—or the swimming pattern of a potential meal.

In addition to the lateral line, most sharks, skates, and rays possess another sense system, which appears as a number of pores scattered about the head. Each pore forms one end of a tube whose other end consists of a group of sensory cells called Lorenzini's ampullae, after the man who first described these organs in 1678. The word ampullae derives from their shape, which is similar to an *ampulla*, a narrow-necked bottle the Romans used in anointing themselves after bathing. Each ampulla is filled with a jellylike substance that appears to react to either pressure changes or temperature fluctuations, or possibly both.

Through these pores in the skin, sharks also can detect the weak electrical charges produced by prey hidden in the sand. The ampullae may be used by some species to communicate using weak electrical signals. Some scientists believe that the ampullae may also detect changes in sea temperatures, pressure, and salinity.

On the back, sides, and lower jaws of many species are "sensory pits," depressions formed by the overlapping of large placoid scales. In the pit is a cluster of what are believed to be sensory cells. They resemble taste buds in sharks' mouths, but their purpose is not fully understood.

Experiments have shown that sharks are so sensitive to weak electric pulses that they may use Earth's magnetic field as an aid to navigation. Dr. A. J. Kalmijn, reporting on studies of the bottom-feeding dusky smooth hound, said that "within the frequency range of direct current up to about eight hertz (cycles per second), sharks respond to fields of voltage gradients as low as a hundred millionth of a volt per centimeter. That would be the equivalent to the field of a flashlight battery connected to electrodes spaced 1,000 miles apart in the ocean." Other experiments have shown that sharks are attracted by sounds in 25 to 100 hertz at distances as far as 820 feet. The lowest note a shark can hear is at 10 hertz (or 1.5 octaves below the lowest key on the piano). The lowest note a human can hear is 25 hertz, so we miss out on some of the very low frequencies that sharks can detect.

In their constant search for prey, sharks seem to use all their senses in succession, picking up a target first by sound. Next, about 100 yards from the prey, the sensitive olfactory system tunes in. Then the lateral line, eyes, and ampullae combine to evaluate the prey. Finally comes the rush to attack, and as the shark bites into the prey, it uses its sense of taste. The final acceptance or rejection comes at that moment. Whitetip reef sharks pursuing the Moses sole have been seen to bite down on the fish, then swim rapidly away. The sole secretes a toxin, pardaxin, which triggers the shark's flight.

Some sharks have nasal barbels that may help them with this final test of taste. Or, for bottom dwellers, long barbels may give a sensation of touch—and knowledge of hidden prey—as the barbels drag along the sea floor.

Most accounts of shark feeding habits start off with the same sweeping remark: Sharks will eat almost anything living in the sea, from mollusks and seabirds to dolphins, seals, and other sharks. Some species seem to have preferences: crabs and lobsters for smooth dogfish, stingrays for hammerheads, other sharks for the bull shark. All sharks are predators. Sharks may also scavenge, but most eat live animals.

When a shark consumes a meal, the food enters a primitive form of alimentary anatomy, the spiral-valve intestine. This simple digestive tract is shaped like a Z. The food enters the mouth at the left end of the upper bar of the Z. From that point to the upper right corner of the Z is the stomach, in which little digestive action takes place. The stomach seems, thus, to be little more than a storage pouch. The food then enters the spiral valve in the large intestine (the long diagonal arm of the Z). This is not actually a valve, but an organ shaped like a corkscrew. The structure, providing a great deal of absorptive surface in a small area, slows down the passage of food. If there were no corkscrew organ, food would rapidly sweep down the tubelike intestine. The spiral valve enables the shark to eat quickly, gulping down big bites of prey, and digest slowly. Shark feces, which are expelled at the bottom right part of the Z, are spiraled. Among the fossils of ancient sharks are spiral **coprolites** (literally "dung that has turned to stone").

In the earliest vertebrates, the stomach was where food was sorted and the intestine was where food was broken down into simple substances that could be absorbed by the intestinal wall for circulation to body cells. Essentially, this primitive system is still present in the shark.

Shark Classification

Superorder Selachii is made up of eight different orders of sharks, found in twenty-eight families. The orders are based on body types:

1. Hexanchiformes: six or seven gills, one dorsal fin

2. Squaliformes: mouth underneath, short snout, no anal fin

3. Pristiophoriformes: sawlike snout studded with teeth

4. Squatiniformes: flattened body, mouth at front, winglike pectoral fins

5. Heterodontiformes: dorsal fin has spines, no anal fin

6. Orectolobiformes: fleshy nasal barbels, eyes behind mouth

7. Lamniformes: no nictitating eyelid

8. Carcharhiniformes: nictitating eyelids, two dorsal fins, no anal fin

Families of similar shark species are gathered in the orders. The Hexanchidae family of cow sharks, six-gill sharks, and seven-gill sharks, for example, is in the Hexanchiformes order. Some families have potential members that have not yet been scientifically classified as species. And some specimens, preserved in museums and marine laboratories, are candidates for admission as new shark species but are still the subjects of taxonomic debates. Anatomical variations that ichthyologists use to differentiate species may seem minor to the nonexpert. As Henry B. Bigelow and William C. Schroeder remark in their monumental study of sharks, it is sometimes difficult to identify some species of skates "without x-ray photographs to show the level at which the tip of the rostral cartilage terminates relative to the anterior rays of the pectorals."

The following list is based on the classification proposed in 1984 by Dr. Leonard V. Compagno. (For detailed descriptions of many species, see chapter 3.)

Class: Chondrichthyes
    Subclass Elasmobranchii
    Superorder: Squalomorphii

Order: Hexanchiformes
    Family: Hexanchidae (cow sharks, sixgills, sevengills)
        Genus: *Heptranchias*
            H. perlo
        Hexanchus
            H. griseus
            H. vitulus
        Notorynchus
            N. cepedianus
            N. maculatum
    Family: Chlamydoselachidae (frilled sharks)
        Genus: *Chlamydoselachus*
            C. anguineus

Order: Squaliformes
    Family: Echinorhinidae (bramble sharks)
        Genus: *Echinorhinus*
            E. brucus
            E. cookei
    Family: Squalidae (dogfish sharks)
        Genus: *Aculeola*
            A. nigra
        Centrophorus
            C. acus
            C. granulosus
            C. harrissoni
            C. lusitanicus
            C. moluccensis
            C. niaukang
            C. squamosus
            C. tesselatus
            C. uyato

Centroscyllium
    C. fabricii
    C. granulatum
    C. kamoharai
    C. nigrum
    C. ornatum
    C. ritteri
Centroscymnus
    C. coelolepis
    C. crepidater
    C. cryptacanthus
    C. macracanthus
    C. owstoni
    C. plunketi
Cirrhigaleus
    C. barbifer
Dalatias
    D. licha
Deania
    D. calcea
    D. histricosa
    D. profundorum
    D. quadrirpinosum
Etmopterus
    E. baxteri
    E. bachyurus
    E. bullisi
    E. carteri
    E. decacuspidatus
    E. gracilispinis
    E. granulosus
    E. hillianus
    E. lucifer
    E. molleri
    E. perryi
    E. polli
    E. princeps
    E. pusillus
    E. schmidti
    E. schultzi
    E. sentosus
    E. spinax
    E. unicolor
    E. villosus
    E. virens

Euprotomicroides
  E. zantedeschia
Euprotomicrus
  E. bispinatus
Heteroscymnoides
  H. marleyi
Isistius
  I. brasiliensis
  I. plutodus
Mollisquama
  M. parini
Scymnodalatias
  S. albicauda
  S. sherwoodi
Scymnodon
  S. ichiharai
  S. macracanthus
  S. obscurus
  S. plunketi
  S. ringens
Somniosus
  S. microcephalus
  S. pacificus
  S. rostratus
Squaliolus
  S. aliae
  S. laticaudus
Squalus
  S. acanthias
  S. asper
  S. blainvillei
  S. cubensis
  S. japonicus
  S. megalops
  S. melanurus
  S. mitsukurii
  S. rancureli
Zameus
  Z. squamulosis
Family: Oxynotidae (rough sharks)
Genus: *Oxynotus*
  O. bruniensis
  O. caribbaeus
  O. centrina
  O. japonicus

O. paradoxus

Order: Pristiophoriformes
 Family: Pristiophoridae (saw sharks)
  Genus: *Pliotrema*
   P. warreni
  Pristiophorus
   P. cirratus
   P. japonicus
   P. nudipinnis
   P. schroederi

Superorder: Squatinomorphii
 Order: Squatiniformes
  Family: Squatinidae (angel sharks, sand devils)
   Genus: *Squatina*
    S. aculeata
    S. africana
    S. argentina
    S. australis
    S. californica
    S. dumeril
    S. formosa
    S. japonica
    S. nebulosa
    S. oculata
    S. squatina
    S. tergocellata
    S. tergocellatoides

Superorder: Galeomorphii
 Order: Heterodontiformes
  Family: Heterodontidae (bullhead sharks, horn sharks)
   Genus: *Heterodontus*
    H. francisci
    H. galeatus
    H. japonicus
    H. mexicanus
    H. portusjacksoni
    H. quoyi
    H. ramalheira
    H. zebra

Order: Orectolobiformes
 Family: Parascyllidae (collared carpet sharks)

Genus: *Cirroscyllium*
  C. expolitum
  C. formosanum
  C. japonicum
  Parascyllium
  P. collare
  P. ferrugineum
  P. multimaculatum
  P. variolatum
Family: Brachaeluridae (blind sharks)
  Genus: *Brachaelurus*
    B. waddi
  Genus: *Heteroscyllium*
    H. colcloughi
Family: Orectolobidae (wobbegongs)
  Genus: *Eucrossorhinus*
    E. dasypogon
  Orectolobus
    O. japonicus
    O. maculatus
    O. ornatus
    O. wardi
  Sutorectus
    S. tentaculatus
Family: Hemiscyllidae (bamboo sharks)
  Genus: *Chiloscyllium*
    C. arabicum
    C. caerulopunctatum
    C. griseum
    C. indicum
    C. plagiosum
    C. punctatum
  Hemiscyllium
    H. freycineti
    H. hallstromi
    H. ocellatum
    H. strahani
    H. trispeculare
Family: Rhincodontidae (whale sharks, zebra sharks, nurse sharks)
  Genus: *Ginglymostoma*
    G. cirratum
  Pseudoginglymostoma
    P. brevicaudatum
  Nebrius
    N. ferrugineus

Stegostoma
  S. fasciatum
Rhincodon
  R. typus

Order: Lamniformes
  Family: Odontaspididae (sand tiger sharks)
    Genus: *Eugomphodus*
      E. taurus
      E. tricuspidatus
    Odontaspis
      O. arenarius
      O. ferox
      O. noronhai
  Family: Mitsukurinidae (goblin sharks)
    Genus: *Mitsukurina*
      M. owstoni
  Family: Pseudocarchariidae (crocodile sharks)
    Genus: *Pseudocarcharias*
      P. kamoharai
  Family: Megachasmidae (megamouth sharks)
    Genus: *Megachasma*
      M. pelagios
  Family: Alopiidae (thresher sharks)
    Genus: *Alopias*
      A. pelagicus
      A. superciliosus
      A. vulpinus
  Family: Cetorhinidae (basking sharks)
    Genus: *Cetorhinus*
      C. maximus
  Family: Lamnidae (mackerel sharks, porbeagles, white sharks)
    Genus: *Carcharodon*
      C. carcharias
    Isurus
      I. oxyrinchus
      I. paucus
    Lamna
      L. ditropis
      L. nasus

Order: Carcharhiniformes
  Family: Scyliorhinidae (cat sharks)
    Genus: *Apristurus* (ghost or demon cat sharks)
      A. abbreviatus

A. acanutus
A. atlanticus
A. brevicaudatus
A. brunneus
A. canutus
A. fedorovi
A. gibbosus
A. herklotsi
A. indicus
A. investigatoris
A. japonicus
A. kampae
A. laurussoni
A. longianalis
A. longicephalus
A. macrorhynchus
A. maderensis
A. manis
A. microps
A. micropterygeus
A. nasutus
A. parvipinnis
A. pinguis
A. platyrhynchus
A. profundorum
A. riveri
A. saldanha
A. sibogae
A. sinensis
A. spongiceps
A. stenseni
A. verweyi
A. xenolepis
Asymbolus
A. analis
A. vincenti
Atelomycterus
A. macleayi
A. marmoratus
Aulohalaelurus
A. labiosus
Cephaloscyllium (swell sharks)
C. fasciatum
C. isabellum
C. laticeps

C. nascione

C. silasi

C. sufflans

C. ventriosum

Cephalurus (lollipop cat sharks)

C. cephalus

Galeus

G. arae

G. boardmani

G. eastmani

G. longirostris

G. melastomus

G. murinus

G. nipponensis

G. piperatus

G. polli

G. sauteri

G. schultzi

Halaelurus (tiger cat sharks)

H. alcocki

H. boesemani

H. buergeri

H. canescens

H. clevai

H. dawsoni

H. hispidus

H. immaculatus

H. lineatus

H. lutarius

H. natalensis

H. quagga

Haploblepharus (shy sharks)

H. edwardsii

H. fuscus

H. pictus

Holohalaelurus

H. punctatus

H. regani

Parmarurus (filetail cat sharks)

P. campechiensis

P. macmillani

P. melanobranchius

P. pilosus

P. xaniurus

Pentanchus

P. profundicolus (onefin cat shark)

Poroderma (barbeled cat sharks)
    P. africanum
    P. marleyi
    P. pantherinum
Schroederichthys
    S. bivius
    S. chilensis
    S. maculatus
    S. tenuis
Scyliorhinus (spotted cat sharks)
    S. besnardi
    S. boa
    S. canicula
    S. capensis
    S. cervigoni
    S. garmani
    S. haeckeli
    S. hesperius
    S. meadi
    S. retifer
    S. stellaris
    S. torazame
    S. torrei
Family: Proscylliidae (finbacked cat sharks)
  Genus: *Ctenacis*
    C. fehlmanni
  Eridacnis
    E. barbouri
    E. radcliffei
    E. sinuans
  Gollum
    G. attenuatus
  Proscyllium
    P. habereri
Family: Pseudotriakidae (false or keelbacked cat sharks)
  Genus: *Pseudotriakis*
    P. microdon
Family: Leptochariidae (barbeled houndsharks)
  Genus: *Leptocharias*
    L. smithii
Family: Triakidae (houndsharks)
  Genus: *Furgaleus* (whiskery sharks)
    F. macki
  Galeorhinus (topes, school sharks, oil sharks, vitamin sharks)
    G. galeus
  Gogolia (sailback houndsharks)

G. filewoodi
Hemitriakis (whitefin tope sharks; "tope" is an elongated
    conical snout)
    H. japanica
Hypogaleus (blacktip tope, zanzibar or lesser soupfins,
    Japanese tope sharks)
    H. hyugaensis
Iago (bigeye houndsharks)
    I. garricki
    I. omanensis
Mustelus (smooth hound sharks, smooth dogfishes,
    gummy sharks)
    M. antarcticus
    M. asterias
    M. californicus
    M. canis
    M. dorsalis
    M. fasciatus
    M. griseus
    M. henlei
    M. higmani
    M. lenticulatus
    M. lunulatus
    M. manazo
    M. mento
    M. mosis
    M. mustelus
    M. norrisi
    M. palumbes
    M. punctulatus
    M. schmitti
    M. whitneyi
Scylliogaleus
    S. quecketti (flapnose houndshark)
Triakis (leopard sharks)
    T. acutipinna
    T. maculata
    T. megalopterus
    T. scyllium
    T. semifasciata
Family: Hemigaleidae (weasel sharks)
    Genus: *Chaenogaleus* (hooktooth sharks)
        C. macrostoma
    Hemigaleus (sicklefin weasel sharks)
        H. microstoma

Hemipristis (snaggletooth sharks, pingal)
    H. elongatus
Paragaleus (sharpnose weasel sharks)
    P. pectoralis
    P. tengi
Family: Carcharhinidae (requiem sharks, ground sharks)
Genus: *Carcharhinus*
    C. acronotus
    C. albimarginatus
    C. altimus
    C. amblyrhynchoides
    C. amblyrhynchos
    C. amboinensis
    C. borneensis
    C. brachyurus
    C. brevipinna
    C. cautus
    C. dussumieri
    C. falciformis
    C. fitzroyensis
    C. galapagensis
    C. hemiodon
    C. isodon
    C. leucas
    C. limbatus
    C. longimanus
    C. macloti
    C. melanopterus
    C. obscurus
    C. perezi
    C. plumbeus
    C. porosus
    C. sealei
    C. signatus
    C. sorrah
    C. wheeleri
Galeocerdo
    G. cuvier
Glyphis (river sharks)
    G. gangericus
    G. glyphis
Isogomphodon (daggernose shark)
    I. oxyrhynchus
Lamiopsis (broadfin shark)
    L. temmincki

Loxodon (slit-eye shark)
    L. macrorhinus
Nasolamia (whitenose sharks)
    N. velox
Negaprion (lemon sharks)
    N. acutidens
    N. brevirostris
Prionace (blue sharks)
    P. glauca
Rhizoprionodon (sharpnose sharks)
    R. acutus
    R. lalandii
    R. longurio
    R. oligolinx
    R. porosus
    R. taylori
    R. terraenovae
Scoliodon (spadenose shark)
    S. laticaudus
Triaenodon (whitetip reef sharks)
    T. obesus
Family: Sphyrnidae (bonnethead sharks, hammerhead sharks, scoophead sharks)
    Genus: *Eusphyra* (winghead sharks)
        E. blochii
    Sphyrna
        S. corona
        S. couardi
        S. lewini
        S. media
        S. mokarran
        S. tiburo
        S. tudes
        S. zygaena

Other Selachians

Sharks are selachians, whose other relatives include skates, rays, and "links"—fish that have some characteristics of sharks. Links include chimaeras, guitarfish (Rhinobatidae family), sawfish (Pristidae family), and angel sharks (see chapter 4).

Skates and rays are batoids, and are sometimes placed in a super-order, the Batoidei (or Batoids). Their families:

Rajidae (skates)

Torpedinidae (electric rays)

Dasyatidae (sting or whip rays)

Gymnuridae (butterfly rays)

Myliobatidae (eagle rays and cow-nosed rays)

Urolophidae (round stingrays)

Potamotrygonidae (river rays)

Mobulidae (devil rays)

Popular Names

Sharks have two names: popular and scientific. Often, a popular name is linked by taxonomists to the scientific name, as in the popular names cited in the classification list that begins on page 29. Some sharks, such as the great white shark, have many popular names. Usually only one is selected as the scientifically recognized popular name. "White shark" has been decreed the official popular name for that shark. But it has not caught on; most people still think of it as the *great* white shark. To eliminate confusion about popular names, scientific names are used for positive identification. Many popular names, however, are used rather than the unwieldy and unfamiliar scientific names.

The leading popular name is given here, and is used throughout this book, so that any mention of the great hammerhead will mean *Sphyrna mokarran*. Whenever there is a possible confusion about a shark, the scientific name will be included. The sandbar shark, for example, is *Carcharhinus plumbeus*, and the sand tiger is *Eugomphodus taurus* (although some recent listings still use the sand tiger's previous scientific name, *Odontaspis taurus*).

CHAPTER 3

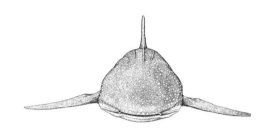

The Great
Shark Gallery

In their magisterial *Fishes of the Western North Atlantic*, Henry B. Bigelow and William C. Schroeder reported in 1948 that 225 to 250 species of shark were known. Ten years later, at a conference on sharks attended by shark experts from the United States, Australia, Japan, and South Africa, the number of shark species was set at "about 350." In 1995 the American Elasmobranch Society reported that 42 species of sharks had been described in the past decade, raising the total recognized by scientists to 390, including 7 previously considered invalid.

Some authorities would lengthen the list to four hundred. The more we learn about the sea, particularly, the sea of great depths, the more we learn about sharks—and the more species are nominated for inclusion in an ever-changing list. At last count in 1995, at least forty-five potential new species were still unidentified and several genera were deemed in need of a thorough revision.

Scientists have divided living things into the kingdom of plants and the kingdom of animals. Within their kingdom, animals are placed in phyla. As noted in chapter 2, sharks are in class Chondrichthyes (having cartilage instead of bone) and in the subclass Elasmobranchii, which is divided into two superorders, the Selachii (or selachians), which are the true sharks, and the Batoidei (or batoids), which include skates, rays, guitarfish, and sawfishes. (The batoids are described in chapter 4.)

Animals are further classified by giving them binomial names in Latin, once the language of science. The first italicized name is the genus, a group of species having some fundamental characters in common. The second italicized name is that of the species itself. Listed systematically, the species fall into orders and families, which are given nonitalicized Latin names usually based on some physical characteristics of all family members. The name for the family Carcharhinidae, for example, comes from *carcharos*, meaning "jagged" or "rough" and *rhina*, meaning "shark," and so it is a family of sharks with jagged teeth (or rough skin). That does not narrow it down much. But a family name does not have to be perfect. The fine-tuning comes with the genus and species names.

Carcharhinus ganges names the Ganges shark: of the family Carcharhinidae and found in the River Ganges. *Carcharhinus obscurus* names the dusky shark, with *obscurus* referring to his sooty color. The most common hammerhead is *Sphyrna zygaena*. *Sphyrna* is derived from the Greek word for hammer and *zygaena* comes from an ancient word for the hammerhead—and that word came from the Greek word for yoke.

Occasionally, an entire family and genus may have only one species, as if the taxonomists have prepared a place for many more species after only one species has been found. The frill shark, *Chlamydoselachus anguineus*, is in that category. Its name breaks down to "frill" (from *chlamys*), "shark" (another Latin word for the animal, *selachos*) and "snakelike" (*anguineus*), a reference to its serpentine body.

The descriptions of sharks in this chapter follow the systematic listing proposed in 1984 by Dr. Leonard V. Compagno, generally accepted as the most authoritative list (see page 29). Because the list is systematic, it does not rank the sharks in terms of potential interest to people. Family Carcharhinidae, for example, contains most of the dangerous species of sharks. But, because the Carcharhinidae are near the end of the classification list, they appear near the end of the chapter.

Classification by name neatly places each species in its own nook. But placing the sharks in the sea is not that neat. Sharks stray out of geographic nooks and are notoriously hard to confine in terms of range and distribution. In the descriptions that follow, distribution is sometimes indicated only in general geographic terms. Wherever possible, however, precise ranges are given for species that are rarely found outside a limited area. The Taiwan gulper shark (*Centrophorus niaukang*) is found only off Taiwan, and the lowfin gulper shark (*Centrophorus lusitanicus*) is known to live only off Portugal. (Its Latin name is derived from the Roman province Lusitania, which became modern Portugal.)

The species presented here have been selected for their importance as representative sharks, for their strange and curious behavior, and for their importance to people—whether they are swimmers or divers or dry observers of the wonders in the natural world.

Most sharks are harmless. In the following species accounts, no mention is made of any danger to humans unless some record suggests that the species is dangerous. When there is potential "danger to humans," that line is added to the account. "Low" indicates that there have been reports of relatively minor injuries—no serious injuries or deaths.

Order Hexanchiformes
Family Hexanchidae (sevengills, sixgills, cow sharks)

Long, slim bodies display vestiges of ancient species: six or seven gill slits and a single dorsal fin. Of the many known species of sharks in the sea today, none resembles its primeval ancestors more than the members of this family. Fossil remains of a shark almost identical to the sevengill have been recorded from the Jurassic period.

Taxonomists generally agree that there are only two sevengill genera: *Heptranchias*, whose species have narrow heads, and *Notorynchus*, whose species have broad heads. Because the species attributed to each genus are so similar, some scientists believe that there are only two species, one for each genus.

Sharpnose Sevengill *(Heptranchias perlo)*

Although comparatively little is known of its habits, the sharpnose sevengill is believed to be a bottom dweller in coastal waters both deep and shallow. Its dull brown or grayish coloring earned it the name "mud shark."

The sevengill of Australia (where it is called the one-finned shark) is considered another species by some scientists.

Also known as: Narrow-headed sevengill, perlon shark, sevengill, cow shark, mud shark.

Maximum known size: 7½ feet; 10-footers reported.

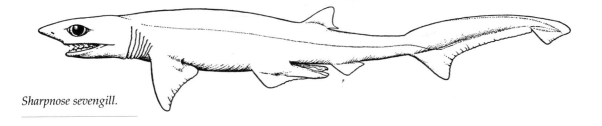

Sharpnose sevengill.

Distribution: Both eastern and western Atlantic and in the Mediterranean; Portugal to the Cape of Good Hope. Relatively rare in U.S. continental waters of the western Atlantic. This species, or one very similar to it, is also found off Japan in the north Pacific.

Sixgill *(Hexanchus griseus)*

A relatively rare shark in U.S. Atlantic coastal waters, the sixgill is abundant enough in the Mediterranean to be considered a nuisance because it drives off more marketable fish. The sixgill lives in deep water and does not normally come in contact with people. Large sixgills, weighing as much as 1,600 pounds, have been hauled up from 4,200 feet off Cuba, where they are frequently caught. One was photographed at 2,500 feet in the South Pacific.

In experiments in the 1990s Dr. Eugenie Clark discovered a new sense organ, located on the head of the sixgill. Diving among sixgills around Bermuda and Grand Cayman Island, she noticed a "transparent window on top of the shark's head." She believed that it was a pineal organ, a light-gathering "third eye" that is similar to an organ found in some primitive fishes, such as the lantern fish.

Divers say that sixgills have threatened them—suddenly coiling as if to strike and snapping at the approaching human. Divers attempting to photograph sixgills have reported that the sharks have attacked strobes after they flashed, perhaps reacting to the electromagnetic field around the strobe. Such provocative encounters have not produced any recorded serious injuries or deaths.

Sixgills give birth to live young. A litter of 108 pups has been reported.

Also known as: Bluntnose sixgill shark, cow shark, gray shark, mud shark, bulldog shark, shovel-nosed shark.

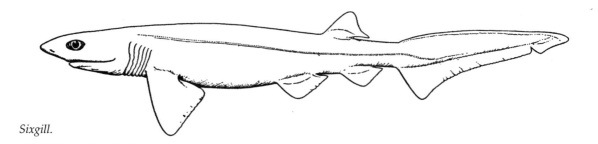

Sixgill.

Maximum known size: 15¾ feet.

Distribution: Throughout the world. In continental waters of eastern and the western Atlantic; Mediterranean; North American Pacific coast from northern British Columbia to southern California, and along the Chilean coast. Also found in the waters of Japan and in the Indian Ocean.

Bigeye Sixgill *(Hexanchus vitulus)*

Found at all levels, but mostly a deep-sea shark.

Also known as: Lesser sixgill, calf shark.

Maximum known size: 5¾ feet.

Distribution: Caribbean, west and southern coasts of Africa, Japanese and Indonesian waters.

Broadheaded Sevengill *(Notorynchus maculatum)*

Appears frequently in San Francisco Bay, site of a nursery where females drop their pups. Pugnacious when caught.

Also known as: Broadnose sevengill, ground shark, cow shark, broad snout.

Maximum known size: 10 feet; 15 feet reported.

Distribution: North American Pacific coast from Alaska to California. This species, or a similar one, is also found in the Mediterranean, off South Africa, in the Indian Ocean, and in the waters off Japan, China, Australia, and New Zealand.

Family Chlamydoselachidae (frilled shark)

Once thought to be "the living representative" of the prehistoric *Cladodus*, the frilled shark does indeed bear a structural resemblance to an archaic form: The frilled shark's first gill opening is a slit that extends across its throat from one side of its head to the other, like a frilled collar. With that frill, its reptilian head, and its long, slender body, the frilled shark looks more like a sea snake than a shark. Its single dorsal fin is small and is placed near its tail, which is practically a single long upper lobe; the lower lobe is almost invisible.

Long thought extinct, frilled sharks were found in Japanese waters in the nineteenth century.

There is only one frilled shark genus and only one known species.

Frilled Shark (*Chlamydoselachus anguineus*)

A deep-water shark that feeds on squid and octopus, the frilled shark is ovoviviparous. The gestation of its young has been estimated to be as long as two years.

A shark known from fossil teeth 12 to 20 million years old, *Chlamydoselachus* was long thought to be extinct until a living specimen was discovered in Japanese waters in the nineteenth century. Dr. Samuel Garman, a Harvard scientist who described and named the shark in 1884, studied it for most of his life. He was particularly fascinated by its teeth, "constructed for grasping and from their peculiar shape and sharpness it would seem as if nothing that once came within their reach could escape them." Its strange appearance, he wrote, "is very likely to unsettle disbelief in what is popularly called the 'sea serpent.'"

Also known as: Frill shark, frilled-gilled shark; in Japan, *rabuka* (silk shark) or *kagura* (scaffold shark, perhaps because its gill slit looks like a noose).

Maximum known size: 6 feet, 4 inches.

Distribution: Waters of Japan and in the eastern Atlantic, from Portugal to Norway. Two recorded catches off California; catches at about 1,800 feet in Scottish and Irish waters.

Order Squaliformes
Family Echinorhinidae (bramble shark)

Only one species is known in this family. The distinctive prickly hide of the bramble shark is liberally sprinkled with denticles topped by one or two small curved spines.

Bramble Shark (*Echinorhinus brucus*)

A bottom dweller, the bramble shark has been caught in waters ranging from 60 to 600 feet. It probably can live in even deeper waters, both tropical

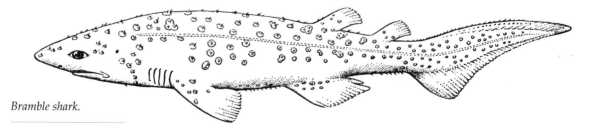

Bramble shark.

and temperate. Its known appearances in American waters are extremely rare. A 62-inch, 100-pound bramble shark was reported caught off Santa Barbara, California, in 1939, and a 6-foot, 5-inch bramble was caught in a gill net off Los Angeles County in 1944. One washed ashore at Provincetown, Massachusetts, in 1898, and the same year a bramble shark nearly 10 feet long was caught near Buenos Aires. Another was taken off Virginia in 1968. In 1995 a female bramble shark, 8½ feet long, was reported as the first taken from the Gulf of Mexico and only the sixth from the western Atlantic. It was captured by bottom long-line at 660 feet.

The prickly shark (*E. cookei*), found mostly in the Pacific, has much smaller prickles.

Also known as: Spiny shark, spinous shark, briar shark, alligator shark, prickle shark.

Maximum known size: 10 feet (caught near Buenos Aires). Other known western Atlantic record, 7 feet.

Distribution: Common in eastern Atlantic; tropical West Africa to Ireland, North Sea, Mediterranean. Reported off South Africa, around the Hawaiian Islands, Japan, Australia, and New Zealand, and in Arabian waters.

Family Squalidae (dogfish sharks)

This vast and varied family includes a six-inch species that is the smallest of all sharks, deep-dwelling sharks, sharks that glow in the sea, and a shark that lives in Arctic cold. The best known, and to fishermen the most notorious species, is the spiny dogfish (*Squalus acanthias*), which names the family. Many are deep-water forms, known only from specimens occasionally hauled from the depth.

Second in size to the Carcharhiniformes, the Squalidae family includes about 80 species. They all have two features in common: they lack an anal fin and projecting before each dorsal fin is a quill-like spine.

Hooktooth Dogfish *(Aculeola nigra)*

A bottom feeder distinguished by its many rows of hooked teeth.
Maximum known size: 2½ feet.
Distribution: Pacific coast of South America.

Gulper Shark *(Centrophorus granulosus)*

Sought for the oil from its enormous liver. Like all members of the genus, the gulper has large green eyes and spends most of its time at great depths.

Maximum known size: 4 feet, 10 inches. (The record gulper shark, according to the International Game Fish Association, weighed 16 pounds, 3 ounces.)

Distribution: Caribbean, North Sea, Mediterranean, west coast of Africa, east coast of Africa, including Madagascar waters.

Black Dogfish (*Centroscyllium fabricii*)

A shark of near-freezing water, the black dogfish, like all members of this genus, is luminescent. *Centroscyllium* means "spiny small shark." This, incidentally, is *not* the "black shark" found in home aquariums. That so-called shark actually is a freshwater teleost (*Morulius chrysophekadion*).

Maximum known size: 3½ feet.

Distribution: Deep-water species. Found off U.S. Atlantic coast and Canadian coast to Nova Scotia; North Sea and Bay of Biscay; west coast of Africa.

Portuguese Shark (*Centroscymnus coelolepis*)

The deepest-living shark known, the Portuguese shark has been caught in traps on the bottom at 8,922 feet. Its name comes from the site of a major fishery specializing in this shark.

Also known as: Portuguese dogfish.

Maximum known size: 3½ feet.

Distribution: North Atlantic, Mediterranean.

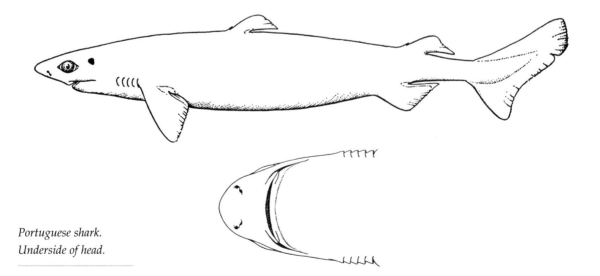

Portuguese shark.
Underside of head.

Kitefin Shark *(Dalatias licha)*

A deep-water dogfish, the kitefin has long been exploited for its skin, which is used as "shagreen" for polishing wood and metal. It is also fished for its oil by Japanese and Portuguese fishermen, who harvest several hundred thousand tons a year. Conservationists consider it vulnerable and potentially endangered because of ever-increasing catches due to the development of more efficient deep-sea fishing techniques.

Also known as: Bonnaterre's deep-water shark, seal shark, black shark.

Maximum known size: 4 feet males, 5½ feet females.

Distribution: Deep seas in the north and central Atlantic, western Indian Ocean, and western and central Pacific.

Caribbean Lantern Shark *(Etmopterus hillianus)*

The Caribbean lantern shark gets its common name from glowing spots on its body. It is about 2½ inches long at birth. One female was caught bearing four young 3½ inches long.

Also known as: Blackbelly dogfish.

Maximum known size: 12½ inches.

Distribution: North Atlantic, from southern Florida to the mouth of Chesapeake Bay; West Indies.

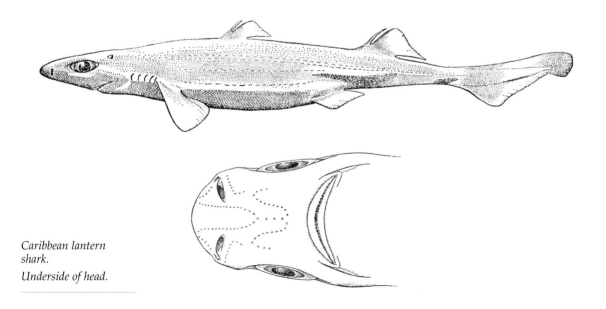

Caribbean lantern shark.

Underside of head.

Luminous Shark *(Etmopterus lucifer)*

The luminous shark is one of many small, luminous *Etmopterus* sharks that have similar features and are under continual analysis by taxonomists. Known principally in Japan, *lucifer*, like other *Etmopterus* sharks, is found in deep seas. It is sometimes confused with a shark once classified as *Acanthidium molleril*. That small shark from Australian and Japanese waters (reclassified as *Etmopterus molleri*) was found off Sydney, at a depth of 780 feet.

Dr. Takashi Yamakawa, who made an epochal review of the *Etmopterus* species in 1985, noted that the species recently had been collected from depths greater than 2,950 feet. His study also showed that these small sharks produce litters of as many as twenty-three pups.

Many of the dwarf sharks glow in the sea, particularly in the deep. Dr. E. Newton Harvey, a leading expert on bioluminescence, wrote in 1957: "Although the purpose of luminescence in fish can hardly be considered a physiological subject, and definite answers are apt to be guesses, the expensive evolution of diverse and complicated luminous organs . . . must have some meaning."

Harvey pointed out that bioluminescence had many potential uses, including identification of the sexes, and illumination of the surroundings to attract a mate or to attract food. As for the ability to switch the light on and off, Harvey suggested that a "sudden flash of light might blind a predator while the prey escapes."

Also known as: Lantern shark, Moller's deep-sea shark, blackbelly shark. **Note:** The cookie-cutter shark (*Isistius brasiliensis*) is also sometimes known as the luminous shark. Other sharks confused with *E. lucifer* include the southern lantern shark (*E. granulosus*), the brown lantern shark (*E. unicolor*), and the New Zealand lantern shark (*E. baxteri*).

Maximum known size: 17 inches.

Distribution: In deep waters off the Atlantic coast of South America and the east coast of Africa. In deep Japanese, Taiwanese, and Chinese waters, and in the South Pacific, including the waters of the Philippines, Indonesia, South China, and Australia.

Dwarf Dogshark *(Etmopterus perryi)*

One of the smallest known sharks, the dwarf dogshark is about 7 inches long at maturity. Discovered in 1985, the palm-size shark was taken at about 1,000 feet. Embryos are about 2.4 inches long. Another recently discovered small shark, also known as the dwarf dogshark (*E. carteri*), was 8.4 inches long.

Distribution: Only known location is in deep water of the Caribbean, off Colombia.

Great Lantern Shark *(Etmopterus princeps)*

The great lantern lives at great depths; one was found at 6,500 feet.
Maximum known size: 1 foot.
Distribution: U.S. Atlantic coast and Canadian coast to Nova Scotia; North Sea and Bay of Biscay; west coast of Africa.

Green Lantern Shark *(Etmopterus virens)*

A tiny, deep-dwelling shark, the green lantern has a brown body striped with pale bluish gray and marked on the belly with bright green iridescence. Some observers have reported seeing groups cooperating to kill large prey. A 9-inch female was found bearing a 1¼-inch embryo nearly ready for birth.
Also known as: Green dogfish.
Maximum known size: 11½ inches.
Distribution: Northern parts of the Gulf of Mexico.

Taillight Shark *(Euprotomicroides zantedeschia)*

The taillight gets its name from the luminescence produced by a gland below its tail. The color of the glow is blue.
Maximum known size: 16 inches.
Distribution: Only two specimens known to science, one from waters off Uruguay in 1966 and another off South Africa in 1980.

Pygmy Shark *(Euprotomicrus bispinatus)*

Vertical migrants of the sea, pygmy sharks live at depths as deep as 4,900 feet during the day and then rise to the surface at night. Like other sharks that live in the deep, they produce a bioluminescence. A description of this phenomenon described it as "an even, pale greenish light, which flared up at the sudden movements of the shark, and faded when the fish became quiet again." The glow probably aids in the maintenance of a school.
Also known as: Slime shark.
Maximum known size: 10½ inches.
Distribution: South Atlantic, Pacific, Indian Oceans.

Cookie-Cutter Shark *(Isistius brasiliensis)*

This most brilliant of all bioluminescent sharks is also a fierce little predator whose strong jaw, razor-sharp teeth, and undaunted hunting techniques

Cookie-cutter shark.
See also color insert.

pit it against huge prey. It gets its name from that technique: It places its mouth against the side of its prey, forming a suction with the aid of its tongue. It then sucks in a cylinder of flesh, rotating its body and tugging, scooping out a bite about the size of a golf ball; the flow of water past the moving victim helps to create the rotation. The shark leaves behind a crater or crescent wound two inches wide. These sharks are rarely seen because they stay in deep water during the day and feed at night.

Discovery of the cookie-cutter's bizarre predation style solved the mystery of the small round holes found on the bodies of tuna, porpoises, whales, and sharks. Also solved was the U.S. Navy's concern about what was putting holes in the neoprene shields around the radar domes of U.S. submarines and in the cover of hoselike antennae unreeled from submerged submarines.

Isistius comes from Isis, the Egyptian goddess of light—an acknowledgment of the light produced by *I. brasiliensis*. The little shark emits what an observer called "a vivid and greenish phosphorescent gleam, imparting to the creature, by its own light, a truly ghastly and terrific appearance." Some scientists believe that the little shark uses this light to attract prey.

Also known as: Cigar shark, luminous shark, Brazilian shark.

Maximum known size: 20 inches.

Distribution: Warm waters of the Pacific, the Atlantic, and Indian Oceans.

Large-Tooth Cookie-Cutter *(Isistius plutodus)*

Its predation technique is the same as *I. brasiliensis,* but the large-tooth can take bigger bites. As *plutodus* (plenty-toothed) implies, it has a mouthful of teeth—they are proportionally the largest of any known shark.

Maximum known size: 16 inches.

Distribution: Warm waters of the Pacific, the Atlantic, and Indian Oceans.

Greenland Shark *(Somniosus microcephalus)*

One of the few shark species to live all year in polar waters, the Greenland shark and other members of its *Somniosus* genus are also among the most somnolent of sharks—and thus the genus name. They have been hauled up from depths as great as 3,960 feet by a solitary Eskimo in a kayak. Eskimos sometimes use a piece of wood for bait, enticing a shark to the surface by slowly pulling in a line, then gaffing or clubbing the shark at the surface. Some Eskimos are ashamed to admit they fish for such easy prey.

The shark meat is boiled three times to remove the poison within. *Hakall,* an Icelandic specialty, can be poisonous if not prepared properly. The symptoms are similar to those of drunkenness. An Eskimo word for being drunk translates as "shark-sick."

Greenland sharks feed on cod and other fish as well as seals. A reindeer (without horns) was found in one. White, and possibly luminous, parasitic crustaceans, which attach themselves to the cornea of the shark's eyes, may act as lures for fish. Fishermen believe that prey, attracted by the lure, swim into the shark's open jaws.

Numerous large eggs—as many as one and a half barrels of them in a single female—have been discovered repeatedly in Greenland sharks, which bring forth their young alive.

The Greenland shark has been taken by Norwegians for centuries, not only in Greenland and along the rim of the Arctic, but also in Norway itself, for it enters the fjords, often destroying the gear of commercial fishermen. They are sought primarily for their liver oil.

Also known as: Gurry shark, sleeper shark.

Maximum known size: 24 feet, more than 1 ton. (The record Greenland shark, according to the International Game Fish Association, weighed 1,708 pounds, 9 ounces, and was caught off Trondheimsfjord, Norway.)

Distribution: Shallow and deep waters in the north Atlantic and Arctic Ocean; also found in the south Atlantic and Antarctica. A close rel-

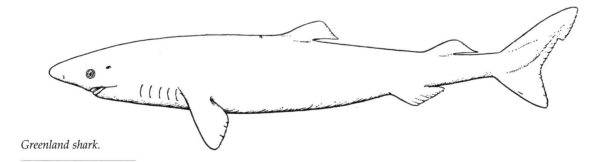

Greenland shark.

ative, the Pacific Sleeper Shark (*Somniosus pacificus*) is found in the north Pacific and the Bering Strait. One slammed into the submersible *Nautile* 4,000 feet down in Suruga Bay, Japan, on September 13, 1989; at more than 23 feet long, it was the largest creature ever seen in the deep. A smaller species, *S. rostratus*, lives in the Mediterranean.

Spiked Pygmy Shark *(Squaliolus laticaudus)*

A candidate for the smallest of all known sharks, it lives at depths of about 1,640 feet by day and at about 650 feet by night. The species was discovered in 1908 when a male was hauled up from a depth of 1,020 feet in Batangas Bay, Luzon, Philippine Islands. The shark measured not quite six inches and appeared to be fully developed. A second was taken from the same bay about a year later. This was a female 4.3 inches long.

These were the only specimens until 1961, when Japanese shrimp fishermen caught five in Suruga Bay. These measured between four and five inches. Its Japanese name translates as "dwarf shark with long face."

The "spiked" in its common name points to the spine on its first dorsal fin. It has a luminescent underside, which may give it an advantage in seas dimly lit, for, when light comes from above, it would be less visible to a predator approaching from below.

Also known as: Cigar shark, spined pygmy shark.

Maximum known size: 5 inches.

Distribution: Although relatively few specimens have been found in Japanese and Philippine waters, it is believed to be found in depths of most tropical seas.

Spiny Dogfish *(Squalus acanthias)*

This is probably the most prolific shark in the sea. Twenty-seven million spiny dogfish were taken in one season off the coast of Massachusetts alone; 20,000 were once caught in a single haul off the Cornwall coast of England. Long Island fishermen used to measure their catch of spiny dogfish in wagonloads. People on Cape Cod once dried, stacked, and burned dogfish as fuel.

When spiny dogfish descend upon fishing grounds, they devour or mutilate netted fish, eat both bait and the catch on long-lines, tear nets to shreds, and raid lobster pots. A long-line with 700 hooks strung along it was once set off Cape Breton, Nova Scotia. When the long-line was hauled up, 690 hooks had spiny dogfish on them. In one of the many campaigns to reduce the spiny dogfish population, fishermen and government officials cooperated in an eradication drive in 1938 in Placentia Bay, near St. John's, Newfoundland. Nearly 10.4 million pounds of spiny dogfish—

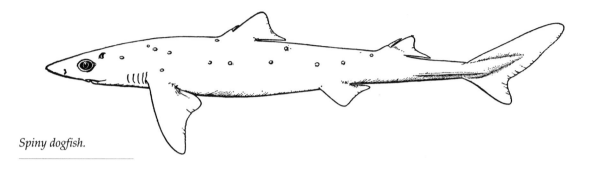

Spiny dogfish.

some two to three million of them—were caught, but a government report on the dogfish drive said that the catching of these millions of dogfish did not result in "any apparent diminution of the supply." Prolific as the dogfish may be, its existence is threatened by overfishing. The Center for Marine Conservation in 1996 issued an "action alert" about the dogfish, citing an increase in catches from 6,000 metric tons in 1989 to more than 22,000 metric tons in 1993 (see chapter 8).

Spiny dogfish are armed with dorsal spines that act as quills. A dogfish wields this weapon by curling its body into a bow, exposing the length of the spines, and then lunging forward. The spine, which is slightly poisonous, can inflict a painful injury, as many fishermen can attest.

Counting the alternating dark and light rings on the second dorsal spine, scientists have estimated that some spiny dogfish may live thirty years.

Spiny dogfish apparently are born in wintering grounds far off shore. Males take eleven years to mature, females between eighteen and twenty-one years. The gestation period of the spiny dogfish is believed to be the longest of any vertebrate animal, at twenty to twenty-four months.

Also known as: Piked dogfish, skittle-dog, thorndog, codshark, spur dog.

Maximum known size: 4 feet.

Distribution: Throughout the Atlantic, from Caribbean to subarctic waters. Also the Pacific, from San Diego to the Aleutian Islands on the west coast, outward to the Hawaiian Islands, beyond to Japan and northern China, southward to New Zealand, Australia.

Piked Dogfish *(Squalus megalops)*

A dogfish with large eyes (thus *megal ops*), the piked dogfish is often filleted and sold as a food fish in Australia. Its gestation period is about as long as that of the spiny dogfish.

Also known as: Shortnose, spurdog, spiky jack, skittle-dog, thorndog, codshark, shortspine spurdog.

Maximum known size: 3 feet.

Distribution: West and east coasts of Africa; Australian, Japanese, Taiwanese, and Chinese waters; also Sea of Okhotsk; South Pacific, including the waters of the Philippines and Indonesia; also the South China Sea.

Family Oxynotidae (rough sharks)

Rough sharks are "among the unloveliest of sharks," as Australian shark specialist Gilbert P. Whitley once wrote. They look as if they are covered with brambles, except for their spongy lips. Their upper teeth are small in the front, large in the back, and the teeth on the lower jaw point backwards. All members of this family are in one genus, *Oxynotus*, derived from Greek words for "sharp-pointed" (*oxy*) and "back" (*noton*), a description of the spines thrusting from each dorsal fin. They have high, sail-like dorsal fins that jut up from stout bodies. There are only five known species.

Prickly Dogfish *(Oxynotus bruniensis)*

A relatively rare shark, it is instantly identified by its extremely rough skin and its odd shape. Humped and stout, it has a first dorsal that sweeps upward like a sail.

Maximum known size: Slightly over 2 feet.

Distribution: Australian and New Zealand waters. A similar species, *O. caribbaeus*, is found in the Caribbean.

Order Pristiophoriformes
Family Pristiophoridae (saw sharks)

Named for their saw-toothed snouts, saw sharks seem obviously related to sawfish, but the latter are batoids (see chapter 4) and are no more related to saw sharks than to any other shark. The saw shark's head is flattened and it has two long barbels, or feelers, that droop on either side of its saw. Saw sharks live at depths of 60 to 1,200 feet, feeding on prey that they dig out with swishes of their saws. The barbels probably detect the vibrations of the prey fleeing from hiding places.

There are five known species of saw sharks, four with five gill openings assigned to the genus *Pristiophorus*; the fifth, *Pliotrema warreni*, has six gill openings.

Saw sharks are eaten in Australia and Japan.

Six-gill Saw Shark *(Pliotrema warreni)*

Found mostly in deep water, ranging from the bottom to mid-water depths. The Latin name comes from *plio* and *trema*—"plentiful openings," meaning gills.
   Maximum known size: 4½ feet.
   Distribution: East coast of Africa.

Long-Nose Saw Shark *(Pristiophorus cirratus)*

Stays close to shore in bays and estuaries.
   Also known as: Common saw shark, little saw shark.
   Maximum known size: 4 feet.
   Distribution: Australian waters.

Japanese Saw Shark *(Pristiophorus japonicus)*

Found in deep water, the Japanese saw shark differs from other species in coloring; it is olive brown whereas the other saw sharks are predominantly gray.
   Maximum known size: 4½ feet.
   Distribution: Japanese, Taiwanese, and Chinese waters.

Short-Nose Saw Shark *(Pristiophorus nudipinnis)*

Like other saw sharks, this one bears live young. So as to not injure the mother, the saw sharks' teeth lie flat against the side of the snout before birth.
   Also known as: Southern saw shark.
   Maximum known size: 4 feet.
   Distribution: Australian waters.

American Saw Shark *(Pristiophorus schroederi)*

The American saw shark is a bottom dweller in warm waters.
   Also known as: Bahamas saw shark.
   Maximum known size: 3 feet.
   Distribution: Off southeastern Florida to the Bahamas.

Order Squatiniformes
Family Squatinidae (angel sharks, sand devils)

The sharks in this family earn many names because of their odd bodies. Their winglike pectorals become angel wings, a devil's cape, or a monk's cloak. An Australian species, ornately dappled with denticles, managed to become an archbishop. In silhouette, they look like fiddles, leading some to believe that they were a form of ray. But, like the saw sharks, these flat-bodied creatures are true sharks.

Bottom-dwelling angel sharks burrow into the sand, wait until a small fish swims by, and then strike, grasping them with needlelike teeth. They also hunt crabs, lobsters, and skates.

All members of the family are ovoviviparous, producing eggs that hatch within the mother. There may be nine to twenty pups in a litter.

Ancient Greeks knew the angel shark as a source for medicine: ash from its burned hide to cure pimples and its flesh to cure swollen breasts—Pliny the Elder and Aristotle both mention it.

In addition to the species described here, others are found in South African waters, and off Australia, Japan, and Korea.

Bishopfish. (Courtesy American Museum of Natural History)

During the Middle Ages, the pious saw the angel shark's pectorals as wings and its tapering body and tail as angelic robes. Others saw it as a monk and dubbed it the monkfish. Writing about this "blessed" shark in 1558, the early ichthyologist Rondelet imaginatively reported:

In our time in Norway a sea-monster has been taken after a great storm, to which all who saw it at once gave the name of monk, for it had a man's face, rude and ungracious, the head smooth and shorn. On the shoulders, like the cloak of a monk, were two long fins in place of arms, and the end of the body was finished by a long tail . . . I have seen a portrait of another sea-monster at Rome, whither it had been sent with letters that affirmed for certain that in 1531 one had seen this monster in a bishop's garb, as here portrayed, in Poland. Carried to the king of that country, it made certain signs that it had a great desire to return to the sea. Being taken thither, it threw itself instantly into the water.

Pacific Angel Shark *(Squatina californica)*

Found in shallows and in deep waters, this is one of three *Squatinidae* species considered dangerous to humans. Although certainly not a killer, it can inflict painful wounds on unwary swimmers and fishermen.

Maximum known size: 4 feet.

Distribution: Western U.S. coast, central American Pacific coast, Pacific coast of South America.

Danger to humans: Low.

Sand Devil *(Squatina dumeril)*

The sand devil earned its common name by snapping at fishermen's hands. It is usually seen close to shore, but has been known to wander seventy-five or eighty miles off the coast.

Also known as: Atlantic angel shark.

Maximum known size: 5 feet.

Distribution: From southern New England to southern Florida, and along the northern coast of the Gulf of Mexico; along the U.S. mid-Atlantic coast in summer, especially the waters of Chesapeake and Delaware Bays, and the bays of the southern shore of Long Island.

Danger to humans: Low.

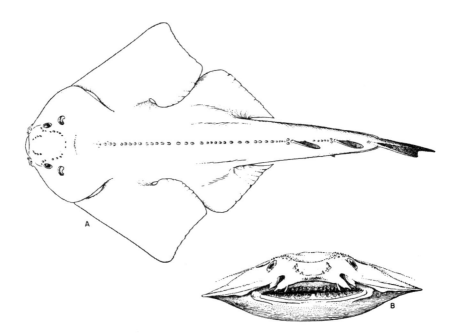

Sand devil.
A—top view;
B—front view.

Monkfish *(Squatina squatina)*

Closely resembling the sand devil and having a similar reputation, the monkfish is made somewhat more sinister by its greater size. This is *not* the gourmet food fish that has the same common name.

> **Also known as:** Smoothback angel shark.
> **Maximum known size:** 6 feet, with some reports to 8 feet.
> **Distribution:** European Atlantic waters, Mediterranean.
> **Danger to humans:** Low.

Order Heterodontiformes
Family Heterodontidae (bullhead sharks, horn sharks)

Bull-like heads give these sharks one of their common names; the other comes from stout spines that resemble horns and jut out from each dorsal fin. Bullheads make their way around the bottom in a kind of crawl, using their paddlelike fins. Their sharp, pointed front teeth grasp their shellfish prey; their back teeth, which look like paving stones, grind up the prey (*Hetero*, "different"; *dontus*, "tooth"). Their jaws resemble those of the long-extinct hybodont sharks, but they do not descend directly from those sharks of some 100 million years ago.

Nighttime hunters, horn sharks spend the day hidden in kelp or amid seafloor rocks. When they hunt, they prey on whatever they can catch: fish, sea urchins, abalone, mollusks, crustaceans. Unknown in the Atlantic or the Mediterranean, they are found in the Pacific and the Indian Ocean, both in surface shallows and a few hundred feet down.

Most horn sharks lay egg cases that are equipped with spiral flanges, giving them a screwlike appearance; scientists have had to "unscrew" capsules to collect them. The female carries the case in her mouth and then wedges it into a rock crevice, where the eggs will mature and hatch in seven to nine months. Female horn sharks have been seen eating other females' egg cases.

Horn Shark *(Heterodontus francisci)*

A sand-colored shark sprinkled with dark spots, *H. francisci* is named for San Francisco (see color insert). Fishermen in those Californian waters frequently find these sharks in trawls. Although the sharks have no commercial value, their dorsal spines are sometimes made into jewelry.

These sharks have done well in captivity. Much knowledge about horn shark reproduction has come from the study of sharks in the Steinhart Aquarium in San Francisco.

When an aquarium visitor reported seeing "a terrific battle" between two horn sharks, staff members went to the tank and discovered that the fight actually was a violent mating ritual. "The female was lying partially on her left side facing the male and did not appear to be making any great effort to get away from him," said a report on the mating. "In a short time he had manipulated his body so that his tail occupied a position over her back immediately in front of the second dorsal fin. By using her second dorsal spine as an anchor and, at the same time, holding on to the left pectoral fin with his mouth—the midregion of his body being in a position to move freely—he was able to thrust his right clasper into her vent. . . . Throughout the entire time of copulation (35 minutes), a gentle rhythmic motion was observed in the caudal region of the male and the female lay motionless on her side."

Also known as: Horned shark, pig shark.

Maximum known size: 4 feet.

Distribution: From Morro Bay to Cape San Lucas, lower California, and into the Gulf of California; Central and South American Pacific coasts.

Danger to humans: Low; has been known to bite harassing divers.

Japanese Bullhead Shark *(Heterodontus japonicus)*

Observers have noted one unusual characteristic of this shark: several females share the same area for the laying of their egg cases.

Also known as: Horned shark.

Maximum known size: 4 feet.

Distribution: Japanese, Taiwanese, and Chinese waters.

Port Jackson Shark *(Heterodontus portusjacksoni)*

This shark gets its name from an inlet in New South Wales, Australia, where one of the first specimens was found by Australian settlers shortly after their arrival in 1778.

Observations and tagging of Port Jackson sharks show that they have wide ranges. They have specific areas where they congregate, apparently for siestas. Hundreds of miles away are other areas for breeding. The female lays spiraled egg cases that sometimes are found wedged between rocks on the sea bottom. The only way to loosen the cases is literally by unscrewing them, as one would a corkscrew.

Also known as: Oyster crusher, bullhead.

Maximum known size: 5 feet.

Distribution: Australian waters.

Order Orectolobiformes
Family Parascyllidae (collared carpet sharks)

Members of this bottom-dwelling family have a chameleonlike ability to change colors to blend into the sea floor. Little is known about the species in this family—scant information on some species is based on observations of relatively few specimens. Only one specimen of *Cirroscyllium expolitum* has ever been found. It was taken in the China Sea.

Taiwan Saddled Carpet Shark *(Cirroscyllium formosanum)*

The basic color of this shark is usually described merely as "pale," but a variety of colors has been noted. They appear as saddlelike patches.
  Maximum known size: 2 feet.
  Distribution: Taiwanese and Chinese waters.

Family Brachaeluridae (blind sharks)

This misnamed family consists of one genus and two recognized species, *Brachaelurus waddi* and *Heteroscyllium colcloughi*, known as the bluegray carpet shark, found off Queensland, Australia. The misnomer comes from the fact that, unlike other sharks, they close their thick eyelids when taken from the water, thus appearing to be eyeless.

Family Orectolobidae (wobbegongs)

These beautifully colored sharks get their common name from *wobbegongs*, the name given them by Australian Aborigines. Characteristics vary among the genera in this family, but each member has three family features: a fringe of fleshy barbels, or feelers, around its mouth; deep grooves connecting each nostril with the mouth; and a coloring pattern that blends in with the rocks and the weeds of the sea bottom. Thus camouflaged, they lurk motionless on the bottom and snatch crabs, lobsters, and fish as they unwittingly pass by. Species that live on weed-covered sea floors often have fringes of flesh around their heads as an additional camouflage. All species have powerful jaws and sharp teeth.

Wobbegongs are found only in shallow waters in the Indo-Pacific and the Red Sea.

Spotted Wobbegong *(Orectolobus maculatus)*

Wiggling along, using its pectoral fins like crutches, this wobbegong has been seen clambering from one rock pool to another. This skill enables it to raid lobster traps, making it an enemy of lobstermen.

Its skin is tanned and used for shoes and handbags.

Maximum known size: 10½ feet.

Distribution: South Pacific; Australian waters.

Danger to humans: Will attack when disturbed or accidentally stepped on and can inflict a painful wound.

Ornate Wobbegong *(Orectolobus ornatus)*

Fringes of flesh hang like tassels from the mouth of this shark. Bits of the wiggling tissue resemble worms, which apparently attract the wobbegong's prey. Eating mostly at night in the shallows, *O. ornatus* feeds on lobsters, crabs, fish, octopus, and shrimp. During the day, the sharks often rest together in retreats under ledges.

The female hatches twenty or more young in her body and gives birth to them alive.

The shark's patterned skin is tanned and used as leather.

Also known as: Carpet shark, banded wobbegong.

Maximum known size: 9 feet.

Distribution: Waters of Australia, New Zealand, and Japan.

Danger to humans: Bites unwary waders.

Family Hemiscyllidae (bamboo sharks)

Bamboo sharks are large, sluggish bottom dwellers of the Atlantic, Indian, and Pacific Oceans. Family members have powerful jaws and distinct barbels on the snout.

Other common names for these species are zebra sharks and long-tailed carpet sharks.

Brown-Banded Bamboo Shark *(Chiloscyllium punctatum)*

Females anchor their egg capsules with silky fibers that are part of the capsule. The fibers are looped around seafloor weeds. An old sea story says that the mother shark weaves the loop with her own lips, but she apparently forms the loop by swimming around the weeds to which she wants the egg capsule attached.

Also known as: Brown-spotted cat shark.
Maximum known size: 3 feet.
Distribution: Japanese, Taiwanese, and Chinese waters; South Pacific, including waters of Philippines, Indonesia; Australian waters.

Epaulette Shark *(Hemiscyllium ocellatum)*

A typically elegant shark of this family, the epaulette gets its name from its white-edged fins. Waders along the Great Barrier Reef are often surprised by epaulette sharks feeding around the waders' feet. Like other members of the genus, it favors shallow tropical waters.
Maximum known size: 3½ feet.
Distribution: Waters of Australia and New Zealand.

Family Rhincodontidae
(whale sharks, zebra sharks, nurse sharks)

For arcane anatomical reasons that only taxonomists and biologists fully understand, nurse sharks, zebra sharks, and whale sharks are all placed in this family. Rhincodontidae is based on *rhiny* ("rasp") and *dontus* ("tooth"), a reference to the flat, prey-clutching teeth of most sharks in this family. Whale sharks, incidentally, have nothing to do with whales, which are mammals. The name refers to their gigantic size.

Nurse Shark *(Ginglymostoma cirratum)*

Sluggish bottom dwellers, nurse sharks often congregate in large schools on the sea floor, much like "well-fed pigs in a barnyard," according to one observer. Unlike most sharks, which take in water to breathe by swimming, the nurse shark often remains motionless, pumping water over its gills by opening and closing its mouth. There is only one genus, its name derived from *ginglymo* ("hinged") and *stoma* ("mouth"). Nurse sharks sometimes use their big mouth to suck in small prey.

Nurse sharks are distinguished by barbels—fleshy appendages that hang below their nose and provide a sense of touch that helps nurse sharks locate food on the bottom. Grooves connect the nurse shark's nostrils to its mouth. The shark uses its small, pavementlike teeth to crush shellfish as it feeds on the bottom, hunting for squids, shrimps, crabs, spiny lobsters, sea urchins, and small fishes (see color insert).

Nurse sharks are not usually dangerous, but they will clamp a vise-like hold on unwary molesters—such as people who grab a nurse's tail, hoping for an underwater ride. Documented attacks, nearly all provoked, have resulted in painful wounds. Nurses that have bitten divers ranged in size from eighteen inches to nine feet. Nurse sharks are no kin to the gray nurse (*Carcharias arenarius*) of Australia, which has been indicted in many fatal attacks.

Nurse sharks do well in captivity. One lived in an aquarium for twenty-five years. In learning experiments, some have been trained to swim to a handler to get food.

They are among the few species whose copulation has been observed. E. W. Gudger of the American Museum of Natural History gave this account:

> Nurse sharks come into very shallow water to mate, and pairs, so engaged, are often seen. External signs of the breeding season may be shown by the tattered hinder edges of the pectoral fins of the females. This is due to the fact that the male, prior to copulation, grasps the posterior edge of one or the other of these fins in his mouth. Due to his smallness and the inferiority of his dental armature, the female not infrequently breaks away, tearing and scarring the edges of her fin in the escape.
>
> Once, however, that a secure hold is attained, she is flipped over on her back and the male then inserts his claspers in the lateral pockets of her cloaca, and the seminal fluid is transferred.

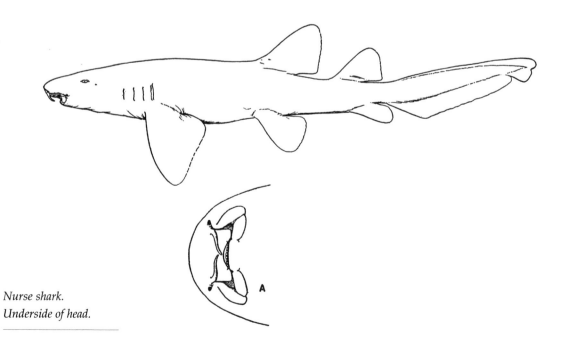

Nurse shark.
Underside of head.

Nurse sharks' litters usually number from twenty to thirty pups.

Also known as: Atlantic nurse shark. The Pacific version is sometimes called the spitting shark or sleepy shark.

Maximum known size: 14 feet, but 10 feet is more typical.

Distribution: Shallow waters of western Atlantic from Rhode Island to Brazil; Caribbean; eastern Atlantic from tropical West Africa to the Cape Verde Islands.

Danger to humans: If provoked, can inflict a painful bite.

Tawny Shark *(Nebrius ferrugineus)*

Because this shark usually lives close to shore, its behavior has long been observed. Thus one of its popular names: spitting shark. Observers have reported seeing it spit when captured, reversing its technique of sucking in prey. After spitting, it is said to grunt. Like nurse sharks, tawny sharks congregate, sometimes in underwater caverns.

Also known as: Spitting shark, giant sleepy shark.

Maximum known size: 10½ feet.

Distribution: East coast of Africa, Arabian Sea and Bay of Bengal, South Pacific, Australian and New Zealand waters.

Danger to humans: Will bite if provoked.

Zebra Shark *(Stegostoma fasciatum)*

A female zebra shark (see color insert) lays an oblong egg capsule whose clusters of tendrils attach themselves to objects on the bottom, where the shark lives. This keeps the capsule anchored while the embryo within it develops.

Also known as: Monkey-mouthed shark, leopard shark.

Maximum known size: 2 feet.

Distribution: Warm shallows off the east coast of Africa; Arabian Sea and Bay of Bengal; South Pacific, including waters of the Philippines and Indonesia; Australian waters.

Whale Shark *(Rhincodon typus)*

The largest shark and the largest fish in the sea, the whale shark was a mystery to science until 1828, when Dr. Andrew Smith, a surgeon to British troops in South Africa, bought the hide of a fifteen-foot shark from local fishermen and sent it to the National Museum of Natural History in Paris. Thus the whale shark, long a creature of myth, became a scientific reality.

The whale shark usually feeds on crustacea and tiny fishes drawn into its enormous mouth (see color insert). "Swimming slowly at the surface

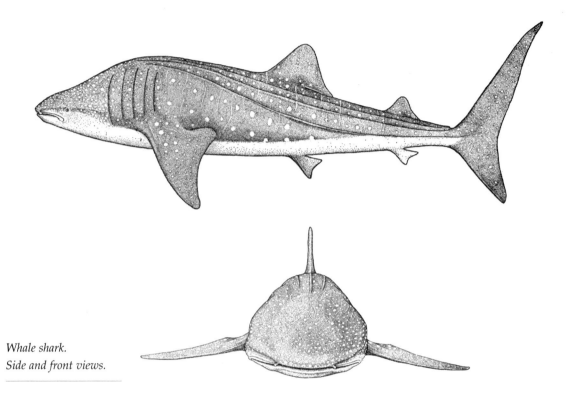

Whale shark.
Side and front views.

toward a dense ball of plankton or anchovies, it speeds up and opens its mouth as it nears the target," Dr. Eugenie Clark, the shark researcher, writes. "As it swims through the massed food, moving its head from side to side . . . it sucks in all or part. . . . Sometimes the shark will come almost to a stop, hanging with its tail down and pumping up and down in the water as it sucks in food. . . ." It has as many as 15,000 tiny teeth, packed into rows that run along the inner surface of each jaw, just inside the lips. The teeth are not used for biting or crushing food but for holding whatever is scooped into the mouth.

As the whale shark swims, a steady current of water passes into its mouth and out the long gills on either side of its head. As the water flows through the gill slits, it is strained by gill rakers so that food particles are swept into the mouth. The food must be small because the whale shark's throat is very narrow and makes an almost right-angle turn to the stomach.

Whale sharks have been observed eating vertically, plunging up and down through schools of small fish. Sometimes during these eating excursions, a whale shark's enormous head breaks the water and fish are seen frantically swimming in the shark's mouth. Tuna feeding on the small fish can be scooped up—some escape, but others are trapped and the whale shark manages to consume them.

Because of their enormous size, whale sharks are almost impossible to weigh accurately. In 1912, a whale shark thirty-eight feet long was caught off Knights Key, Florida. Dr. E. W. Gudger, who made a lifelong study of whale sharks, measured the shark and estimated its weight at 26,594 pounds, based on his formula: Multiply the length in inches by the square of the girth in inches (216) and divide by 800. After this scientific examination, an enterprising promoter skinned the shark, had it stuffed, and toured the country with it, billing it as "The Only Creature of the Kind in the World."

Gudger believed that thirty-two feet was about the average length of the whale shark and that it could reach a length of seventy to seventy-five feet. A whale shark caught near the mouth of Havana Harbor and weighed piecemeal was approximately nine tons. Its heart weighed forty-three pounds and its liver 900 pounds.

Numerous collisions between ships and whale sharks have been recorded in ship logs throughout the world. It happens often enough to be a recognized maritime hazard. The U.S. Navy Hydrographic Office devoted the entire back of its June 1948, issue of *Pilot Chart* of the North Pacific Ocean to record collisions between ships and whale sharks. Here is one account of a schooner's collision, near Cape San Lucas, at the tip of Baja California:

> The vessel was struck on the starboard side by an immense shark. The wheel was wrenched out of the hands of the man at the wheel. The tail of the fish rose 8 feet above the rail of the ship and about 14 feet above the waterline. The engine was stopped [since] the fish struck the propeller. The fish was distinctly seen when it went astern, was a mottled color and was at least 30 to 35 feet long. After going into drydock, it was found that considerable damage had been done to the hull and rudder of the ship.

Whale sharks are amazingly docile. Conrad Limbaugh of Scripps Institution of Oceanography was once with a group of divers who happened upon one. "We clambered on the shark, looking it over closely, even looking into its mouth," he reported. "It showed no signs of concern except when we bothered its face. Then it slowly dived out of sight. But it would return to the surface, and we would climb aboard again."

Little is known about the whale shark's breeding habits. In 1910, a female examined in Ceylon had sixteen egg cases in one of her oviducts. In 1955, J. L. Baughman of the Texas Game, Fish and Oyster Commission reported the discovery of an egg case, 27 inches long by 16 inches wide, in 31 fathoms of water 130 miles south of Port Isabel, Texas. The egg case contained an embryo of a whale shark, identified by the conspicuous checkerboard pattern of white dots and bars on its back. Baughman's discovery showed that the whale shark brings forth its young in egg capsules.

Whale sharks are pelagic in the tropical seas of the Atlantic, Pacific, and Indian Oceans, usually in a worldwide range roughly between 30

THE GREAT SHARK GALLERY

degrees north and 35 degrees south. But they have been caught as far north as Long Island, New York, and one collided with a ship about 380 miles east of Cape Cod, Massachusetts.

An ecotourist industry has sprung up at Ningaloo Reef on the northwest coast of Western Australia, the biggest marine park in the country. Whale sharks aggregate here in large numbers from March to late April. Divers snorkel with these sharks at Ningaloo. Scientists there are studying the sharks' behavior from data collected by acoustic telemetry and tagging.

Japanese fishermen call the whale shark *ebisuzame*, a good-luck symbol (and thus immune to being fished), which the fishermen try to avoid killing.

Whale sharks also gather in the Seychelles in August and November. Many whale sharks are seen off East Africa, but the greatest concentration of the sharks appears to occur off Mozambique and the northern coast of South Africa, from October through March. Ninety-five whale sharks were observed in a 68-mile stretch of water between Durban and Umtentweni, South Africa, on a single January day in 1994, during an aerial survey conducted by the Shark Research Institute. Large numbers of whale sharks have been seen off Mexico, from Cabo San Lucas to Acapulco, from March to August, and there are frequent sightings of the sharks off Australia's Queensland coast in November and early December. Newborn whale sharks measuring 21 to 25 inches long have been caught in the Pacific Ocean off the coast of Central America, and in January 1996, according to one report, newborn whale sharks were found in the Marshall Islands. Newborn whale sharks have also been caught in the Gulf of Guinea in the Atlantic Ocean, and in the Persian Gulf.

Maximum known size: 60 feet, according to the estimate of a whale shark caught in the Gulf of Thailand in 1925. Largest accurately measured whale shark: 40 feet, 7 inches; caught in Bombay, India, in 1983. Its mouth was 4 feet, 6 inches wide, and its pectoral fins were more than 6 feet, 6 inches long.

Distribution: Tropical and warm temperate waters throughout the world.

Danger to humans: Not aggressive to divers but occasionally bump boats that are reeling in game fishes. Not considered dangerous, despite its great size.

Order Lamniformes
Family Odontaspididae (sand tiger sharks)

A small family found in tropical and warm waters, members of Odontaspididae are the only sharks known to gulp air to increase their buoyancy. As aplacental viviparous sharks, they produce eggs within temporary shells from which the embryos hatch inside the mother. There they are nourished by a yolk sac and a secretion known as "uterine milk." The embryos are not connected to the womb. Usually, the mother gives birth to only two live pups at a time because the developing young sharks also feed on the eggs that their mother continues to produce. After a year in the mother's oviducts, the two sharks turn around and are born headfirst so that their denticles, which point toward the tail, will not scrape the birth canal.

Members of the family are easily identified. A sand tiger shark's body is light gray-brown, darkest along its back, snout, and upper sides of its pectoral fins, paling on its sides. Its belly is grayish white. It has many roundish or oval yellow-brown spots on its sides. The species are so alike that some taxonomists wonder if they may all well be variations of the same species.

Sand Tiger Shark (*Eugomphodus taurus*)

Sand tiger sharks are voracious eaters; captured sharks sometime have as much as 100 pounds of fish in their stomachs. A group of sand tigers will sometimes surround a school of bluefish and attack them from all sides in a feeding frenzy.

In aquariums, their fierce look and ceaseless swimming draw spectators who want to see "a real shark" (see color insert). The name "sand tiger" was supposedly attributed by promoters of aquariums who felt that an earlier popular name, "sand shark," did not sound dangerous enough. Captive sand tigers drastically cut down on their diet, eating only a pound or so of fish a day.

From Delaware Bay to Cape Cod, they are among the most abundant summer sharks. They disappear from the seaboard as soon as the water temperature falls below about 67°F. The year-round sand tiger shark residents of the east coast of Florida apparently do not migrate.

These sluggish sharks have been involved in several abortive, non-fatal attacks on people. Christopher W. Coates, director of the New York City Aquarium, once said of the sand tiger shark: "They can bite like hell and we don't trust them." They have been known to steal speared fishes from divers without attacking the divers.

The sand tiger once was known as the Spanish shark in the United States—a name inspired by the baseless belief that it had been a tropical shark driven into temperate waters by the cannonading during the Spanish-American War.

In Africa, *Eugomphodus taurus* is known as the ragged-tooth shark. Divers, who encounter this shark frequently on coastal reefs, report that they are only dangerous if provoked. Studies there show that their first mammalian prey are usually small harbor seals. As the sharks grow, they eat sea lions, elephant seals, and small toothed whales. They usually launch a surprise attack from below, inflicting a large, potentially fatal bite. The pinniped often bleeds to death while the shark swims off to immobilize another prey. Sometimes, however, the swift bites may be superficial and the pinniped escapes, bearing scars as testimony to the attack.

After a gestation period of nine to twelve months, these sharks usually give birth to two pups, survivors of interuterine cannibalism: as embryos, they eat siblings or feed on unfertilized eggs.

Also known as: Sand shark, shovel-nose shark, ragged-tooth shark, raggy (in South Africa), gray nurse shark (erroneously for another species; see below).

Maximum known size: 6½ feet.

Distribution: Tropical and warm temperate waters throughout the world.

Danger to humans: Should be considered dangerous.

Australian Gray Nurse Shark (Odontaspis arenarius)

Unrelated to the bottom-dwelling nurse shark, this shark may have gotten its name from an ancient English word, *nusse*, which meant "great fish." In both Australia and South Africa, the gray nurse is regarded as dangerous to swimmers and divers.

Dr. J. L. B. Smith, an authority on the shark of South Africa, wrote of the gray nurse: "Probably most shallow water attacks in South Africa are due to this shark, which also penetrates far up estuaries. The jaw of a ten-foot specimen would easily sever a human head or thigh; those of the largest would easily cut a man in half."

The gray nurse's teeth are long, slender, and curved inward. When it seizes prey, its upper jaw suddenly shoots out and the teeth erect.

In Australia, gray nurse sharks have been seen lying on the bottom in neat rows close to shore in "nurse grounds." They seem to segregate by size—"lying on the bottom as if they had been selected of one length," as an Australian observer wrote. Fishermen also noted that usually when they catch several gray nurse sharks at one time, all are the same size. Great schools have been seen in Australia chasing shoals of fish toward the beach, there to be cornered and slaughtered.

Also known as: Ragged-tooth shark.

Maximum known size: 11 feet, but usually 6 to 7 feet.

Distribution: Australian and New Zealand waters, Japanese coastal waters. Known as the blue nurse or Indian sand tiger in Indian, Chinese, and South African waters, it is given the species name *O. tricuspidatus*.

Danger to humans: Considered dangerous; blamed for fatal attacks in Australia and South Africa.

Family Mitsukurinidae (goblin sharks)

The entire family Mitsukurinidae consists of one species, and for a time it consisted of one specimen. This was caught by a Japanese fisherman and given to Alan Owston, an amateur naturalist in Yokohama. He saw it as a prospective new species and gave it to Kakichi Mitsukuri, a zoologist. Mitsukuri took it to the United States in 1897 and showed it to David Starr Jordan, president of Leland Stanford University, who decided it was not only a new species but worthy of a new family. The name he gave it, *Mitsukurina owstoni*, honored its two discoverers.

A year later, a British scientist, recognizing the new shark as a very old one, proposed the name *Scapanorhynchus owstoni*, placing it in the fossil family of *Scapanorhynchus*, whose sharks had been extinct some 70 million years. The original name was later restored after taxonomists discovered differences in the fins and teeth of the fossil shark and the goblin shark.

Goblin Shark *(Mirtsukurina owstoni)*

Sharp-snouted with long, needlelike teeth, the goblin shark lives in deep water and is rarely seen. The snout is covered with ampullae of Lorenzini, sense organs used to detect weak electrical charges produced by prey.

According to an 1989 accounting by Dr. Victor Springer of the Smithsonian Institution, only thirty-six goblin shark specimens are known to science; twenty-three were found in Japanese waters. Most were taken in waters more than 1,150 feet deep, and one in Australia was found at 3,150 feet. At twelve and a half feet, the Australian goblin was the largest ever recorded.

Also known as: Elfin shark.

Maximum known size: 12½ feet.

Distribution: Very deep waters off Japan, Portugal, India, and Australia.

Family Pseudocarchariidae (crocodile sharks)

There is one genus and one species in the family.

Crocodile Shark *(Pseudocarcharias kamoharai)*

This shark is one of the smallest species in the large order Lamniformes. It has been found far at sea and on the bottom close to shore. Its tendency to stay on the bottom may have inspired its common name.

The embryos, developing in two uteruses, are cannibals. The cannibalization continues until there are two embryos in each uterus. If each tried to eat the other, perhaps neither would be physically fit for birth and the world outside the womb. So they cease their cannibalizing and two are born alive from each uterus.

Maximum known size: 3½ feet.

Distribution: Central American Pacific coast, west coast of Africa, east coast of Africa, including Madagascar waters; Japanese, Taiwanese, and Chinese waters; South Pacific, including waters of the Philippines and Indonesia; also South China Sea.

Danger to humans: Can inflict serious bites on hands of unwary captors.

Family Megachasmidae (megamouth sharks)

There is only one species in the family Megachasmidae, which was created—along with the genus and the species—in 1976 when the first megamouth was discovered. The family name is a natural choice for a shark with a mouth so wide and deep. The name was given the shark by newspapers after the report of its discovery. In a rare bow to a popular name, scientists accepted it as the basis for the classification name, rendering it in Latin: *mega* ("big"), *chasma* ("gape" or "yawn").

Megamouth Shark *(Megachasma pelagios)*

This remarkable shark was introduced to science in November 1976 when the U.S. Navy research ship *AFB-14* delivered an unusual fish to a naval facility in Hawaii. There, Dr. Leighton Taylor of the Waikiki Aquarium tentatively decided that he was looking at a new shark species.

The *AFB-14*, working in deep water off the northern shore of Oahu, Hawaii, had found the huge fish entangled in a parachutelike dragger, used as a sea anchor. At about 500 feet below the surface, the fish had tried to swallow the dragger. Ashore, it was lifted out of the water by a Navy crane and kept frozen at the Hawaiian Tuna Packers in Honolulu. Later taken to a National Maritime Fisheries Service dock at Kewalo, it was thawed and injected with formalin to preserve it.

The shark, already called "megamouth," was a male fourteen and a half feet long and weighed 1,653 pounds. Its stomach contents showed that it was obviously a plankton eater. What seemed to be luminescent tissue inside its mouth indicated that it might cruise with its mouth open, luring plankton and other prey, such as deep-sea shrimp, with the faint light. (Shrimp were found in its stomach.)

Not until 1984 was another megamouth found. This one was hauled out of water off southern California. A third was found off Western Australia in 1988. A fourth, which was badly decomposed, washed ashore in Japan in 1989.

In 1990 a commercial fisherman captured a fifteen-footer in a gill net off Dana Point, California, and towed it into the harbor by its tail. After it was photographed and measured (see color insert), it was released with a tracking device attached. For the next several days, marine biologists tracked it, but little was learned about its life.

All of the megamouths discovered up to 1993 were male. Then, in November 1994, a megamouth washed ashore in Japan. It was a female, nearly 16 feet long and weighing more than 1,700 pounds. With the capture of a megamouth by three intrepid Filipino fishermen in Macajalar Bay, Cagayan de Oro, in February 1998, the count of known megamouths grew to eleven. The Filipino megamouth, which was eaten by villagers, was a male. Of all the megamouths known by then—after captures off Hawaii, California, Japan, Senegal, Brazil, and the Philippines—seven were male and two female; the sex of the others, discarded by fishermen, is unknown.

Maximum known size: Nearly 16½ feet.

Distribution: Known only from specimens cited above.

Family Alopiidae (thresher sharks)

"The so-called fox-shark," wrote Aristotle, "when it finds it has swallowed the hook, tries to get rid of it. . . . It runs up the fishing-line, and bites it off short. . . ." Ancient Greeks named this shark after the fox (*alopex*), as did the Romans (*vulpes*) because they believed it was so cunning. The Greek name has endured as the source of the family name; the Roman name appears as a species name.

Myths about thresher sharks usually are inspired by their enormous tails, which are typically as long as the bodies they are attached to. Down the years have come numerous eyewitness reports of the sharks using their tails as tools: to round up fish, to flip fish into their mouth, to stun fish—or even water birds—by slapping them, killing prey by wielding the tail like a scythe. Scientists generally have been skeptical about such reports, but threshers, whose jaws and teeth are relatively weak, surely must use their tails for obtaining food.

Threshers seem to stay near the surface, probably because they are constantly in search of prey. They have been seen making spectacular leaps out of the sea, but the reason for this maneuver is unknown.

Members of this family are ovoviviparous. Embryos are cannibals, feeding on each other and on unfertilized eggs. Threshers usually give birth to two to four pups after a gestation period believed to be nine months.

Pelagic Thresher *(Alopias pelagicus)*

The pelagic thresher resembles the other threshers but is shorter and has smaller teeth, according to a description of a specimen captured off Durban, South Africa.

Also known as: Small-tooth thresher.
Maximum known size: 11 feet.
Distribution: Worldwide, mostly well offshore.

Big-Eye Thresher *(Alopias superciliosus)*

Large green eyes—one fifth the size of the head—indicate that this species inhabits deep water.

Maximum known size: 18 feet.
Distribution: Offshore in tropical and temperate waters worldwide.

Thresher Shark *(Alopias vulpinus)*

A pelagic fish, the thresher often comes near to shore when it is corralling prey. The thresher pursues schools of mackerel, bluefish, shad, menhaden, bonito, and various herrings. When it nears a school of fish, it splashes the water with its tail, driving the fish into a pack and making smaller and smaller circles around them. Then, when the fish are jammed together in a frightened mass, the thresher darts among them, mouth agape, and swallows them. Twenty-seven mackerel were found in one thirteen-and-a-half-foot thresher. They also feed on squid, octopus, and an occasional seabird.

Around the end of June, when the porgies are running near Block Island, Rhode Island, threshers are usually the most common shark found in those waters. In the Southern California Bight, threshers have a nursery, bringing forth their young there and keeping them in the area through their puppyhood.

In *The Forgotten Giants*, a study produced in 1997 by the New England Aquarium for the Ocean Wildlife Campaign, thresher sharks were reported to have declined in abundance by about 67 percent in U.S. Atlantic waters from 1976 to 1994. Declines have also been noted in U.S. Pacific waters. "There is little doubt that thresher shark abundance off the west coast of the United States has been dramatically reduced from what it was in the 1970s," the study said.

Also known as: Fox shark, sea fox, swingletail, thrasher, whip-tailed shark.
Maximum known size: 20 feet, 1,000 pounds.

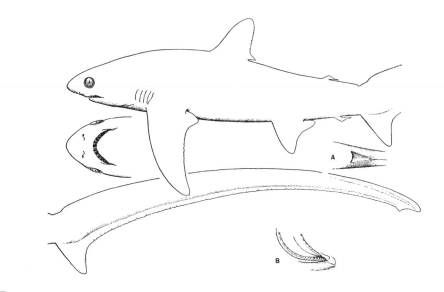

*Female thresher shark.
A—view of caudal
peduncle showing
precaudal pit;
B—corner of mouth,
lips parted to show
labial furrow (see page
12 for terminology).*

Distribution: From Ireland to the Cape of Good Hope and the Mediterranean on the east, and from Nova Scotia and the Gulf of St. Lawrence to northern Argentina on the west.

Danger to humans: Suspected of attacks on fishermen in boats.

Family Cetorhinidae (basking sharks)

A family consisting of one genus and one species.

Basking Shark *(Cetorhinus maximus)*

Second in size only to the whale shark, the basking shark feeds by cruising through the sea with mouth agape and scooping in a continual torrent of water that is strained from food by gill rakers in gill slits extending from high up on their backs to the middle of their undersides. Up to 2,000 tons of water pass through these bristlelike rakers each hour as the shark takes in planktonic organisms, small crustaceans, invertebrate larvae, and fish eggs and larvae, much as a whale uses its baleen to extract food.

The basking shark gets its name from its habit of lying on the surface, back awash and first dorsal fin riding the water like a small black sail. Sometimes the tip of its tail—and more rarely its snout—also break water.

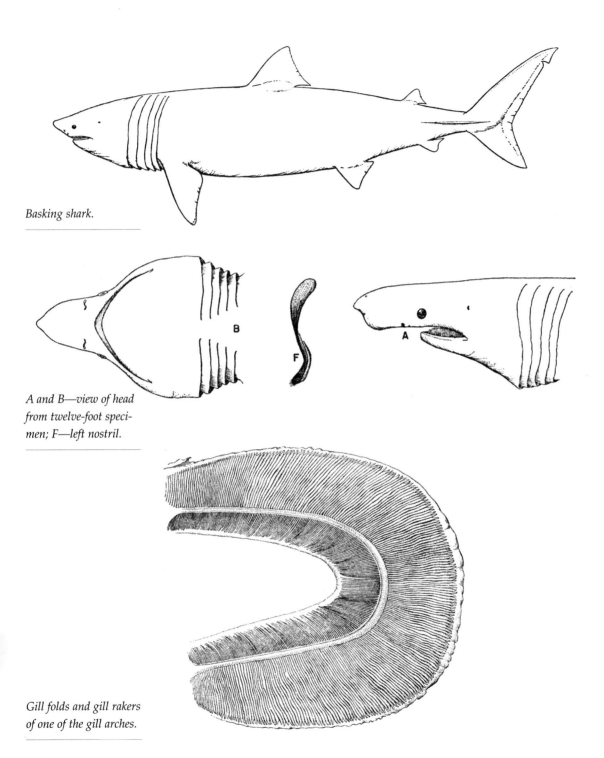

Basking shark.

A and B—view of head from twelve-foot specimen; F—left nostril.

Gill folds and gill rakers of one of the gill arches.

The size of an adult is about twenty-two to twenty-nine feet. Scientists usually dissect specimens to weigh them. A twenty-nine-footer had about one ton of semidigested plankton in its stomach. These were the other weights: head, one ton; liver, 1,850 pounds; fins, one ton; tail, half ton; skin, one ton; meat and back, 3,000 pounds; guts, half ton; contents of stomach and intestines, half ton to one ton; total: not quite seven tons.

One theory holds that the basking shark feeds on the surface when plankton is abundant, then sheds its gill rakers and hibernates in the deep. Dr. Eugenie Clark found evidence to support this theory when she examined a dead basking shark in Japan and found that its stomach was empty of plankton and its gill rakers missing. "Probing beneath the tissue covering the cartilage that normally supports the huge strainers," she wrote, "I discovered a new set of gill rakers in the process of development but apparently ready to break through soon."

Baskers have been spotted swimming in pairs and in schools of 100 or more. Occasionally, a basking shark leaps from the sea, a lifting feat of unimaginable strength. This leaping habit may be an attempt to get rid of the vast colonies of parasites that infest its massive body.

Of the countless basking sharks landed by commercial shark hunters, not one female is known to have carried an embryo. The most widely accepted theory is that basking sharks are viviparous, conceive their young while basking at the surface, and bring them forth in the sunless privacy of the deep after a gestation of possibly two years or longer. Biologists do not know the age at which female sharks reach reproductive maturity, the length of the gestation period, or the size of the young when born.

In colonial times, basking sharks were abundant in the Gulf of Maine, and many were caught off the tip of Cape Cod to provide oil for the lamps of the colonists. But the great sharks have long since vanished from New England waters, except for occasional strays.

Until the 1950s, fishermen in northern Europe harpooned basking sharks and extracted copious quantities of oil and vitamin A from the sharks' enormous livers. Basking sharks still are harvested off the coast of Japan and China for their meat and fins. Although they are not hunted in the western Atlantic, many die after becoming entangled in fishing nets and lobster pots. A major fishery for basking sharks persists in the Firth of Clyde in Scotland, where a fisherman harpooned as many as 122 in one season. There are also fisheries in Iceland, Peru, Ecuador, China, and California. The liver oil is sold, mostly to Japan, as an aphrodisiac, a health food, and a lubricant in cosmetics.

In Japan itself the basking shark is relentlessly hunted by fishermen who take advantage of the shark's surface-feeding habits. They approach it in small boats and harpoon it. Towed to a processing plant, a typical four-ton, twenty-seven-foot basking shark yields a ton of meat, which is further processed for distribution by food companies. Some of the meat will be sold for smoked products, some for frying, and some will be minced for use in a kind of fishburger. About 100 gallons of oil will be extracted, mostly for medicinal use. The fins will be cut off and dried for shark fin soup, and the cartilaginous skeleton will be processed into fertilizer and animal feed.

Norway has had a basking shark fishery since the sixteenth century. In modern times Norwegians caught about 2,500 basking sharks a year. By 1981, the annual catch had dropped to about 750, but the fishing of these depleted stocks continues.

In 1993 the Pelagic Shark Research Foundation (PSRF) reported that the global population of the basking shark had dropped by 80 percent since the 1950s. At that time they were seen by the thousands in populations around the world. In California, the PSRF said, recreational anglers often hook basking sharks and tow them behind their boats. The basking shark is protected in the Monterey Bay Sanctuary in California, and the PSRF, founded in 1990 to protect sharks, believes that the basking shark particularly needs federal protection in U.S. waters.

Since the early 1980s an organization called The Basking Shark Project has been gathering information about basking sharks in British waters, home to one of the world's largest populations of the species. Project surveyors report that the basking shark is gradually disappearing from areas where they were previously common. They also estimate that 95 percent of the basking sharks captured by hunters are females.

"A creature as large as it is like a canary in an oceanic coal mine," Dr. John McCosker, a shark researcher with the California Academy of Sciences, observed in 1995. "As their numbers decrease, it's a sign that if we're not causing direct reduction, we're probably causing indirect reduction because of water quality."

Also known as: Elephant shark, bone shark, sailfish shark, sunfish.

Maximum known size: 40 feet, perhaps 50 feet, and up to 3.6 metric tons (7,938 pounds).

Distribution: Temperate and boreal waters, centering west and south of Iceland, along western Ireland, among the Hebrides, and off southwestern Norway. In the Pacific, between November and February, it ranges around Monterey and San Simeon Bays, California. It has also been seen off Peru, Ecuador, Australia, New Zealand, Japan, and China.

Little is known about its reproductive behavior. Estimated gestation periods of its young range from three to five years.

Danger to humans: May attack boats when harpooned, but is not aggressive to divers and not considered dangerous, despite its great size.

Family Lamnidae (mackerel sharks, porbeagles, white sharks)

Large, powerful, and streamlined with strong caudal keels, sharks of this family look like "real sharks"—the kind that swimmers see in their nightmares. There are three genera—*Lamna, Isurus,* and *Carcharodon,* the latter consisting of one species, *Carcharodon carcharias,* derived from *carcharos* ("ragged") and *odon* ("tooth").

Those large, triangular, serrated teeth—sharp enough to saw wood—set *Carcharodon carcharias* apart from all other members of the family. This is the world's most feared shark, the star of the movie *Jaws:* the great white shark.

White Shark *(Carcharodon carcharias)*

In the 1970s the book and movie *Jaws* introduced millions to the great white shark, making it the most feared and loathed animal in modern history. But in the 1990s the white shark (as it is now officially known) was becoming an animal recognized not for its rare attacks on human beings but for its key role in the oceanic ecosystem. South Africa, most of Australia, the state of California, and the U.S. government have even made the great white a protected animal. The great white shark is an "apex predator," the ultimate link in the food chain. White sharks eat anything they want, and nothing eats them. As the apex predator, a white shark is the final grim reaper, keeping the ecosystem balanced by keeping down prey populations. If, for example, white sharks were killed off in an ecosystem that included seals, the seal population would build up—to the detriment of mollusks that are the prey of seals.

In the spring, female white sharks in some California populations head south from northern California toward the Channel Islands. There, and at sites farther south, they give birth to their pups. Near the end of summer, they head north again.

In the El Niño years of abnormally warm water, white sharks are more plentiful off central California because both they and their prey shift northward. During 1984 to 1985 and 1991 to 1992—the warmest oceanic

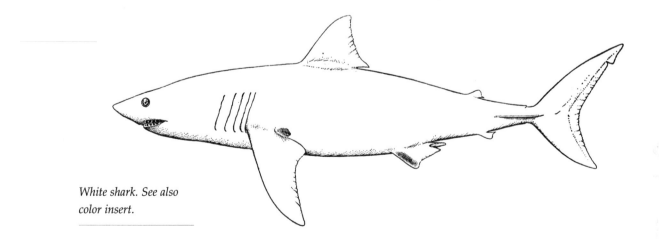

White shark. See also color insert.

seasons in recent history—researchers noted a sharp increase in white shark populations. But those populations are always low, with perhaps fewer than 100 adult animals in the state's waters.

California gave protected status to the white shark in 1992, after research established that along the state's coastline adult white sharks are an important predator of marine mammals, especially elephant seals. Juveniles feed mostly on fish. When white sharks reach approximately 1,000 pounds, they switch to marine mammals.

The waters off central California offer a rich bounty of food for white sharks, and every summer and fall they feed off shore. The Farallon Islands, a national wildlife refuge about twenty-seven miles off San Francisco, is a major feeding ground. The food consists of northern elephant seals, California sea lions, Steller sea lions, and harbor seals that live around and breed on these islands. The coastal waters along central California, especially around the Año Nuevo State Reserve and along the Marin Headlands, is another feeding area. In the summer the sharks feed on seals and sea lions along the coast as far north as Oregon and occasionally the Gulf of Alaska, and in the fall, they turn south and feed along the offshore islands.

Hunting elephant seals off the California coast, a white shark cruises near the bottom, its dark upper body blending into the rocks. Above, on the surface, are the seals. The shark picks out a prey, then swims swiftly upward and rams into the seal, stunning it. Then its jaws open and its mouth moves forward, its snout bending up and out of the jaws. As the shark closes in on the seal, the shark cannot see what it is about to grasp. Relying on its electronic-field sensors, it knows exactly where its prey is. At this point, the shark's triangular and serrated upper teeth cut into the prey and extract large chunks. Shifting the chunk in its jaw, the shark holds it with its narrow, unserrated bottom teeth in a kind of "plucking" move.

Occasionally the seal fights back. Researchers have seen deep scarring on sharks' heads from the teeth and claws of elephant seals. But the shark inevitably wins, gets its first chunk of prey, then leaves the dying seal for a leisurely later meal. Often other white sharks arrive to feed off the kill, with no apparent interference from the killing shark. (White sharks, however, can be aggressive toward each other. Observers of white sharks in South Africa have seen them jumping completely clear of the water and inflicting wounds on each other while in combat, for unknown reasons.)

Researchers, relating white shark feeding behavior to data about attacks on human beings, theorize that the white shark is not a "man-eater" but a "man-biter"—attacking a swimmer or a surfer with a massive first bite that causes huge blood loss—and then leaving the victim until the shark returns to feed on the carcass. (Of the some 100 worldwide shark attacks each year, about thirty are fatal, and an estimated half to a third of those fatal attacks are made by white sharks.)

One of the pioneer researchers on shark behavior, Dr. Eugenie Clark, got a closeup view of white sharks during a dive in a steel-and-mesh cage in South Australia, in an area known as Dangerous Reef. She wrote this account in the August 1981 *National Geographic* magazine:

> One fish came straight toward me with mouth so wide open I could see past the awesome teeth and peer down its gullet. Seconds later I saw and heard the massive jaws crunch down on the mesh as the tip of the shark's nose thrust through the space between the bars. I plastered myself against the opposite side of the cage, only to find another shark brushing against my back! . . .
>
> Most of the time they merely cruised by our cages, so stream-lined, so graceful, so magnificent that I was completely awestruck by their beauty. Soon I no longer backed against the far side of the cage when a shark came at me, but aimed my camera in its face or down its throat if it swam head-on. At other times I reached through the bars and managed to stroke or pat a passing body.

A rare observation of an encounter between a white shark and a killer whale was witnessed in October 1997 off the Farallon Islands by biologist Peter Pyle of the Point Reyes, California, Bird Observatory. A killer whale, or orca, was biting down on a shark four and a half to five and a half feet long when Pyle approached in a boat. The orca was a calf whose mother was nearby. Apparently, the mother had already killed the shark and given it to the calf. "About five minutes after we got there," Pyle later reported, "part of the liver popped out of the shark. The gulls were in a feeding frenzy on the liver and other bits of the shark floating to the surface. . . . We saw the calf drop the shark carcass and head for the liver."

Elsewhere than the California coast, whites usually feed on fish (especially tuna), squid, other sharks, dolphins, whales, seals, and sea lions. They also feed on the carcasses of whale sharks and the fat-rich blubber in the carcasses of large whales. One 1982 study showed that a fifteen-foot shark could live for about forty-five days on sixty-six pounds of whale blubber.

Other sharks four to seven feet long have been found whole in the bellies of white sharks. A sea lion weighing 100 pounds was found in a white shark taken off California, and one caught in Florida waters had in it two sharks, each of which was six to seven feet long. They also eat sea turtles, easily crunching through the shells. Seals cleanly bitten in two have been found in their stomachs.

White sharks are theoretically pelagic, but many have been taken in fish traps within a few yards of the beach in the vicinity of Woods Hole, Massachusetts, and on Cape Cod. They have been harpooned in ten feet of water off Provincetown, Massachusetts, and within two miles of a bathing beach in Boston harbor. A white shark once attacked a fisherman in a dory on St. Pierre Bank, south of Newfoundland. The species was determined by teeth left behind on the dory's scarred hull.

Little is known about the mating behavior of white sharks. Embryos are cannibals, with about seven to nine surviving for birth after a gestation period of at least a year and possibly as long as two. Estimates of gestation are based on the relatively large size of pups. (The smallest known free-swimming white shark measured fifty-one inches and thirty-six pounds.) A female may only reproduce a few times in a lifetime.

The biggest recorded white sharks include a twenty-nine-footer caught in 1978 off the coast of the Azores. A twenty-one-foot white shark was caught off Cuba. The average size is around fifteen feet, but there have been unconfirmed reports of sharks as large as twenty-five feet.

Also known as: Great white shark, man-eating shark, white pointer, blue pointer, white death.

Maximum known size: 25 feet reported; 21 feet and 2,658 pounds recorded.

Distribution: Worldwide, along coasts and around islands, especially where there are seals; temperate coastal waters in the Pacific and Atlantic. In North American waters, it has been reported from Newfoundland to Florida, and from southeast Alaska to southern California. Nowhere in its range is it very common.

Danger to humans: Extreme. Known for fatal attacks on swimmers, divers, and surfers; has even attacked small boats.

Note: For more information about great whites and attacks on humans, see chapter 5; for more information about protection for great whites, see chapter 8.

Shortfin Mako *(Isurus oxyrynchus)*

A large, swift, and dangerous shark, the mako has been clocked swimming at twenty miles per hour, the fastest speed ever recorded for a shark. Pound for pound, it is one of the strongest of sharks. At ten feet in length, a mako may weigh more than 1,000 pounds, and the mako may reach a length of thirteen feet or more (see insert).

The mako is beautifully colored. Its upper body is a deep purplish indigo, turning silvery on its sides and fading to snow white below. In Polynesian legends, the mako is a reincarnated human being and must be treated with respect. This would be good advice for divers, for this mako can be aggressive. Divers who have encountered the mako say that it should be particularly treated with caution when it swims in a figure-eight pattern and approaches with jaw agape—a possible prelude to an attack. The Maori of New Zealand apparently believed it was a "man-eater," roughly a translation of the Maori *mako-mako*.

The mako is a fierce, tireless fighter, leaping again and again to shake off the hook. Western writer Zane Grey called the mako "the aristocrat of

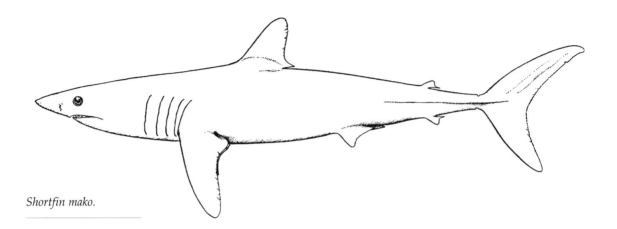

Shortfin mako.

all sharks. His leaps are prodigious, inconceivably high. The ease and grace . . . is indescribable." As a "sporting fish," he wrote, it is "as game as beautiful, as ferocious as enduring." Ernest Hemingway also fished for the mako. It is a marauding mako that consumes the marlin in Hemingway's *The Old Man and the Sea*.

Like Hemingway's fisherman, three Australian fishermen had their fishing dramatically spoiled by a mako one day in 1988. The ten-foot shark leaped into their boat, knocking two of the fishermen into the sea. The third man radioed for help while the shark thrashed around. When rescuers arrived, the shark was dead and the boat wrecked.

The mako's usual fare includes bluefish, mackerel, tuna, and other pelagic species of fish, as well as squid. Large makos will attack swordfish and small cetaceans. Captain Nathaniel E. Atwood, a New England fisherman and amateur naturalist, exhibited before the Boston Society of Natural History in 1866 the jaws of a large shark believed to have been a mako. "In the stomach of this specimen," he said, "nearly the whole of a full-grown swordfish was found, and some ten or twelve wounds in the skin of the shark gave evidence of the contest which must have occurred."

In modern times, a 120-pound swordfish was found, with sword still attached, in the stomach of a 730-pound mako taken near Bimini.

A duel between the razor-toothed mako and the toothless swordfish would appear to be one that the shark was sure to win. But the swordfish's sword is a weapon that can be wielded with incredible power. There are many documented accounts of swordfishes thrusting their swords through a foot or more of solid oak in the hulls of ships.

A food fish in many areas around the world, the mako is sometimes marketed in California as a swordfish. Since the 1980s, mako populations have been decreasing because of over-fishing. A fishery for makos, off California, reported a catch of about 244 metric tons in 1982. After the catch sharply declined—to about 98 metric tons in 1985—the commercial fishing stopped. But sport fishing accelerated, with mako tournaments being second only to marlin tournaments in southern California and the mid-Atlantic. The number of angler trips for mako in southern California rose from 41,000 in 1986 to an estimated 410,000 in 1989.

According to 1995 U.S. fisheries statistics, the species experienced about a 47 percent decline in abundance from 1987 to 1997 and a 68 percent decline in U.S. Atlantic waters from 1978 to 1994.

Little is known about the reproduction of the shortfin mako. Litters usually number eight to ten pups. Females are believed to gather in nurseries to give birth; the waters of Long Island Sound and the California Bight are believed to serve as nurseries. Females abort embryos during capture.

Makos are "warm-blooded," in the sense that heat from blood is kept within the body and not dispelled through the gills. This phenomenon, similar to a process in tuna, gives makos an advantage as swift swimmers.

Also known as: Bonito shark.

Maximum known size: 13 feet and 1,000 pounds.

Distribution: Tropical and warm temperate seas worldwide, following warm waters toward the polar regions at the extreme northern and southern ends of their range.

Danger to humans: Blamed for nonfatal attacks on swimmers and boats, particularly when hooked.

Longfin Mako *(Isurus paucus)*

The longfin resembles the shortfin mako, but has larger pectoral fins and larger eyes, an indication that it lives in deep waters. The longfin mako is not well known. It was not described as a separate species until 1966.

Maximum known size:. 13½ feet.

Distribution: Tropical waters; the Pacific; U.S. Atlantic and Canadian coasts; both coasts of Africa.

Danger to humans: Not indicted in an attack, but it should be treated as potentially dangerous because of its size and large teeth. Possibly more sluggish than the shortfin mako.

Salmon Shark *(Lamna ditropis)*

This shark gets its common name from a fondness for salmon—and an ability to catch them in swift chases. *Ditropis* means "two-keeled," a reference to a small keel in addition to the strong caudal keels found on all members of this family. (The porbeagle shark, *L. nasus,* also has a second keel.) *Lamna* comes from a Greek word for a man-eating monster that Greek parents threatened to sic on naughty children to make them behave.

Also known as: Bonito.

Maximum known size: 13 feet.

Distribution: Abundant in the waters of the Pacific Northwest, from Alaska to northern California, common off southern California; Central American Pacific coast; Japanese, Taiwanese, and Chinese waters.

Danger to humans: Should be respected because of its size; divers have encountered the salmon shark in California waters without incident.

Porbeagle Shark (*Lamna nasus*)

Originally a British name for this shark, porbeagle is now the preferred common name over mackerel shark. "Porbeagle" seems to have been coined from the *por* of "porpoise" and *beagle*, an old English word for small dog. A fast, sleek shark, it is renowned in the Atlantic as a predator that follows the mackerel on their migrations.

Like the other species in the family Lamnidae, porbeagles are "warm-blooded," in the sense that they can keep their bodies warmer than the surrounding water. This ability gives them the chance to hunt in relatively cold waters as they pursue prey in the North Atlantic. Small groups of porbeagles have been seen herding prey into dense schools and taking turns plunging into the school, mouths agape.

Porbeagles are known to mate in the western North Atlantic during September and October. Pups—typically four, each about two feet long—are born after an eight-month gestation period. U.S. Coast Guardsmen who hooked a porbeagle in the mid-Atlantic reported in 1965 delivering thirty young by cesarean section. The pups died in two days.

Both Norwegians and Canadians operated porbeagle fisheries off Atlantic Canada in the 1960s and again in the early 1990s.

Also known as: Mackerel shark, herring shark, blue shark (in Maine).

Maximum known size: 13 feet.

Distribution: Continental waters of northern Atlantic—on the eastern side from the North Sea to South Africa and on the western side from the Newfoundland Banks to New Jersey, with sightings reported in South Carolina. Also found in the Mediterranean, South Pacific, and southern Indian Ocean.

Danger to humans: Probably not dangerous because it prefers waters that swimmers avoid: 65°F or lower.

Order Carcharhiniformes
Family Scyliorhinidae (cat sharks)

These cat-eyed sharks, about twenty inches long, live on or near the bottom in nearly all seas; they have been found more than 6,500 feet down.

Typically, they hunt on the bottom at night, swimming after or ambushing small fish and crustaceans.

The largest shark family in number of genera and species, it is also among the lesser known. But new information comes in from virtually every exploration of deep-water habitats.

Cat sharks are shy, harmless, and bother people only when they foul fishermen's nets.

The large genus *Apristurus*, commonly known as ghost or demon cat sharks, includes five species whose description is based on a single specimen. They are the longfin cat shark, *A. herklotsi;* the longhead cat shark, *A. longicephalus;* the pale cat shark, *A. sibogae;* the south china cat shark, *A. sinensis;* and the borneo cat shark, *A. verweyi.*

Among the other sharks in this genus are:

Atlantic Ghost Cat Shark *(A. atlanticus)*

Well named because so little is known about it.

Brown Cat Shark *(A. brunneus)*

Named for its chocolate-brown color, the brown cat shark is found from Alaska to southern California. It grows to about three feet and is usually hauled up from very deep water. One was caught in British Columbia's Howe Sound at 1,020 feet. It is colloquially known as the brown shark.

Japanese Cat Shark *(A. japonicus)*

Well known in Japan; abundant in deep waters off Japan.

Smalleye Cat Shark *(A. microps)*

Found off the west coast of Africa; its skin has a fuzzy feel.

Two large genera in this large family—*Atelomycterus* and *Aulohalaelurus*—include beautifully marked cat sharks found around coral reefs in the western Pacific. Some representative species:

Australian Spotted Cat Shark *(Asymbolus analis)*

Lives on the bottom of the sea, has russet spots, and is found off southern Australia.

Australian Marbled Cat Shark (*Atelomycterus macleayi*)

Prefers shallows; one was found twenty inches down in Australian waters.

Draughtsboard Shark (*Cephaloscyllium isabellum*)

A shark with a distinctive checkerboard coloring, the draughtsboard is found in Australian, New Zealand, Japanese, and Taiwanese waters.

Swell Shark (*Cephaloscyllium ventriosum*)

The swell shark's scientific name means "shark with a big head and large stomach." It can inflate its stomach with water and air when disturbed. As the air is released, the noise of air leaving it sounds like the barks of a dog.

The swelling works defensively in two ways: It frightens off a potential predator by its size, or it can so jam itself into a rock crevice that it cannot be dislodged (see color insert).

It is relatively common in southern California inshore waters and is also found along the continental shelf of Mexico and South America and in the waters of Japan and Australia.

Lollipop Cat Shark (*Cephalurus cephalus*)

A shark with a large head and a fanciful name, this cat shark also has a large gill region, a possible adaptation for bottom living.

Mud Cat Shark (*Halaelurus lutarius*)

A member of the "tiger cat shark" genus—so called because many species are striped—-the mud shark gets its common name from its propensity for muddy sea bottoms.

Skaamoong Shark (*Haploblepharus edwardsii*)

Also called "shy eyes" or the shy shark, the skaamoong gets that common name because it curls its tail over its eyes, as if to shield them, when taken from the water. Found off the east coast of Africa.

Salamander Cat Shark (*Parmarurus pilosus*)

One of the filetail cat sharks, so called because of their slim bodies (compared to their large heads), the salamander gets its scientific name *pilosus* ("hairy") because of the appearance of the cluster of denticles on its tail fin. Its common name comes from its long-bodied resemblance to a salamander.

Onefin Cat Shark (Pentanchus profundicolus)

Known from one specimen caught off the Philippines in 1913, the onefin cat shark's single fin gives it a physical, but no taxonomic, resemblance to the frilled shark.

Barbeled Cat Shark (Poroderma marleyi)

A black-spotted cat shark found in deep waters off the east coast of Africa. Some of the other species in the genus are striped.

Narrow-Tail Cat Shark (Schroederichthys maculatus)

Found along the U.S. Gulf Coast and in Caribbean waters, all members of this genus are deep-water cat sharks. Little is known about them.

Chain Cat Shark (Scyliorhinus retifer)

Also known as the chain dogfish (although it is not in the dogfish family), the chain cat shark gets its name because its body is crisscrossed by narrow dark stripes, making it appear that the body is wrapped in chains. (This is in contrast to other *Scyliorhinus* species, which generally are spotted.) *S. retifer*, which grows to about two and a half feet, lives at or near the bottom along the continental shelf from Cape Lookout, North Carolina, to northern New Jersey. Small pebbles have been found in the stomachs of some specimens, leading to speculation that the pebbles are used for ballast.

Like other known members of the Scyliorhinidae family, it is oviparous. Its brownish-amber egg cases are about two inches long.

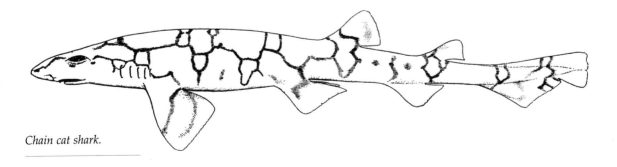

Chain cat shark.

Family Proscylliidae (finbacked cat sharks)

Research into this family has been scant. One species, the harlequin cat shark (*Ctenacis fehlmanni*), is known only from a specimen taken off Somalia in 1973. But one species, the slender smooth hound (*Gollum attenuatus*), has yielded some information about its reproduction.

Cuban Ribbontail Cat Shark *(Eridacnis barbouri)*

Found in deep water between Florida and Cuba, the Cuban ribbontail is about thirteen inches long.

Pygmy Ribbontail Shark *(Eridacnis radcliffei)*

One of the smallest sharks known, the pygmy ribbontail gives birth to pups about four inches long. Females mature at about six inches and its maximum size is about eight inches. It is found off the east coast of Africa, in the Arabian Sea, and in the South Pacific.

Slender Smooth Hound *(Gollum attenuatus)*

The slender smooth hound has a slim body and bell-shaped snout. Reproductive studies were made on about 740 specimens caught with a bottom long-line from a seamount in deep New Zealand waters. In a typical egg capsule with fifty to eighty ova, only one embryo developed. The other ova were probably used as nutrients for the single surviving embryo.

Family Pseudotriakidae (false or keelbacked cat sharks)

This misnamed family has only one genus and one species (though taxonomists in the past have recognized two species, one for the Atlantic and one for the Pacific).

The species is the false cat shark (*Pseudotriakis microdon*), misnamed because the sharks are more like the sharks of Scyliorhinidae than they are of the family Triakidae. So they are not pseudo at all, just in the wrong family.

The first specimen known to science washed ashore at Amagansett, Long Island, on February 8, 1883. At first glance, the ten-foot fish appeared to be a nurse shark. But it had a long, low first dorsal fin that

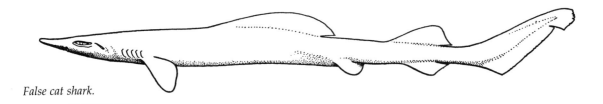

False cat shark.

was about the size of its tail fin, and it did not look like any other shark. It was temporarily dubbed the "small-toothed nurse shark" because it was flat-bodied and had about 400 rows of tiny teeth in its large jaw.

Since 1883, only a small number of them have been found in Atlantic waters; there have been rare finds of a similar shark in Japanese waters.

Most have been caught in deep water. One was taken at a depth of nearly 5,000 feet. Another was photographed at a depth of 2,100 feet off East Africa.

The assumption is that they are rare, deep-water sharks, prowling the depths in a range that includes at least Iceland (where three have been recorded) and the Cape Verde Islands (where one was taken).

Family Leptochariidae (barbeled houndsharks)

The family consists of one genus and one species: *Leptocharias smithii*. About two feet long, it is found in the eastern Atlantic, particularly at the warm waters of river mouths.

Family Triakidae (houndsharks, leopard sharks, and others)

These small (five feet or less) coastal sharks have the typical bodily outline of a shark with the pavement-like teeth of flat, bottom-dwelling sharks. The teeth are used to crush crabs, lobsters, and other crustaceans that form most of their diet.

Some of the most abundant sharks on both the Atlantic and the Pacific coasts of North America are members of this family. Species of this large family are found in shallow waters of all temperate and tropic seas. All species bear their young live and many migrate away from cool water and toward warm, with the seasons.

Included in the family are whiskery sharks, sharks known as topes (a "tope" is an elongated conical snout), houndsharks, soupfin sharks, smooth hound sharks, smooth dogfishes, gummy sharks, and leopard sharks.

93

Whiskery Shark *(Furgaleus macki)*

The whiskery shark gets its name from the appearance of its nasal barbels.

Tope Shark *(Galeorhinus galeus)*

The tope is the largest inshore native shark in British waters, staying mainly in coastal shallows all year. Packs of tope have been seen chasing shoals of small fish and trapping them against a harbor wall, or driving them on to a rocky shore.

Topes mature at about ten years of age and are believed to produce young every two years, with a gestation period of a year. In the summer, females give birth to twenty or more live young that measure up to fifteen inches.

Tagging studies showed that some topes migrated as far as the Azores; one reached the Canary Islands in 268 days. One tagged tope shark lived forty years. Another was observed swimming thirty-six miles in one day.

Once sought extensively for its liver oil (thus the common names oil shark and vitamin shark), the tope is now hunted in some areas as a game fish.

In Australia, it is known as the school shark and, while harmless to humans, is a pest. As Gilbert P. Whitley wrote in *The Fishes of Australia*, "[T]his shark delights to bite the bodies and tails off snapper and other fish as the anglers are hauling them in. Thus the fishermen's only reward is a series of fish heads and the doubtful satisfaction of knowing that they have afforded the sharks a pleasant afternoon's amusement."

Also known as: School shark, oil shark, vitamin shark; in England as toper, penny dog, miller's dog, rig.

Maximum known size: 6½ feet for females; 6 feet for males. (The record all-tackle toper shark, according to the International Game Fish Association, weighed 98 pounds, 8 ounces, and was caught off Santa Monica, California.)

Distribution: Western U.S. coast; Pacific and Atlantic coasts of South America; North Sea and Bay of Biscay; Mediterranean; west and east coasts of Africa; Australian and New Zealand waters.

Blacktip Tope *(Hypogaleus hyugaensis)*

An important food fish in Japan.

Also known as: Zanzibar or lesser soupfins, Japanese tope sharks.

Maximum known size: 4 feet.

Distribution: East coast of Africa; Arabian Sea and Bay of Bengal; Japanese, Taiwanese, and Chinese waters.

Bigeye Houndshark *(Iago garricki)*

A large gill structure indicates that this houndshark has adapted to water that is high in salt and low in oxygen.
Maximum known size: 2 feet; males are two-thirds the size of females and weigh one-sixth as much.
Distribution: Arabian Sea and Bay of Bengal.

Gray Smooth Hound *(Mustelus californicus)*

A common shark in the shallow estuaries of central California during the spring and fall, it grows to about two and a half feet. Surfers often see it finning the surface in the shallows of Moss Landing.

Commercial fishermen often catch and discard these sharks. Around California's Elkhorn Slough Wildlife Reserve, archers habitually have used them as targets, inspiring protests from environmental and surfer organizations.

Smooth Dogfish *(Mustelus canis)*

The smooth dogfish, or smooth hound, is so called because it does not have a spine on its dorsal fin.

Second only to the spiny dogfish (*Squalus acanthias*) in abundance along the southern New England and mid-Atlantic coasts, the smooth dogfish is the bane of fishermen. Someone once calculated that 10,000 smooth dogfish could devour 60,000 lobsters, 200,000 crabs, and 70,000 other fish in a single year.

The migration of the Atlantic smooth dogfish begins in May when they arrive by the thousands at the entrance of Long Island Sound, starting a summer sojourn along the coasts of New Jersey, New York, and southern New England. Between early May and mid-July, their thirteen- to

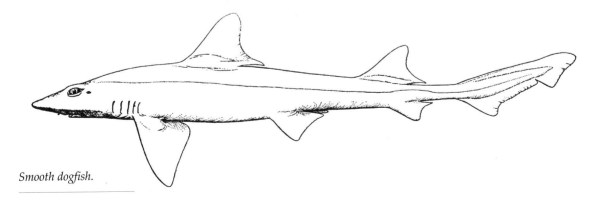

Smooth dogfish.

fourteen-inch young are born. Many are scooped up in nets along the coast of southern New England. The dogfish winter between the southern half of North Carolina and the offing of Chesapeake Bay. A sudden chill in these winter waters can kill a smooth dogfish.

The smooth dogfish's small size and the ease of dissecting it to study its sensory and reproduction systems have made it a popular specimen in zoology and biology classrooms. So large numbers are caught and preserved each year.

The smooth dogfish stays fairly close to shore and is normally found in waters of less than sixty feet. It is aided in its bottom search for lobsters and crabs by its ability to change its color to blend in with the background—to an extent unusual for sharks. Its color ranges from pearl to dark gray.

Smooth dogfish have been known to enter river mouths and swim upstream. They have, for example, been reported in the Calcasieu River of Louisiana, as far inland as Prien Lake.

Also known as: Smooth hound in England, hound in South Africa.

Maximum known size: 5 feet.

Distribution: From Cape Cod, and occasionally the Bay of Fundy, southward to Brazil and Uruguay in the western Atlantic; along the coasts of Great Britain. A similar species (*M. norrisi*) is found in the Florida Keys and off the west coast of southern Florida. Other similar species (*M. mustelus* and *M. asterias*), are known in the Mediterranean and the eastern Atlantic.

Brown Smooth Hound (*Mustelus henlei*)

Similar to the gray smooth hound, the brown version is distinguished by its coloring: darker reddish brown to blackish brown. These smooth hounds live in shallow coastal waters and can be seen foraging just beyond the breakers. It is also common in tidal flats and around oyster beds, where it feeds on crabs, shrimp, and small fishes.

Maximum known size: 3 feet.

Distribution: From northern Oregon to Peru, but rare south of the Gulf of California. Common and sometimes abundant in San Francisco, Tomales, and Humboldt Bays. Estimates in the 1960s made it the most abundant shark in San Francisco Bay and perhaps along the entire California coast. But its populations have dropped off sharply since that time.

Sicklefin Smooth Hound (*Mustelus lunulatus*)

A five-foot, eight-and-a-half-inch sicklefin was recorded in San Diego, which is believed to be the northern limit of its range. To the south it extends as far as Colombia. The sicklefin differs principally from *M. californicus* by having slightly longer pectoral fins.

Leopard Shark *(Triakis semifasciata)*

This is an unmistakable shark with a striking color pattern—dark bars over a golden brown, sometimes tinged with iridescence. It is commonly found near shore, often in large schools. Leopards feed on a wide variety of small fishes and crustaceans.

Females reach maturity at forty inches, males at a slightly smaller size. Gestation lasts approximately one year. There may be as many as forty pups in a litter.

Maximum known size: 83 inches; average size is 59 inches for males, 71 inches for females.

Distribution: From the Oregon coast to the Gulf of California.

Danger to humans: Generally considered harmless, but did make an unprovoked attack in 1955 on a diver in Trinidad Bay, California. The diver was not seriously injured.

Family Hemigaleidae (weasel sharks)

Coastal tropical sharks found in the Eastern Hemisphere. Similar sharks, twice as big, lived in seas throughout the world during the Tertiary period.

Hooktooth Shark *(Chaenogaleus macrostoma)*

Found in shallows and moderately deep waters of the Arabian Sea; Japanese, Taiwanese, and Chinese waters; South Pacific.

Snaggletooth Shark *(Hemipristis elongatus)*

Largest of the weasel sharks, at eight feet the snaggletooth should be considered dangerous. But it has not been implicated in any attacks. It gets its name from long teeth that protrude when its mouth is shut.

A food fish in India, it is found in shallow waters around both coasts of Africa, the Indian Ocean, and along island coasts in the South Pacific.

Family Carcharhinidae (requiem sharks, ground sharks)

This largest of the shark families—some sixty species—is also the most important, even though the arcane demands of taxonomy place it near the bottom of the muster of shark families. Most of the sharks dangerous to humans are in this family, as are many sought by fishermen around the world. Carcharhinidae species are usually found in tropical and warm temperate seas, both along the coast and far at sea.

The sharks of this family are sometimes known as requiem sharks, supposedly because of their reputation for causing death. The funereal name still persists in the French word for shark, *requin*—but it seems likely that this is a case where one word that long ago simply meant "shark" happened to be almost the same as a word that suggested the Latin *requiem*, the Catholic Mass for the dead.

Blacknose Shark *(Carcharhinus acronotus)*

Found in the Caribbean and along the Atlantic coasts of the United States and South America, the blacknose has a dark-tipped snout, dark-tipped fins, and grows to about six feet. It is a suspect in attacks, probably because specimens in captivity have acted aggressively toward shark researchers.

Gray Reef Shark *(Carcharhinus amblyrhyrnchos)*

The most common sharks in tropical Pacific reef waters, gray reef sharks are often suspected of attacks on divers (see insert). One fatal attack has been recorded, as has an assault on a submersible. When they act aggressively, they appear to be defending the territory of the reef. Often a reef shark performs threat postures—humping and twisting its body—before attacking.

Reef sharks have been seen in schools of 20 to 100. Groups often cooperate to ambush schools of small fish, swimming up to them from below.

Females gather together at birthing times after a gestation period of about twelve months. They give birth to four to six pups about two feet long.

Translation of the Latin name: "sharp-nosed shark with blunt snout."
Also known as: Longnose blacktail shark.
Maximum known size: 7 feet.
Distribution: Shallow tropical waters in the South Pacific and Indian Ocean.
Danger to humans: Sometimes extremely aggressive; involved in several attacks on people, at least one fatal; will snatch fish from spearfishing divers.

Spinner Shark *(Carcharhinus brevipinna)*

An aggressive shark that has been blamed for attacks on divers and swimmers, the spinner gets its name from its habit of pursuing schools of prey

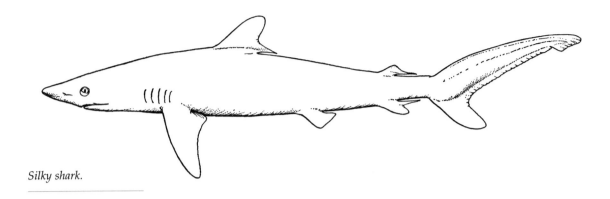

Silky shark.

from beneath the school and then spiraling upward, snapping up prey, and sometimes leaping out of the water.

Also known as: Longnose gray shark, smooth-fanged shark.
Maximum known size: 9 feet.
Distribution: Shallow and deep tropical waters throughout the world.
Danger to humans: Involved in several unprovoked attacks.

Silky Shark *(Carcharhinus falciformis)*

A large, aggressive pelagic shark, the silky shark has unusually smooth skin, which gives it its popular name. The leading edge of its first dorsal fin is curved, giving it another name: sickle shark.

Maximum known size: 8 feet.
Distribution: Tropical and subtropical seas worldwide; Massachusetts to Brazil in the western Atlantic.
Danger to humans: Dangerous or potentially dangerous, although it has not been blamed for any specific attack; it may, like the oceanic whitetip shark, have been involved in attacks of victims of air and sea disasters.

Galapagos Shark *(Carcharhinus galapagensis)*

The Galapagos is a large, dangerous shark found around the Pacific islands. Its body is darkish gray on top with an off-white belly and a black-edged tail (see color insert). It has a large first dorsal fin with a nearly vertical rear edge. It was made a species in 1905 on the basis of specimens found near the Galapagos Islands.

Galapagos sharks frequently swim in schools, feeding in the depth for bottom-dwelling deep-sea fishes, squids, and octopuses. Females give birth to six to sixteen pups, each 22–32 inches long. For a time after birth, the pups live in shallow waters, away from the cannibalistic adults.

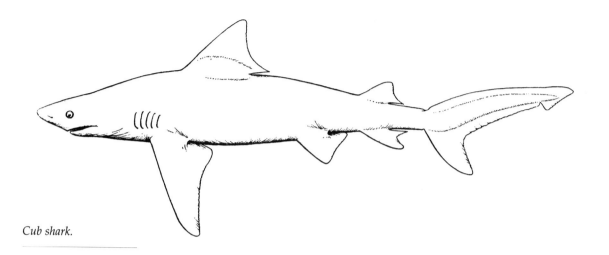

Cub shark.

Also known as: Gray reef whaler.
Maximum known size: 12 feet.
Distribution: Tropical seas around Pacific islands.
Danger to humans: Responsible for at least one fatal attack on a swimmer. Aggressive young sharks often harass divers.

Cub Shark *(Carcharhinus leucas)*

A shark that ascends rivers and lurks in shallows close to shore, the cub shark is extremely dangerous because it favors places that people share. These sharks, which have many local names, have been blamed for several widespread fatal and nonfatal attacks, especially in the tropics and in the River Ganges, where they attack pilgrims and feed on corpses consigned to the sacred waters. (See also Ganges shark, page 107.)

In the United States, the mouth of the Mississippi River is a favored birthing site for cub sharks, which gather there from May through July—brackish waters are frequent nursery sites for cub sharks. They also have been found in the Miraflores Locks of the Panama Canal, where the waters of numerous lakes mingle with the waters of two oceans, and have been taken in Lake Yzabal, Guatemala.

Cub sharks roam shoal waters, loiter around wharves and docks, patrol passages between islands, and explore estuaries. They have been seen far inland in the roadside canals of south-central Florida and are suspects in many reported attacks in Florida.

A slow swimmer that rarely shows itself at the surface, the cub shark scavenges for most of its food, taking practically any offal tossed into the sea. When the innocuously named cub shark does hunt, it is as lethally efficient as any other shark in the Carcharhinidae family.

Cub sharks in Lake Nicaragua were once thought to be a separate species, but research now indicates that cub sharks can reach the lake by ascending the winding, rapids-laced 130-mile San Juan River, which flows into the Caribbean on the eastern coast of Nicaragua. Natives fear the shark of the river as much as the shark of the lake. In the spring of 1944, a single shark attacked three persons near Granada, the lake's principal town. Two died. At least one person a year is reportedly claimed by the sharks. Numerous dogs have been devoured by the sharks, which are locally notorious for their voracious appetites. Cub sharks have also been seen 2,300 miles up the Amazon River.

An African population of *Carcharhinus leucas* is known as the Zambezi shark, which grows to about ten and a half feet and 660 pounds and is able to survive in both salt and fresh water. It has been seen at many places along the Zambezi River, 120 miles and more from the sea. The shark also has a lethal reputation along many other rivers that empty into the southern and eastern shores of Africa. In a six-month period in 1961, the Zambezi shark was blamed for three attacks at the mouth of the Limpopo River. In 1970, a prawn fisherman in water five feet deep, about twelve miles from the sea in Mozambique, was attacked by a shark, which tore off an arm, swam off, returned, and reportedly ripped off the man's head. In Africa, these sharks frequent dirty water, and, as elsewhere in its range, are often found around river mouths and close inshore. Attacks on swimmers, once attributed to the white shark, were actually made by Zambezi sharks.

Also known as: Shovelnose shark, bull shark, ground shark, requiem shark; local names: Nicaragua shark, Ganges shark, Zambezi shark; freshwater whaler, Swan River whaler, river whaler (in Australia).

Maximum known size: 11 feet, 400 pounds.

Distribution: Western Atlantic from southern Brazil to North Carolina and occasionally as far north as New York; abundant in the West Indies and the Gulf of Mexico, particularly off the Texas coast.

Danger to humans: Considered extremely dangerous and blamed in many attacks, including fatal ones, where the shark was not positively identified.

Blacktip Shark (*Carcharhinus limbatus*)

The conspicuously black-tipped fins of this shark are often seen in tropical and subtropical seas. Fishermen have watched groups of blacktip sharks soaring upward in the sea to hit a school of prey from below. Occasionally, a shark will leap into the air, somersault, and fall back into the sea. The antics seem to accompany feeding, which the swift, gregarious sharks turn into a frenzy.

They feed on smaller fishes, such as menhaden in the Atlantic and sardines in the Pacific, and stingrays, whose stingers are found imbedded in the sharks' jaws. Blacktips are often found in the stomachs of larger oceanic sharks such as the tiger shark.

A report on their feeding techniques comes from a diver who dove with other thrill seekers in a commercial "shark feeding tour" off an island in French Polynesia. The divers gathered on the bottom, about sixty feet down, when the tour guide opened a cask of fish and attracted fifteen blacktips. "One at a time the sharks come [and] grab pieces of fish," he noted. "They sink their teeth into the food, and shake their heads violently from side to side to tear off pieces." In their quest for the dead fish, they ignored nearby live fish—and the divers.

Dark gray, dusky bronze, or ashy blue above, the blacktip's trim body is pure white or yellowish white below, with a band of dark upper color extending backward along each side, and the pale color of its lower parts extending forward. Its pectoral fins are black-tipped. The dorsal and anal fins and the lower lobe of the tail fin are black-tipped in the young, but the color usually fades with age. Its eye is catlike: greenish yellow, bisected by a black band.

Also known as: Small black-tipped shark, spotfin shark, gray shark, blackfin.

Maximum known size: 8 feet.

Distribution: Worldwide in tropical and subtropical waters.

Danger to humans: Blamed for at least one nonfatal attack; considered potentially dangerous, especially around spear fishermen carrying fish.

Oceanic Whitetip Shark (Carcharhinus longimanus)

A big, bold, and dangerous shark of the open seas, the whitetip was blamed for attacks on survivors around the waters of torpedoed ships during World War II. An analysis of shark attack says the whitetip "has approached divers in the open ocean and stubbornly persisted in investigating and circling them, showing little fear in response to their defensive actions. Probably one of the more dangerous sharks."

The white-tipped shark's coloring is not always so distinctive as its name implies. Its body is light gray or pale brown to slaty blue above; yellowish or dirty white below. The tips of its dorsal fins are sometimes pure white and sometimes grayish (see color insert).

Males and females may take five years to reach maturity. After a gestation period of unknown duration, the female gives birth to one to five young, each about two feet long.

Also known as: White-tipped shark.

Maximum known size: 13 feet.

Distribution: Warm waters of the Atlantic, Gulf of Mexico, Caribbean, and Indo-Pacific.

Danger to humans: Considered one of the more dangerous sharks.

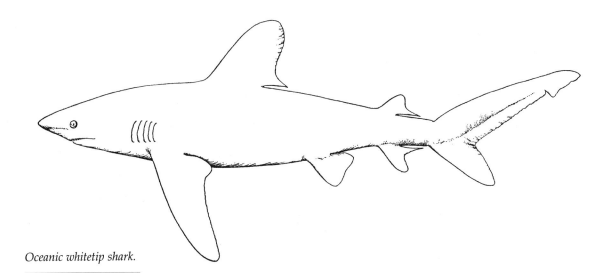

Oceanic whitetip shark.

Blacktip Reef Shark *(Carcharhinus melanopterus)*

Common in shallow waters around coral reefs, the blacktip reef shark is frequently encountered by people diving or even wading. It has been seen wriggling across the seafloor, with fins exposed, in inches of water; and it has been reported occasionally entering river mouths in Malaysia and Madagascar, where it has also been found in brackish lakes.

Females give birth to two to four young after a gestation period of about sixteen months.

Also known as: Black shark, whaler.

Maximum known size: 7 feet.

Distribution: East coast of Africa; Arabian Sea; Japanese, Taiwanese, and Chinese waters; shallow and close coastal waters of the tropical Indo-Pacific. Its Mediterranean range seems to have been extended by sharks that transited the Suez Canal.

Danger to humans: Several known attacks on spear fishermen and on the legs of waders in shallow water on coral reefs—the attacks caused neither major injuries nor deaths and may have been cases of mistaken identity for usual prey.

Dusky Shark *(Carcharhinus obscurus)*

Although often mistaken for other sharks, the dusky has a distinctive coloration: gray or pale gray above and white below, with the lower surfaces of its pelvic fins grayish and sooty toward the tips. The dusky is a powerful shark. The strongest shark bite ever recorded—thirty-two pounds of force—was measured between the jaws of a dusky.

The dusky is often seen around people, making them uneasy when it follows a ship (as it frequently does) or approaches a bathing beach. (It is the species most often found entangled in antishark nets off South African beaches.)

In Australia, the shark is known as the dusky whaler and is a major commercial fish.

Duskies eat many kinds of fish, cephalopods, crustaceans, and smaller sharks.

Mating apparently occurs in the spring and the gestation period is believed to be sixteen months. Birthing takes place in nurseries, which include Chesapeake Bay and areas off Durban, South Africa.

Also known as: Black whaler, bay shark, lazy gray shark, shovelnose shark, dusky ground shark.

Maximum known size: 12 feet.

Distribution: Both sides of the Atlantic—at sea and close to shore—on the western side from southern Massachusetts to southern Florida; on the eastern side from the Mediterranean coast of Spain to South Africa. Also found in the Gulf of Mexico.

Danger to humans: Has a bad reputation but has not been blamed except for a few specific attacks, including one off Natal, South Africa, and another off Bermuda.

Caribbean Reef Shark *(Carcharhinus perezi)*

A shark that grows to about nine and a half feet, the Caribbean reef shark is abundant around coral reefs in Caribbean waters. It is considered dangerous and has been implicated in at least two attacks.

Sandbar Shark *(Carcharhinus plumbeus)*

Sandbar sharks are brownish gray or slate gray above, shading to a pale tint of the same color or whitish below. They are found throughout the world, including the canals of Venice. They are the most abundant sharks in Hawaiian waters.

Great South Bay and other sheltered waters around Long Island have long been nurseries for sandbar sharks. Studies reported in 1996, however, cloud the historic record of sandbar pupping grounds around Great South Bay. In the studies, no sandbar sharks were caught in New York's Great South Bay, Shinnecock Bay, Peconic Bay, or in Barnegat Bay, New Jersey. But many were caught in Great Bay, New Jersey, leading to the new belief that Great Bay is now the northern boundary of sandbar nurseries and pupping grounds.

During birthing times, males leave the nursery areas, heading for deeper waters. The pups—usually eight to twelve in a litter—are born from June to August. At other nurseries in Chesapeake Bay, births take place in September. The pups remain in the nursery waters until cooler weather sets in. They then move offshore. There are also nurseries in shallow seas off Virginia, in numerous shallow waters along the western Atlantic, in the northern waters of the Gulf of Mexico, and in the Gulf of Gabes in the Mediterranean Sea.

The sandbar's common name comes from its habit of appearing as it crosses a sandbar, then disappearing again on the other side. Another name, New York ground shark, establishes it as a shark well known in New York waters. Early in the century, hundreds were seen at a time in Great South Bay, Long Island, between Lindenhurst and Great River. It still is probably the only sizable shark that regularly visits the small bays on the populous north shore of Long Island. Among its prey are smooth dogfish and small bottom fishes.

Carcharhinus plumbeus is the latest name for what once was thought to be several species, each with its own set of common names, Latin names, and ranges. "A most extraordinary snarl has developed over the years in the determination of the scientific name to be applied to the sandbar shark," shark authority Stewart Springer wrote in 1960. After examining several thousand records over a twenty-five-year period, he recommended *plumbeus* as a worldwide species name.

Also known as: Brown shark, ground shark, New York ground shark, northern whaler, Gambuso shark.

Maximum known size: 7½ feet.

Distribution: Worldwide along temperate coasts; in the Pacific, found abundantly around the Hawaiian Islands.

Danger to humans: Considered potentially dangerous because of its abundance, but never implicated in an attack.

Tiger Shark (*Galeocerdo cuvier*)

Even more a threat to swimmers and divers than the white shark, the tiger shark is probably the most dangerous shark in the world. Parts of human bodies have been found in tiger sharks captured off Florida. People in the West Indies regard the tiger as the most dangerous of the many species of sharks in those waters, where it is an important food fish. Australians blame many attacks on tiger sharks. In India, tigers are accused of lethal attacks along both eastern and western coasts.

Tiger sharks also eat each other. U.S. Fish and Wildlife Service workers on a cruise in Philippine waters reported seeing a large female tiger shark eat a smaller one struggling on a hook. Then, still hungry, she immediately

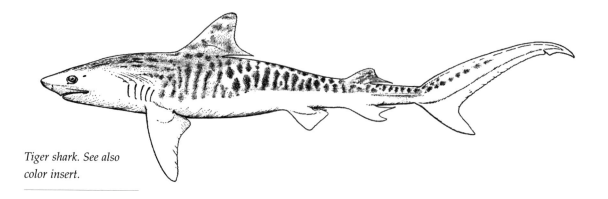

Tiger shark. See also color insert.

grabbed at a baited hook and was captured herself. Tigers caught on this cruise had in their bellies turtles, squid, crabs, sea birds, poisonous sea snakes, other sharks—and an unlucky black cat.

Tigers caught in the Gulf of Mexico off Texas had cormorants and small migratory birds in their stomachs. A fourteen-footer landed at Durban, South Africa, had in its stomach the head and forequarters of a crocodile, the hind leg of a sheep, three seagulls, two (unopened) two-pound cans of green peas, and a cigarette tin. Tiger stomachs have also contained nuts and bolts, coiled wire, lumps of coal, boat cushions, clothing, a tom-tom, and an unopened can of salmon. Objects that cannot be digested remain intact in the stomach for some time and finally are regurgitated.

The omnivorous tiger bites with a rolling motion of its powerful jaws, so that its big, saw-edged teeth chop large prey into several pieces. In this way, a twelve-foot tiger was able to devour another shark ten feet long. Tigers can also bite in half the carapace of a sea turtle. A tiger seen in Australia with a portion of a thresher shark's tail protruding from its jaws was probably in the process of chopping the thresher into bite-size pieces. Another was found with a horse's head in its stomach.

A fourteen-foot tiger shark that died in captivity in Australia had in its stomach two intact dolphinfish (*Coryphaena*), each about four feet long. The shark had been captured about a month before, and during that time had been fed only horseflesh. So it had managed to keep the dolphins preserved for at least a month. Another tiger, a thirteen-footer captured in Australia, had thirty-two fish, averaging fifteen inches in length, packed—and undigested. Dr. Russell J. Coles, describing sharks he caught off Cape Lookout, North Carolina, told of finding in one tiger shark eleven chunks of shark meat, weighing one to five pounds each and representing at least three shark species.

Embryonic tiger sharks are intrauterine cannibals, eating their lesser developed siblings. Brilliantly striped when young, the survivors of cannibalism are born alive and struggle to work their way free of water-filled sacs that contain them. Litters of thirty to fifty embryos are common; eighty-two young were found in one eighteen-footer caught off Cuba.

Tiger sharks seem to hunt mostly at night, coming closer to shore and eating almost anything that floats. The tiger swims slowly, then turns on speed as it approaches prey.

Tigers get their name from their stripes, which fade with age and finally disappear. They are sandy to dark gray on the upper body, off-white below. Some tiger sharks have dark smudges along their sides and black fin tips. A tiger's head is broad, its snout blunt.

Also known as: Whaler shark.

Maximum known size: 21 feet; 30-footer reported in Indochina waters. (The record tiger shark, according to the International Game Fish Association, weighed 1,314 pounds, and was caught in Cape Moreton, Queensland, Australia.)

Distribution: All tropical and subtropical seas; frequently in temperate seas. Tigers are the most common large shark in the tropics, particularly the Caribbean and the Gulf of Mexico. Found along the U.S. Atlantic coast in warm months. The tiger often appears close to shore and sometimes enters river mouths and enclosed sounds.

Danger to humans: Extremely dangerous, implicated in attacks in many areas.

Ganges Shark (Glyphis gangericus)

Pilgrims bathing in the sacred waters of the River Ganges frequently are attacked by sharks. In a single year, twenty people were attacked and only ten survived. But no one can say how many people were victims of bull sharks and how many were struck down by Ganges sharks. Numerous bodies, cast into the rivers for burial in sanctified waters, are devoured by sharks.

Maximum known size: 7 feet.

Distribution: Arabian Sea and Bay of Bengal.

Danger to humans: Extremely dangerous.

Speartooth Shark (Glyphis glyphis)

Smaller than the Ganges shark, the speartooth has been taken off Papua, New Guinea, and Queensland, Australia, and has been reported up rivers. But the extent of its range is not known.

Borneo River Shark *(Glyphis sp.?)*

Once thought to be extinct, this extremely rare shark was rediscovered in 1997 in the Kinabatangan River of Sabah, in Northern Borneo, Malaysia.

Until this rediscovery, the only specimens were sharks found in the nineteenth century and preserved in museum collections under the name Borneo River shark, classified as *Glyphis*, with species unknown.

The quest for the Borneo River shark was conducted by volunteers working with the Shark Specialist Group of the World Conservation Union, with assistance from the World Wildlife Fund. Dr. Leonard V. Compagno, a member of the group and head of the Shark Research Center at South African Museum, gave a cautious assessment: "We have very little idea of the geographic distribution of these sharks, much less their general biology. They show up like ghosts, few and far between, in a handful of scattered localities. . . . I'd hesitate to place the Kinabatangan shark to species without examining it, but whether it is the Borneo River shark or another species of *Glyphis*, this is a remarkable discovery."

Lemon Shark *(Negaprion brevirostris)*

This shark is sometimes confused with the cub shark, but the lemon shark's coloring is a distinguishing difference: Its underside is yellowish and the source of its name. Its snout is very short and its second dorsal fin is almost as large as the first. It is frequently seen near shore.

Lemon sharks, favored by researchers and aquarium operators, do well in captivity, especially since, unlike many pelagic sharks, they do not need to swim to breathe. They are the only large, pelagic sharks whose mating has been observed. They mate side by side, united in such a way and swimming so perfectly synchronized that, as Dr. Eugenie Clark wrote, "they gave the appearance of a single individual, a two-headed monster." They mature late and do not seem to mate until they are twelve years or older. Some authorities believe that they may be as old as twenty before they mate.

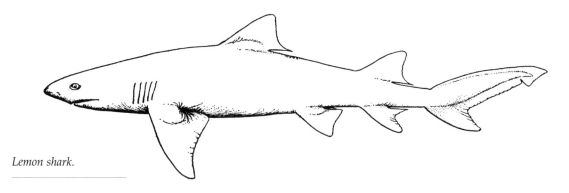

Lemon shark.

Intelligence experiments performed on lemon sharks showed that they could be taught to press their snouts against targets to get food. In food-intake studies, the average shark ate about three percent of its body weight each day.

In the wild, young lemon sharks eat worms, crabs, shrimp, and small fish. As they grow older, their diet changes to include larger fish, lobsters, stingrays, and seabirds.

Photographs of the birth of lemon sharks show ten to twelve pups emerging tail-first, tugging at the umbilical cord until it snaps, and then swimming off. They may stay in their birth area for four years.

Maximum known size: 11 feet, but usually 6 to 8 feet, with the female slightly larger.

Distribution: Tropical coasts of the Western Hemisphere; the eastern Atlantic coast from New Jersey to Brazil, sometimes entering rivers—common along the southeast coast of the United States, in the Florida Keys, and up the west coast of Florida to Tampa and Pensacola.

Danger to humans: Suspected of nonfatal attacks in Florida waters.

Blue Shark *(Prionace glauca)*

The strikingly beautiful blue shark holds the record for longest distance traveled: 3,716 miles across the Atlantic, averaging nearly forty-four miles a day. Another blue, tagged off New York City, was found 3,740 miles off the coast of Brazil, establishing for the first time that blue sharks in the Western Atlantic cross the equator.

The world's most abundant oceanic shark, the blue is a migrant in both the Atlantic and Pacific, but little is known about its migrations. Research based on blue shark tagging has indicated that they travel with the seasons as water cools. They also appear to have mating grounds in several areas, including the north Pacific and off Portugal.

Blue shark. See also color insert.

Migration undoubtedly is tied to the reproductive cycle. Nearly all the blue sharks that sports fishermen catch in the spring off Cornwall, England, for example, are gravid females about to drop their pups. On the western side of the North Atlantic blue sharks at that time are almost invariably males. Separation of the sexes at calving time has been noted among many species of sharks. The most likely explanation is to prevent males from eating the females at the vulnerable time of birthing and to protect the pups from being eaten.

Mating, which has not been observed, apparently is rough. Females have skin that is twice as thick as a male's—thicker than his teeth are long. What appear to be scars of bites have been found on females but not on males. Mating occurs in late spring or early winter. Blue sharks usually mature around the age of five. When they first mate, the female stores the sperm in oviducts until the following spring. Fertilization then occurs and the female's first pups are born when she is seven years old.

Like most oceanic sharks, blues give birth to live young. After a gestation period of nine months to a year, a blue gives birth to as many as 135 young. A blue less than ten feet long can give birth to 50 young, each about one foot in length.

A medical doctor who was also a fisherman once reported on the posthumous birth of pups to what was apparently a blue. As the shark died,

> the tail of the first baby shark presented itself. This was rapidly followed by a further four babies and two spherical bright yellow objects which were enclosed in loose folds of membrane and which were taken to be placentae. . . . Each of the first five baby sharks born was alive and made swimming movements in the fluid which was escaping from the mother and which had changed in appearance and become far less viscous and clear. Palpation of the abdomen suggested that there were more to come and, by exerting slight pressure, a further six or seven babies were born. It was noticed with interest that each one arrived tail first. During the course of a few minutes the remainder of the babies—there were 22 in all—were born, and at no time was any movement of the mother noted, nor was there any contraction of the abdominal muscles or waves of uterine contraction, such as seen in a human.

By the time the ship reached shore, all the newborn sharks were dead. A dead shark emerged while the 100-pound mother was being weighed, and a postmortem examination revealed two more dead pups.

An important food fish in many places, the blue shark is also caught frequently on long-lines and drift nets set for tuna, swordfish, and other commercial fish. An estimated 6.2 to 6.5 million blue sharks are caught each year. Most are killed and thrown back into the sea or used for fish meal.

Blues were particular villains to whalers. Marine scientists John Treadwell Nichols and Robert Cushman Murphy gave a vivid description of blue sharks seen during a 1916 whaling expedition: "Whenever a whale was killed, the sharks would uncannily begin to congregate, like hyenas round a dead lion, assembling so rapidly that the sea would be fairly alive with them. . . . When the water for an acre around the ship was stained a ghastly yellow from outpouring blood, the scrambling sharks would make the sea a living mass as each fish tried to bury its teeth into the exposed surfaces of dark red muscle."

Sailors used to claim that a blue will appear astern of a ship when a man aboard died. Nichols and Murphy wrote that when a seaman died aboard the whaler, two or three blues did appear, along with another species of shark. But, the scientists reported, "the sharks paid no attention when the dead man was consigned to the waters, and they followed uninterruptedly in our wake for several days."

Blues eat great quantities of squid and bluefish. They can digest nearly three pounds of fish a day.

Along the North American Pacific coast, from British Columbia to the Gulf of California, blue sharks are found both on the high seas and in waters close to shore. They are easily spotted, for they often swim with both their dorsals and their tail fins exposed. The blue shark's big, sickle-shaped pectoral fin is as long as its head. The electric blue gleams just beneath the surface as a curious shark circles a boat or a diver. The color shades to dark indigo, then to snow white on the underside.

Also known as: Great blue, blue pointer (Australia).

Maximum known size: 13 feet.

Distribution: Worldwide in tropical and temperate seas.

Danger to humans: Usually seems merely inquisitive and shy, circling around divers and swimmers, but it has attacked people; also blamed for feeding frenzies on survivors of World War II ship sinkings.

Milk Shark *(Rhizoprionodon acutus)*

In India, the flesh of this shark is eaten by nursing mothers to improve their milk flow.

Found in shallows and offshore both coasts of Africa, the Arabian Sea and Bay of Bengal, and throughout the Pacific.

Caribbean Sharpnose Shark *(Rhizoprionodon porosus)*

A shark about three and a half feet long that is abundant in the Caribbean and along both coasts of South America, this sharpnose is caught as a food fish in inshore areas of its range.

Australian Sharpnose Shark *(Rhizoprionodon taylori)*

Although common in Australian waters, this sharpnose has been the subject of little research. But a recent study, which examined sharks off Townsville in northern Queensland, provided a large amount of new information.

Mating occurred in midsummer. After fertilization, the embryos entered a seven-month state known as diapause, during which little or no development took place. The young were born shortly before the mating season, after an eleven-and-a-half-month gestation period. The litters ranged from one to ten young, about nine inches long.

The Queensland sharks were found to be eating mostly small fish, prawns, crabs, and squid.

Maximum known size: Males 2¼ feet, females 30 inches.
Distribution: Australian waters.

Atlantic Sharpnose Shark *(Rhizoprionodon terraenovae)*

Found in the Caribbean and the Bay of Fundy to Yucatán, the Atlantic sharpnose reaches about three and a half feet in length. It has been found in the Pascagoula River in Mississippi, but it normally lives in coastal waters, as does the Pacific coast sharpnose *(Rhizoprionodon longurio)*.

Whitetip Reef Shark *(Triaenodon obesus)*

A relatively listless shark—often seen lying motionless in caves and crevices in coral reefs, rousing itself only to grab an octopus—the whitetip reef shark is more active as a night hunter. Small fish are also in its diet. Perhaps its propensity for grabbing octopuses is the basis for its habit of stealing dead fish from spearfishers.

Maximum known size: 5 feet.
Distribution: Indian Ocean, Red and Arabian Seas, Australian waters, and around Pacific island groups.
Danger to humans: Occasionally attacks divers, especially spearfishers, but not considered dangerous because of its timidity and small teeth.

Family Sphymidae (hammerheads)

No sharks are more easily identified than the aptly named hammerheads (*sphyrna* means "hammer"). They live in all temperate and tropical seas, from close to shore to deeper water. The head, or cephalofoil, may serve as a bowplane for greater maneuverability. With the shark's eyes at the ends of the hammer and a set of enlarged nostrils, the shark theoretically spreads the two senses, probably expanding the amount of information pouring into the predator's brain (see color insert).

Another theory about the purpose of the elongated head suggests that it increases the hammerhead's electroreception. Marine biologist A. Peter Klimley of the University of California at Davis, studying hammerheads around a deep-sea mountain off the Baja Peninsula, found that the mountain, Espíritu Santo, is surrounded by a strong electromagnetic field. He believes that the hammerheads use Espíritu Santo for navigation. Hammerheads are often seen swimming along and moving their heads from side to side, as if using it like a metal detector in the hands of a beachcomber. Hammerheads have a specially developed muscle that allows precise up and down movements of the head.

Experiments by Dr. Stephen M. Kajiura on young scalloped hammerheads showed that the sharks had an extraordinary ability to locate a buried dipole whose current simulates the current that would be produced by buried prey. Sharks rapidly found the hidden dipole and even bit it repeatedly before losing interest. But it is still unknown whether hammerheads have better electroreception than other species do.

Large species—the scalloped hammerhead, the great hammerhead, and smooth hammerhead—have been blamed for fatal and nonfatal attacks. But divers have frequently seen scalloped and great hammerheads and labeled them unaggressive.

The species, differentiated by size and varying head shapes, are sometimes difficult to identify. In all species, young are born alive; their heads are so flexible at birth the lobes fold against the body to ease their passage into the world. Litters of thirty or forty are common.

Winghead Shark *(Eusphyra blochii)*

The widest-headed hammerhead, the winghead may have a body only twice as long as the head is broad. This shark, which grows to about five feet, is found in the Arabian Sea and Bay of Bengal, the Red Sea and Persian Gulf, and the coasts of northwestern Australia and islands throughout the tropical Pacific.

Scalloped Bonnethead *(Sphyrna corona)*

At a maximum size of five feet, this is the smallest hammerhead. Its rounded head is more mallet-shaped than hammer-shaped. Bonnetheads often form schools numbering in the thousands.

Studies of captive bonnetheads by Dr. Arthur Myrberg and Dr. Samuel Gruber of the University of Miami showed that the ten sharks under study formed a hierarchy based on size and sex.

One of the most abundant species of shark along the U.S. Gulf Coast, the bonnethead sometimes appears near wharves.

Also known as: Shovelhead, shovel-nosed shark, bonnetnose.

Maximum known size: 5 feet.

Distribution: Southern Brazil to the southern shores of North Carolina, with occasional strays to New England; along the Pacific coast, from southern California to Ecuador; also the Gulf of Mexico.

Scalloped Hammerhead (*Sphyrna lewini*)

Several research scientists have learned about scalloped hammerheads by swimming with them in the Gulf of California. The scientists discovered that the hammerheads often formed large schools, consisting mostly of females, with the larger sharks along the outside ranks. Odd behavior by individuals—such as suddenly swimming in circles or shaking their great

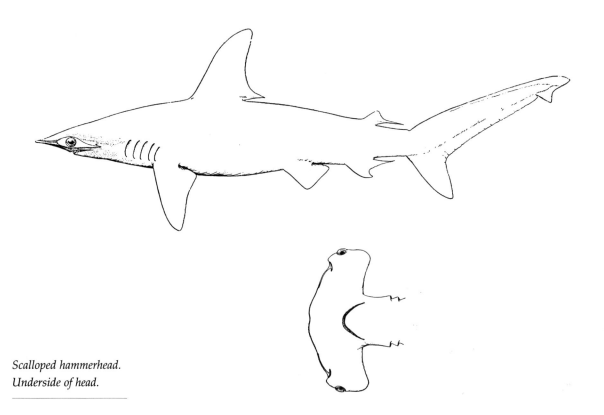

Scalloped hammerhead.
Underside of head.

heads for no apparent reason—seemed to have to do with courtship and perhaps aggression.

That aggression, however, does not seem to be directed toward swimmers and divers. Any attack blamed on the scalloped hammerhead is probably a case of mistaken identity.

In an experiment conducted by the Hawaii Institute of Marine Biology, juvenile scalloped hammerheads, which are usually light tan in color, were found to be sunbathers. Experimenters believed that the sharks chose waters where ultraviolet rays were high, increasing the melanin content in their skin. They had distinct "tan lines" from their exposure to sunny waters. As pups, they had used murky waters as a refuge from predatory adults. As adults, they would spend more time in clear, sunlit waters. The researchers speculated that the darkening of their skin through suntanning might aid them when they became adult predators themselves.

Also known as: Bronze hammerhead, kidney-headed shark.

Maximum known size: 13½ feet.

Distribution: Tropical and warm temperate waters worldwide, close to shore and far at sea.

Danger to humans: Not aggressive, according to divers able to identify it, though potentially dangerous because of its size.

Great Hammerhead *(Sphyrna mokarran)*

Of all the hammerheads, this large and aggressive shark is probably the guilty species involved in attacks blamed on hammerheads.

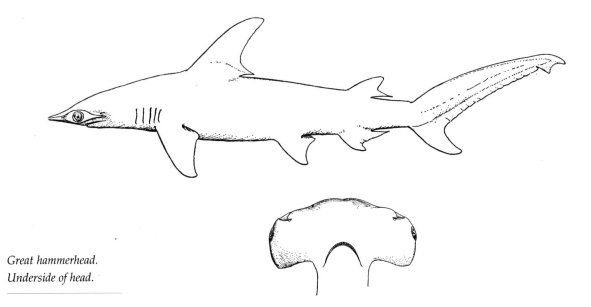

Great hammerhead. Underside of head.

The hammerheads' reputation as killers traces back to a day in 1805 when three sharks, identified only as hammerheads, were landed in one net at Riverhead, Long Island. In the largest hammerhead was a man's body and a tattered striped cotton shirt.

Since then there have been repeated claims that hammerheads were responsible for attacks on swimmers and divers in the Virgin Islands, Florida, Australia, and Guyana. Although the attacking species is rarely named, suspicion inevitably falls upon *Sphyrna mokarran* because of its great size—up to nearly twenty feet.

Its eating habits have added to its ferocious reputation. Off Cape Lookout, North Carolina, Russell J. Coles once caught a thirteen-foot, ten-inch female hammerhead that had "just eaten four of her own species from my net, two of which had been swallowed whole, except the heads. . . ."

These hammerheads eat stingrays—even though the stingers stick into the shark's stomach and jaws. An almost perfect skeleton of a stingray was found in the stomach of a hammerhead (believed to be of this species), and imbedded in the shark's jaws were more than fifty stings. Hammerheads that eat stingrays apparently have developed an immunity to the poison secreted in the ray's sting.

Far at sea, these hammerheads are often seen in large schools.

Also known as: Horned shark (in Africa).

Maximum known size: 20 feet reliably reported; 15 feet more typical.

Distribution: Tropical and warm waters worldwide, inshore, sometimes in very shallow water, and at sea.

Danger to humans: Although not positively identified as an attacker, should be considered extremely dangerous.

Smooth Hammerhead *(Sphyrna zygaena)*

Another suspect in attacks on swimmers, and even boats, the smooth hammerhead is big enough and aggressive enough to have earned that suspicion. A fast, lively shark, it is often seen virtually skimming along the surface, its tail and dorsal fins visible.

In the summer, great schools migrate northward along the Atlantic seaboard. Many linger around Charleston, South Carolina; others continue on to Maryland, New Jersey, and New York waters, sometimes entering New York Harbor. Most of these sharks are small and were probably born shortly before the beginning of the summer migration to warm water. Fishermen find numerous newborn hammerheads—each about thirty inches long—in nets along the outer shore of Long Island in August.

The hammerhead migrants linger in New York waters from July to October, disappearing suddenly when the water temperature falls below 67°F. They then presumably head for warm water, though the rest of their migratory pattern is not known.

Also known as: Black hammerhead, balance fish.

Maximum known size: 13 feet.

Distribution: Except for Atlantic migration, worldwide in tropical and subtropical waters; seen occasionally in the British Isles.

Danger to humans: Should be considered extremely dangerous.

CHAPTER 4

Shark Kin and Companions

Skates and rays have bodies resembling sharks, reproduce like sharks, and, by living in virtually all the seas of the world, equal the cosmopolitan range of sharks. Batoids, as skates and rays are collectively known, live everywhere in the sea inhabited by sharks, from shallows along the coasts to great depths far from shore.

Batoids are in fact enough like sharks to be used as biological stand-ins for sharks by researchers. The batoid stand-in role was first discovered by researchers at the Mote Marine Laboratory in Florida. They had long used sharks as research subjects, but, as a laboratory report noted, scientists who want to experiment with sharks must capture them and then use them for research without knowing what they have been exposed to, what they have eaten, how old they were, or even their general health. Shark biologists in research facilities throughout the world often have tried to breed sharks in captivity, hoping to produce a controlled population analogous to laboratory rats. All attempts ended in failure.

Then, in 1981, Mote Marine scientists found the answer: the clearnose skate (*Raja eglanteria*), one of the most common skate species found along Florida's west coast. The scientists worked successfully to maintain clearnose skates in an artificial environment without impeding the skates' natural breeding instincts. As a result, researchers obtained considerable information about the reproduction of the skate. And, because skates are so like sharks, this information could be extrapolated for studies of shark reproduction.

After mating with a laboratory male, a female skate was found to be able to store sperm and fertilize eggs continually throughout the three- to four-month egg-laying season. An egg-bearing female, the laboratory reported, will lay a pair of eggs every three to five days and may produce between thirty and forty pairs of fertilized eggs throughout the season.

Each fertilized egg is protected by an egg case, commonly known as a "mermaid's purse." Encapsulated in the tough black case is a yolk that resembles a hen's egg yolk. And, like a chick developing in a hen's egg, a skate embryo gets nourishment from the yolk and develops into a miniature skate. Embryonic development takes about twelve weeks. When the skate hatches, it is a perfect replica of an adult, but only about six inches long and four and a half inches wide.

Skates begin their laboratory careers as embryos. Researchers follow the development of systems and organs or, according to a Mote report, use chemicals to "assess altered development." Other studies cover growth and reproduction.

Skates in general are bottom dwellers, feeding on crabs, shrimps, lobsters, and other small crustaceans, as well as polychaete worms, bivalve mollusks, and small fish. Skates have little commercial value to U.S. and Canadian fishermen, but skate is a popular dish elsewhere, particularly in France.

Classification of Skates, Rays, and Others

In the scientific classification of selachians, the panorama of shark orders and families ends with order Pristiformes, family Pristidae, the saw sharks—saw-nosed sharks whose flattened bodies would seem to place them among the skates and rays. Similarly, the flat angel sharks of the order Squatiniformes, family Squatinidae are sometimes lumped among the rays because angel sharks have lateral gill slits, which continue under their pectoral fins. Rays have gill slits only on their undersides. (Saw sharks and angel sharks are described in chapter 3.)

Skates and rays are evolved shark forms that enable these selachians to feed easily along the sea floor. In the course of evolution, the cylindrical body of the shark became flattened, the pectoral fins became greatly enlarged, and their basal attachments gradually widened until they became united to the sides of the head.

The evolutionary process is reflected in the embryonic development of skates and rays. The embryo goes through a number of sharklike stages until it concludes its gestation as a disk-shaped form.

Batoids range in size from little skates less than a foot long to giant rays whose winglike disks span more than twenty feet. Many batoids are wider than they are long. Their flattened bodies have a long pedigree: Cartilaginous fish arose in the late Silurian period, but the earliest batoid fossils date to the Jurassic period, and the ancestral flattened body form appears little changed in modern species.

There are more batoid species than shark species. Counts of batoid species range from 494 to 572, compared to the 390 shark species currently recognized by science. There are also 30–50 other hard-to-classify species—guitarfish and sawfish, chimaeras, ratfish, and elephant fish—with physiological ties to selachians.

Taxonomists have differed for decades on the most rational way to classify skates, rays, and other selachians that are not sharks. The most widely accepted system in current use was developed in 1996 by Joseph J. Cech, Jr., and Peter B. Moyle of the University of California at Davis:

Order Pristiformes
    Family Pristidae (sawfishes)

Order Torpediniformes
    Family Torpedinidae (electric rays)
    Family Narcinidae (electric rays)
    Family Potamotrygonidae (river stingrays)

Order Rajiformes (skates and rays)
    Family Rhinobatidae (guitarfishes)
    Family Platyrhinidae (thornbacks)
    Family Rajidae (skates)
    Family Anacanthobatidae (smooth skates)

Order Myliobatiformes
    Family Dasyatidae (stingrays)
    Family Gymnuridae (butterfly rays)
    Family Myliobatidae (eagle rays and cow-nosed rays)
    Family Urolophidae (round stingrays)
    Family Potamotrygonidae (river stingrays)
    Family Mobulidae (manta rays and devil rays)
    Family Hexatrygonidae (six-gill stingrays)
    Family Plesiobatidae (deepwater stingrays)

The classification gives a hint of the vastness and variety of the non-shark selachians. The new addition of the Hexatrygonidae family was based on the finding off South Africa of one previously unrecorded deep-water stingray, which in 1981 was given the name *Hexatrygon bickelli.* From that single specimen a separate family was created. A second possible candidate for the *Hexatrygon* genus was reported from the Indian Ocean in 1995. The Plesiobatidae family is similarly tiny, consisting of a single genus, *Plesiobatis.*

The sequence of species accounts in this chapter does not follow the classification list. Rather, the accounts begin with skates, which are widespread, and provide an introduction to these flat-bodied, cartilaginous fishes that are related to sharks without actually being sharks. In another departure from scientific classification, descriptions of guitarfishes, sawfishes, and electric rays follow accounts about skates and rays. This is done so that readers meet all the skates and rays before reading about the odder forms. Skates usually live in temperate waters, stingrays in tropical and warmer waters. Sawfish, of course, are often mixed up with saw sharks. They are two distinct types, each placed in its own classification niche— saw sharks among the sharks, sawfish among the rays—but they share the same odd organ: a saw-toothed snout.

Guitarfishes and sawfishes are often called "links," an overly simple label that portrays them as creatures that somehow tie the sharks to the skates and rays. But the scientific classification actually looks upon them as part of the continuum of the selachians, primarily because all of them have the same basic characteristic: a cartilaginous skeleton, distinguishing them from all fish species with bones.

Family Rajidae (skates)

Skates resemble rays at first glance, but their tails are lobed and fleshier and heavier than in rays and do not have poison stingers. Few skates grow to large size. They have fleshy, moveable fins, usually attached to the anterior margin of each pelvic fin, on which they can "walk" across the bottom (see color insert).

Skates' egg cases, which range in size from about seven and a half inches long and five and a half wide to about two and a half by one inch, are found on beaches throughout the world. American beachcombers know them as "mermaids' purses."

Dried skates, cut and twisted into weird shapes by sailors and merchants, have long been sold as miniature sea monsters. The curios, peddled as monkey fish, dragons, basilisks, mermaids, or sea eagles, were sometimes called "Jenny Hanivers" by seafarers.

Naturally malformed skates, whose pectoral fins failed to fuse with their heads while they were embryos, have fooled even ichthyologists. These mistakes of nature were sometimes hailed as strange new species.

Skates mate venter-to-venter (lowerside-to-lowerside), and mating pairs are sometimes caught by fishermen on hook and line. Observations

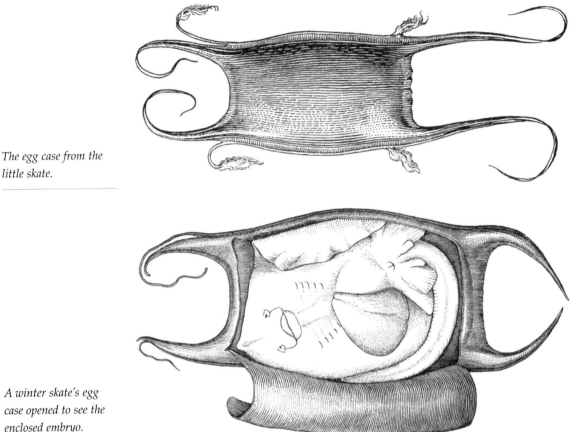

The egg case from the little skate.

A winter skate's egg case opened to see the enclosed embryo.

of mating include reports on a large skate found in European waters, *Raja batis*. Males and females of that species hold their disks flat while mating. The female of the smaller *Raja asterias*, according to a report by Henry B. Bigelow and William C. Schroeder, "curves her pectorals ventrally, while the male, rolling the outer corners of his pectorals out of the way ventrally, then bends the fins inward around her back, which brings his alar spines [claw-like retractile spines on the dorsal side of the outer part of each pectoral] in position to fasten to her. At least for some of the larger species it is reported that only one clasper is introduced into the cloaca of the female at a time, but for other species it is said that both are introduced simultaneously."

Skates are oviparous, and their oblong egg capsules are essentially the same as the oviparous sharks' capsules. But, instead of tendrils, the skate's capsules have stiff, pointed horns projecting from all four corners. The capsules are generally coated on one side with a sticky substance. Small pieces of shells, stones, or seaweed adhere to it and help to keep it

This is an old, old Jenny, which appeared in Gerner's Icones Animalium, *published in 1560. The skate's head has been bent forward and its "wings" trimmed. (From an old print)*

on the bottom. Sometimes, too, the horns imbed themselves in the muddy or sandy bottom.

Embryos incubate in the capsule for about six to twelve months. Either by osmosis or by tiny perforations in the capsule, sea water enters and leaves, bathing the embryo with oxygen and carrying off carbon dioxide. The embryo feeds on albumen in the egg case and probably some nutrients carried in by the sea. In some species, a plug of albumen seals the slits in the shell. After a while, the albumen is absorbed, thus unsealing the slits. In other species, a delicate membrane temporarily seals the slits. When the slits (located in the horns of the skate's capsules) open, a current of water flows freely through the capsule. When its incubation is completed, the skate slips out and begins its free life in the sea.

Skates swim by undulating their pectoral fins in a graceful movement that more resembles flying than swimming. Skates spend much of their time half buried in the sand or mud, awaiting prey. Since its mouth is on the bottom of its body, the skate appears not to be able to catch moving prey by dashing forward; it swims over its victim, then suddenly drops down upon it and devours it. The skate's usual diet includes crabs, shrimps, lobsters, clams, and smaller shellfish.

Many skates, including some that are common on the U.S. Atlantic, Gulf, and Pacific coasts, have electric organs in their tails. The output of these organs is feeble and their value to skates is not known.

Skates are found in the warm, temperate, and boreal latitudes that gird the earth. They are particularly abundant from southern New England to New Jersey. Skates are not known to undertake large-scale migrations, but they do move inshore and offshore in response to seasonal changes in water temperature, generally offshore in summer and early autumn and vice versa during the winter–spring period, according to studies by the Northeast Fisheries Science Center (NFSC).

Old fisheries records show daily catches of enormous size. One boat off New Jersey claimed 10,000 pounds of skates in one net haul. They are also abundant in California waters. Skates are sometimes sold in fish markets as "Rajafish," but they are also frequently caught as by-catch and discarded.

Landings of skates off the northeast United States were 8,100 metric tons in 1993, a 34 percent decrease from the 12,300 metric tons landed in

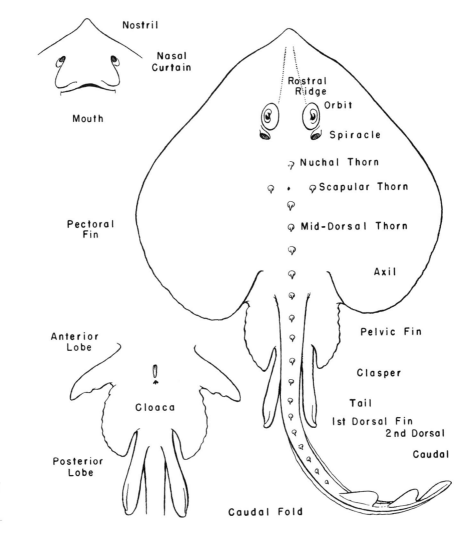

Nostril

Nasal
Curtain

Mouth

Rostral
Ridge

Orbit

Spiracle

Nuchal Thorn

Scapular Thorn

Mid-Dorsal Thorn

Pectoral
Fin

Axil

Anterior
Lobe

Pelvic Fin

Clasper

Tail
1st Dorsal Fin
2nd Dorsal

Cloaca

Caudal

Posterior
Lobe

Caudal Fold

Terminology of a typical skate.

1992. The largest haul of skate, 9,500 metric tons, was recorded in 1969, when a swift decline began. Landings bottomed out at 500 metric tons in 1981. But, largely due to the demand for lobster bait and for the "skate wings" export market, landings have increased again, threatening skate populations. Winter and thorny skates have been the principal targets of skate wing fishermen, who seek little skates for bait customers.

Barndoor skates, caught in nets and discarded over the years, have been rapidly disappearing. Some scientists fear that the barndoor, one of the largest marine rays, is nearing extinction. Canadian scientists in 1998 reported that one population, off southern Newfoundland, dropped from 600,000 in the 1950s to about 500 in the 1970s—to "basically nothing" in the 1990s.

"Recent increases in skate landings and the potential for rapidly expanding export markets bring into question the level at which sustainable fisheries for these species can be maintained," said a NFSC report posted in 1998. "Skates have a limited reproductive capacity, and stock size could be quickly reduced through intensive exploitation. In areas of the world where skates are more fully utilized, their numbers have been reduced to extremely low levels (e.g., in the Irish Sea). Similarly, particularly vulnerable species in the Northwest Atlantic (e.g., barndoor skate) appear to show signs of recruitment overfishing. The abundance of winter skate has declined in recent years on Georges Bank."

Anglers who reel in skates are frequently surprised—and disappointed—at what they have caught. For the skate has the habit of depressing the outer edge of its body when hooked, thus forming a kind of vacuum cup on the bottom. Anglers have to use so much effort to dislodge the stubborn skates that they think they have a heavier fish than the lightweight they finally land.

Although there is no evidence that any skates live permanently in fresh water, strays have been caught in river water far enough from the sea to be called fresh.

Skates, generally found in shallow water and in depths of less than 100 fathoms, also dwell in the great depths. At least seven species have been recorded below a depth of 6,560 feet.

Seven skate species live along the North Atlantic coast of the United States:

1. Brier (clearnose) skate (*R. eglanteria*)

2. Little skate (*Raja erinacea*)

3. Leopard skate (*R. garmani*)

4. Barndoor skate (*R. laevis*)

5. Winter skate (*R. ocellata*)

6. Thorny skate (*R. radiata*)

7. Smooth-tailed skate (*R. senta*).

For skates of West Coast, see CALIFORNIA SKATE (*R. inornata*).

Clearnose Skate *(Raja eglanteria)*

One of the most abundant skates along the Atlantic coast from New Jersey to Florida, the clearnose is frequently caught close to shore, where it is believed to breed. Sometimes called the brier skate because of a row of thorns that runs down the middle of its back, it appears in April between Chesapeake and the Delaware Bays. It is common around New York and

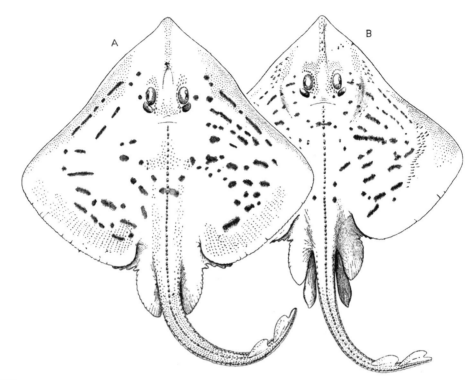

Clearnose skates:
A—female; B—male.

New Jersey from mid-May to October. From July until September, it is usually off southern Massachusetts, where it sometimes is called the summer skate. In cold weather, it retreats as far south as Florida.

Its egg cases are two to three and a half inches long (not including horns), and one and a half to two and a fourth inches wide.

Also known as: Brier skate, summer skate.
Maximum known size: 3 feet.
Distribution: Western Atlantic from New England to Florida.

Little Skate (*Raja erinacea*)

A common skate along the Atlantic coast, the little skate is often used as bait in eel and lobster traps, was once so plentiful that a trawler once reported hauling in an average of 98.8 pounds of little skates per hour in Long Island Sound. Still relatively plentiful, the little skate is one of several Atlantic species that are caught and discarded by commercial fisheries.

Its tail and the midridge of its back are thorny. Its upper surface is grayish or dark brown, usually with small, darker spots; its lower surface is white or pale gray.

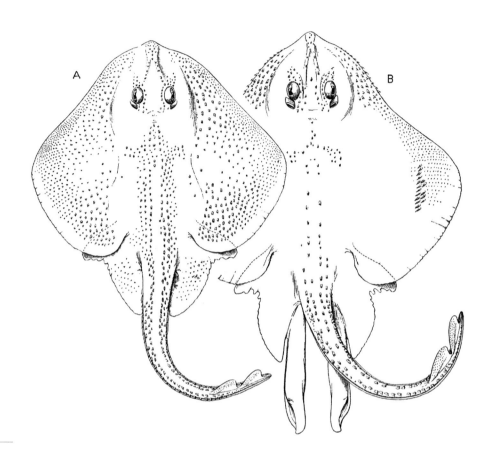

Little skates:
A—female; B—male.

These skates mate year round. The egg case is black, about two inches long (not including horns) and about one to one and a half inches wide. Incubation is six to nine months.

Also known as: Hedgehog skate, common skate, tobacco box skate.
Maximum known size: 21 inches.
Distribution: Close to shore along the western Atlantic, from North Carolina to Nova Scotia and on the southern side of the Gulf of St. Lawrence. The center of distribution is Georges Bank and southern New England.

Barndoor Skate *(Raja laevis)*

This big skate is one of the few skates known to attack fish, including spiny dogfish, herring, and cod.

The barndoor's yellowish or greenish brown egg case is about five inches long and about two and a half inches wide. Juveniles do not reach sexual maturity until they are at least twelve years old.

It is a close relative of the common skate (*Raja batis*) of the eastern Atlantic. The largest common skate recorded in Great Britain was seven feet across.

The barndoor has all but vanished from its North Atlantic waters. "It's as though the bald eagle disappeared and no one noticed," says Ransom A. Myers, a Canadian scientist studying the disappearance of the barndoor. "This shows how remarkably little we know about the oceans." The drastic drop, Myers believes, is due to the inadvertent trapping of the big ray in commercial fishermen's nets. Also contributing to the vanishing of the barndoor is its own low reproduction rate, a characteristic common to many sharks, skates, and rays.

Also known as: Sharpnose skate.

Maximum known size: 5 to 6 feet.

Distribution: Continental shelf of the North Atlantic, from the Grand Banks of Newfoundland to North Carolina; commonly found in the Gulf of Maine.

Winter Skate (*Raja ocellata*)

This skate gets its scientific species name from the eyelike spots scattered about the upper surface of its body.

An inhabitant of relatively cool water and sandy or gravelly bottoms, the winter skate tends to disappear from shallow water along southern

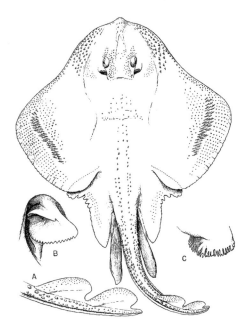

Winter skate.
A—close-up of tail;
B—nostril;
C—nasal curtain.

New England in the early summer, and then reappears there and in New York waters in early autumn. This habit gives it its common name: winter skate.

The greenish brown or brownish olive egg case is about two or three inches long and one to two inches wide, excluding horns.

Also known as: Eyed skate, big skate.

Maximum known size: 32 inches.

Distribution: Continental waters of the western North Atlantic—from northern North Carolina to northern Nova Scotia, the southern side of the Gulf of St. Lawrence, and the Newfoundland Banks. The center of distribution is Georges Bank and southern New England.

Thorny Skate (Raja radiata)

An Atlantic skate that in recent years has been the target of commercial fisheries satisfying an Asian export market for skate wings.

Maximum known size: 2 feet.

Distribution: Western North Atlantic; common in the Gulf of Maine.

Western Skates

California Skate (Raja inornata)

One of the most abundant skates on the western coast of the United States, it is pale above and duskily mottled below. Small prickles line its midback, larger ones on the snout and between the eyes, and there are three to five rows of prickles on the back of its tail.

The California skate has been found in waters ranging in depth from sixty feet to a mile.

Maximum known size: 2½ feet.

Distribution: From the Straits of San Juan de Fuca (Washington) south to Bahia Tortugas, central Baja California.

Other West Coast skates:

- Big skate (*Raja binoculata*), 8 feet wide. Bering Sea and southeastern Alaska to central Baja California.

- Longnose skate (*Raja rhina*), 4.6 feet wide. Southeastern Alaska to central Baja California.

Starry Skate (Raja stellulata)

A beautifully ornamented skate, whose upper side is a constellation of black spots.

Also known as: Prickly skate.
Maximum known size: 2½ feet.
Distribution: Bering Sea to northern Baja California, usually in fairly deep water.

Abyssal Skate (Raja bathyphila)

The abyssal skate dwells in the depths, and is rarely caught. The few specimens that have been brought to the surface were hauled from depths of a mile or more in the North Atlantic. It is known to grow to eighteen inches in length.

A similar creature of the depths, the deep-sea skate of the Pacific (*Raja abyssicola*), is known from a single specimen pulled from a depth of about 9,525 feet in the Pacific, west of Moresby Island, British Columbia. It was a male four and a half feet long.

Several other West Coast abyssal skates are listed by the Love Lab of the Biological Resources Division of the U. S. Geological Survey. Following are their names, size, distribution, and the deepest depth from which a specimen was taken:

- Deepsea skate (*Bathyraja abyssicola*), 4 to 5 feet wide. Japan and Bering Sea; Queen Charlotte Island, British Columbia to Islas de Los Coronados, northern Baja California; 9,528 feet.

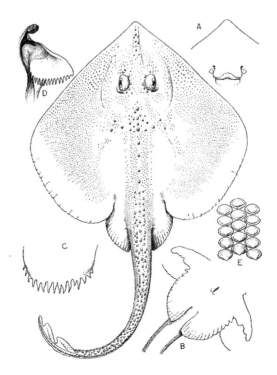

Female abyssal skate. A—underside of head showing nostrils and mouth; B—under view of pelvic fins, cloaca, and base of tail; C—nasal curtain; D—left nostril with curtain; E—upper teeth.

- Aleutian skate (*Bathyraja aleutica*), 4 to 5 feet wide. Northern Japan to Aleutian Islands, and southeast Alaska; 2,296 feet.

- Sandpaper skate (*Bathyraja interrupta*), 2.8 feet wide. Alaska to Cortes Bank, southern California; 4,554 feet.

- Flathead skate (*Bathyraja parmifera*), [no size given]. Bering Sea; Oregon to Point Arguello, central California; 5,128 feet.

- White skate (*Bathyraja spinosissima*), [no size given]. Tillamook Head, Oregon to Eureka, California; 9,695 feet.

- Black skate (*Bathyraja trachura*), [no size given]. Bering Sea to north of Isla Guadalupe, central Baja California; 6,540 feet.

Texas Skate *(Raja texana)*

This skate is spectacularly marked by a single eyelike spot on the upper side of each "wing" or pectoral.

Maximum known size: 20 inches.

Distribution: West coast of Florida and the coasts of Mississippi, Louisiana, and Texas.

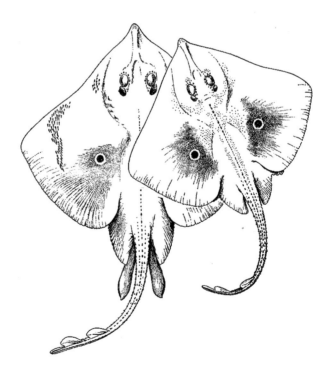

Texas skate.

Order Myliobatiformes (rays)

Typically, rays are shaped like a kite, complete with tail. In many species, the tail is armed with one or more barbed points, known as spines or stings. Looked upon from above, a ray appears to be blinking. But the "eyes" on its topside are the spiracles that are part of its respiration system.

A ray seems to "fly" along, its winglike pectoral fins flapping like a bird, touching the sand or silt and fanning small crustaceans, starfish, and other food off the bottom so that they can be more easily eaten.

Rays resemble skates, but several anatomical differences set the two apart. (In North American waters, skates are generally long-nosed whereas rays are not.) Among fishermen and nonexperts, the two are often thought to be the same. Even their names are from the same root. "Skate" is a Norse word. The creatures the Norse called "skates" were christened "rays" (*raie*) by the French, ray meaning "striped" or "streaked," a characteristic that doesn't apply to all species.

Unlike the skates, which produce their young oviparously in egg cases, rays are all believed to be ovoviviparous, bringing forth their young alive (after they have hatched from eggs within their mother). In some rays, there is a connection between the mother and the uterine-hatched embryo that is more direct than is found in ovoviviparous sharks. The female rays of this type have a uterus whose walls are densely lined with long filaments, called villi. The villi, passing into the spiracles of the embryo, carry a milky nutritive fluid that the embryo absorbs as food.

Some rays give birth to young fantastically large in comparison to the mother. E. W. Gudger of the American Museum of Natural History reported that "the size of these young, flat, wide-pectoral raylets, when ready for birth, is the thing that makes their parturition a matter of seeming impossibility."

Gudger reported the capture off Beaufort, North Carolina, of a ray (*Rhinoptera bonasus*) twenty-four inches wide, which, "on being clubbed on the head in the small boat to keep her quiet, gave birth to two young, each 8.5 in. long (tip of nose to end of ventral fin), and 13.5 in. wide." Another ray (*Dasyatis sayi*) from the same location was, Gudger reported, "36 in. wide by 35 in. long. From her were obtained two young of about equal size. The one measured was 14.75 in. wide and 5.75 in. long. In addition the tail was 9.5 in. long."

The female ray is able to accomplish the birth of such proportionally huge young because the flat-bodied embryos are tightly rolled; they resemble a cigar in shape. At birth—its passage eased by the milky uterine fluid in which it has been immersed—the ray pup leaves its mother's body, immediately unrolls in the sea, and swims away.

Compared to skates, rays have a much wider distribution and a wider diversity of forms to suit them to their environments, including freshwater thousands of miles from the sea.

Family Dasyatidae (stingrays)

Ancient Greeks were quite familiar with Mediterranean stingrays, which they called *Trygon.* Aristotle is quoted as saying, "Nothing is more terrible than the spine that arms the tail of Trygon." Telegonus, son of King Ulysses of Ithaca, supposedly killed his father with a spear bearing as its tip a Trygon stinger. Stingers have been used as weapons in many cultures.

Whips made from the thorny, stinger-bearing tails of an African type of stingray have been reported along the Congo and in tropical West Africa. In Ceylon, stingray tails were used, until recent times, as whips for punishing criminals. Men also used them in the Seychelles Archipelago of the Indian Ocean to whip their wives.

In his *Generall Historie* of Virginia, Captain John Smith, writing of himself in the third person, tells how he captured a stingray with "a most poisoned sting . . . which she stucke into the wrist of his arme near an inch and a half; no blood nor wound was seene, but a little blewe spot, but the torment was instantly so extreme, that in foure houres had so swollen his hand, arme and shoulder we all with much sorrow concluded his funerall, and prepared his grave on an island near the mouth of the Rappahannock River by himself directed; yet it pleased God, by a precious oyle Dr. Russell at the first applyed to it with a probe, ere night his tormenting paine was so well asswaged that he eate of the fishe to his supper."

This large, worldwide ray family includes about 190 species, both large and small. These rays have rounded pectoral fins and slim, usually whiplike tails that are generally longer than the body. They breathe by taking water into spiracles on the upper bodies and expelling the water through gill slits on the lower body. The large spiracles are behind each eye on the upper surface. Their small teeth are arrayed in many rows. All females in these species are ovoviviparous, retaining their young within the body until it is fully developed.

BEWARE OF STINGRAYS

If you think stingrays are around, shuffle your feet when you walk into the water. This lessens the likelihood of accidentally stepping on one and also drives them away by stirring up the bottom.

If you are wounded by a stingray, let the wound bleed for a few moments to flush out as much poison and sand as possible. Then wash the wound thoroughly, apply a mild antiseptic, and get to a doctor.

Some old-time fishermen suggest applying very hot water as an immediate remedy for the pain. In a Florida case, benadryl hydrochloride, penicillin, and an antitetanus drug were all administered by hypodermic thirty minutes after a man was struck on the left palm by a stingray. But the treatment had no apparent effect. The victim reported soreness around the wound for more than a month.

Most stingrays bear only a single venomous sting, or spine, on the upper part of the tail, but several have two, or even three or more. The point, which may be eight to fifteen inches long, is covered by a thin sheath that is pushed back toward its base when it is thrust into a victim. The stinger is hard and stiletto-shaped, with a sharp point. Its edge is fringed with tiny barbs that point back toward the base of the sting. Thus, when it enters, the barbs hold it in the wound and thwart easy removal. Along both edges of the underside of the stinger run two deep grooves. Within the grooves flows the venomous secretion, whose chemical composition is little understood.

Stingray poison produces excruciating pain and even paralysis. One victim, "slightly scratched" on the thumb, suffered intense pain, high fever and, for three months, slight paralysis of the arm. Another, scratched on the arm, was in pain for two days.

Stingrays are found usually near to shore, usually in warm waters; species have been known to ascend rivers. They feed on mollusks, worms, crustaceans, and small fishes. They often burrow into the bottom and remain unseen. If an unwary bather or wader steps on a stingray, the ray usually tries to stab the assailant, producing a painful wound.

About 1,500 stingray attacks are reported in the United States each year. Most victims are attacked after stepping on a stingray lying partially hidden in the mud near shore.

Divers have made a popular pastime out of playing with large stingrays. But, as Scott W. Michael warns in his *Reef Sharks and Rays of the World*, "most of these rays present a potential hazard to humans. The large sting(s) on the tail, which is ensheathed in venomous tissue, is used as a defense weapon. When provoked, these fish thrust the tail over their bodies and into the offender. . . . A number of fatalities have resulted from physical damage or loss of blood."

Some stingrays live in fresh water. One species, *Himantura chaophyra*, is known to inhabit the Borneo and Kinabatanga Rivers in Borneo. Stingrays are plentiful in the fresh waters of Thailand, where they are known as *pla kaben nam chuet*—"the freshwater ray fish."

Southern Stingray (*Dasyatis americana*)

Roughly diamond-shaped, the Southern stingray has a narrow, whiplike tail with a low ridge and one or two sharp serrated stingers on the upper surface. The sting is known to carry a potent toxin. This ray often digs into the soft sea bottom in search of food, leaving shallow craters in its wake. It feeds on fish, crabs, clams, and shrimp—usually at night. When threatened, it strikes a scorpionlike pose, raising its stinger tail over its head.

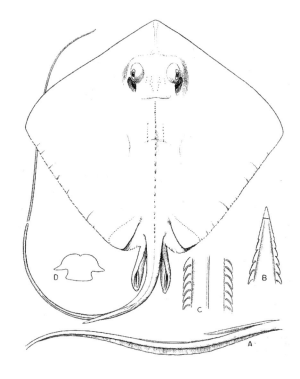

*Male Southern stingray.
A—tail showing
stinger; B—tip of
stinger; C—middle
section of tail;
D—cross-section
of stinger.*

Maximum known size: 5 feet wide, 5 feet long.
Distribution: Western Atlantic, New Jersey to Brazil.

Shorttail Ray *(Dasyatis brevicaudatus)*

One of the largest stingrays in the world, it was first discovered by Captain James Cook, who saw so many stingrays while exploring Australia in 1770 that he named one of the bays, a few miles south of what was to become Sydney, Stingray Bay (later changed to Botanists', and finally, Botany Bay).

This may be the species responsible for the death in 1938 of an eighteen-year-old girl in Auckland, Australia. She was struck by a large stingray whose sting, whipped by its powerful tail, stabbed her left thigh and then her heart.

It feeds on crustaceans, squid, fish, and bivalves and is often seen in large groups.

Also known as: Captain Cook's stingaree.
Maximum known size: 7 feet wide, 14 feet long.
Distribution: New Zealand and Australian waters.

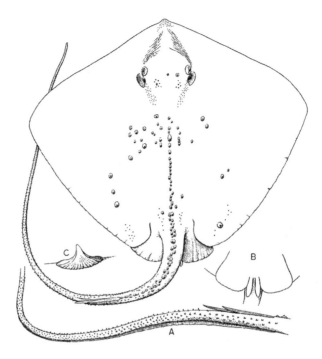

Male roughtail stingray. A—tail, showing stingers; B—under view of pelvic fins and claspers; C—thornlike tubercule on tail.

Roughtail Stingray *(Dasyatis centroura)*

A big stingray of the coastal waters of the western North Atlantic, the roughtail is known to reach five feet in width and more than ten feet in length. One caught in New Jersey was described as nearly seven feet across and, had its tail been complete, it would have been thirteen to fourteen feet long, but official reports do not recognize the specimen. It has spiny thorns on its tail.

Maximum known size: 5 feet wide, 10 feet long.

Distribution: Western North Atlantic from Georges Bank and Cape Cod to Chesapeake Bay, Cape Hatteras, and possibly Florida. Also reported as far south as Brazil.

Hawaiian Stingray *(Dasyatis hawaiiensis)*

The arrangement of its pectoral fins gives this ray a squarish look. The long, slender tail is usually longer than the smooth-skinned body. The upper body is brown, with pale outer edges and a white underside.

Maximum known size: 4 feet.

Distribution: Known records in Hawaii, California, and Peru; probably found in other tropical Pacific waters.

Brown Stingray *(Dasyatis latus)*

The brown stingray's slender tail is usually longer than the body. Brown on the upper body and white below, the ray has brown markings on the edges of its pectoral fins. It feeds mostly on shellfish which it digs up, using its head as a spade.
Maximum known size: 3 feet long.
Distribution: Hawaii and Australia; reported elsewhere in tropical Pacific waters.

Marbled Ribbontail Ray *(Taeniura melanospilos)*

A beautifully marked ray, the marbled ribbontail has a tail longer than its body. It is usually found in rocky reefs.
Maximum known size: 5 feet wide.
Distribution: Western Pacific, Indian Ocean, Red Sea, and around the Galapagos Islands and Cocos Island. A similar species (or populations of *T. melanospilos* itself) have been reported in the Mediterranean and the Red Sea.

Atlantic Stingray *(Dasyatis sabina)*

A small ray, the Atlantic stingray often feeds by digging a hole with its undulating fins, then, facing into a current, it eats what the water brings, including polychaete worms, tiny crustaceans and fishes.

Like many species of stingrays, it ascends rivers. The Atlantic stingray has been caught more than 200 miles up the Mississippi River, and in Lakes Pontchartrain and Borgne in Louisiana, and in the lakes of the St. John River, Florida.
Maximum known size: 20 inches wide.
Distribution: Shallow Atlantic coastal waters from Chesapeake Bay to Florida and the Gulf of Mexico.

Thorntail Stingray *(Dasyatis thetidis)*

This prickly stingray has been seen in caves and in large reef caverns in New Zealand, along coastal shallows, and in water 1,200 feet deep. Groups have been seen, gathering apparently for mating. Its diet includes conger eels, worms, crabs, and shrimp.

Maximum known size: 6½ feet.
Distribution: Waters of New Zealand, Australia, and South Africa.

Family Gymnuridae (butterfly rays)

Flapping its wide pectorals like wings as it glides through the sea, the butterfly ray has the look of grace and beauty that inspired its name. Gray, brown, purple, or green markings lace its topside like filigree. On the bottom, its colors change, darkening on a black background, paling on a light background. And there, on the bottom, prowling for food, sluggishly moving with the tides, its colors muted, the butterfly ray is as dull to behold as a butterfly still locked in its cocoon.

Usually, young develop in only one of the mother's two oviducts and only one embryo develops. But sometimes two or three embryos will be developing at the same time. After a time in a membrane, the embryo is released into the uterus, where it is nourished by the contents of a yolk sac and by fluid secreted from glandular villi (mucus membranes lining the inner uterine walls). The villi reach into the spiracles of the embryos, which essentially suckle from the villi. Young are born after a gestation period of unknown length, their winglike fins rolled up. As the butterfly ray enters the sea, the wings unfurl and it swims away.

The family includes two genera: *Gymnura*, whose species, found in the Red Sea, the Atlantic, the Pacific, and the Mediterranean, have no dorsal fins on their tail, and *Aetoplatea*, whose species are found off South Africa, in the Red Sea, the Indian Ocean, and the East Indies, and have small dorsal fins.

Lesser Butterfly Ray (Gymnura micrura)

Found along the coastal waters of the western Atlantic, this ray has a tail that lacks a sting.

These rays have shown a variety of colors when taken from the water: gray, brown, light green, purple, with vermicular patterns of paler or darker dots. They seem to prefer a sandy bottom; this is the source of their erroneous common name, sand skate.

Large numbers of them have been seen moving in with the tide on tidal flats and withdrawing with the ebbing tide.

Also known as: Sand skate.
Maximum known size: 4 feet long.

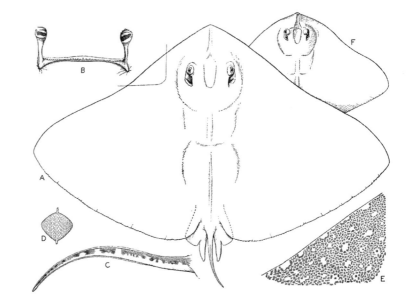

Male lesser butterfly ray: A—upper view; B—nostrils, with nasal curtain over mouth; C—tail showing folds; D—cross-section of tail; E—part of disk showing color pattern; F—under view of head showing gills, nostrils, mouth covered by nasal curtain.

Distribution: Coastal waters from Brazil to Maryland, occasionally as far north as southern New England; in the lower parts of Chesapeake Bay; off Galveston, Texas.

California Butterfly Ray (*Gymnura marmorata*)

Unlike *G. micrura*, this butterfly ray does have one or more stings in its diminutive tail, thus earning the name butterfly stingray.

Maximum known size: 5 feet long.

Distribution: Point Conception, California to Peru.

Family Myliobatidae (eagle rays and cow-nosed rays)

Eagle Rays

The lozenge-shaped eagle rays make up a large family that has members in tropical and temperate seas throughout the world. They bear as many as five venomous stings in their long, whiplike tails, and they are large. Some reach seven to eight feet in breadth and weigh up to 800 pounds.

Eagle rays earn their name by a kind of swimming that looks like the flight of a great bird. Sometimes they soar out of the sea and glide through the air, using their winglike pectoral fins as sails.

Using their long snouts and rounded pectoral fin tips as a tool, they dig holes in the sandy sea floor and nose out prey. They eat small crustaceans by grinding the shells with pavement-like teeth. They are looked upon as varmints by California clammers.

Young are nourished by "villi food" similar to that of the butterfly rays.

Spotted Duck-Billed Ray *(Aetobatus narinari)*

A big, speckled creature, this ray has been seen in large schools, numbering as many as several hundred. Perhaps this is a "herd defense" against pelagic sharks, which follow the rays, particularly during the time when females give birth, eating the young as soon as they are born. Russell J. Coles, who studied the sharks and rays in North Carolina waters for many years, reported that "in giving birth to its young, the female ray leaps high in the air."

Ichthyologists are generally skeptical about suggestions that these rays—or any others—must leap into the air to give birth. But there is no

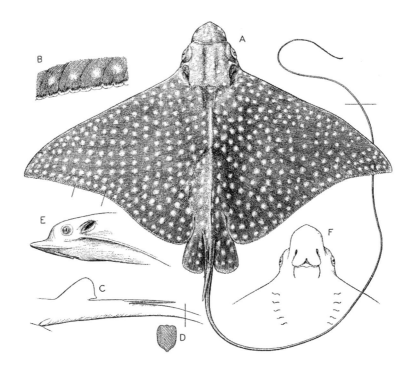

Spotted duck-billed ray. A—upper view; B—part of disk, showing color pattern; C—view of tail showing dorsal fin and stinger; D—cross-section of tail; E—side view of head; F—under view of head showing gills, nostrils, mouth covered by nasal curtain.

doubt about the spotted duck-billed ray's prowess as a jumper. In fact, in Australia it is sometimes called the jumping ray.

In the species' underside-to-underside mating, a male bites a pectoral fin on a female, flips beneath her, and inserts one clasper. Within an hour, the female may mate with as many as four males. Gestation is about one year. One to four young are born at a time.

These rays are powerful swimmers. One towed a twenty-two-foot boat "wherever it wished." With as many as five stings in a long tail, it is a formidable animal. Cole tells of one that "suddenly threw its body against me and drove its poisoned sting into my leg above the knee for more than two inches, striking the bone, and producing instantly a pain more horrible that I had thought possible that man could suffer." He treated the wound immediately and recovered.

This ray uses its projecting mandible as a spade to dig out shellfish from sandy bottoms. With its powerful jaws, it cracks clamshells and extracts the clams so efficiently that it can swallow the clams intact and spit out the shells. Like several other species of ray, it sometimes lets out a sound resembling a bark when captured.

Also known as: Spotted whip ray, spotted eagle ray.

Maximum known size: 7½ feet wide, more than 500 pounds.

Distribution: Both sides of the Atlantic; Pacific and the Indian Oceans; Red Sea.

Danger to humans: People wounded by stingers—and unable to get immediate medical attention—have lost a leg or arm. Some victims have died.

Bat Ray (Myliobatis californicus)

Similar in its eating habits to the eagle ray of the Atlantic, this Pacific ray has long been treated as a menace by West Coast oystermen. To protect their oyster beds they erected antiray fences, made by driving stakes about six inches apart so that the wide-winged rays could not squeeze through. Like the eagle ray, bat rays swim along the bottom, searching for the feeble but steady water currents expelled by the siphons of clams. By flapping its pectoral fins it can create a suction that digs out the clams.

Bat rays often travel in large schools. Aggregations estimated at several thousand have been reported occasionally in the waters off Lower California.

Studies of the embryo of *M. californicus* have solved the puzzle of how female stingrays bring forth their sting-bearing young without being gored themselves: The pup's sting is pliable and covered with a sheath that is sloughed off soon after birth.

Bay rays live in a narrow region, from the intertidal zone to depths of about 200 feet.

Also known as: Bat stingray.

Maximum known size: 6 feet wide.

Distribution: Pacific coast, Oregon to the Gulf of California.

Eagle Ray *(Myliobatis freminvillii)*

Fishermen know captive eagle rays as dangerous cargo, lashing out with a whiplike tail studded by one or two stings. Females taken near Cape Lookout, North Carolina, carried as many as six embryos "folded together in pairs, the heads and tails of each pair in reversed position." (This would give each embryo an opportunity to feed from uterine wall villi.)

They are gray, reddish chocolate, or dusky brown above, whitish below, with pectoral fins dusky toward their tips.

Also known as: Hedgehog skate, common skate, tobacco box skate.

Maximum known size: 34 inches wide.

Distribution: Western Atlantic from Cape Cod to Brazil, appearing in the northern end of its range in the warmer months; probably lives year-round in West Indies and Caribbean waters.

Eagle ray. A—tail showing dorsal fin; B—head; C—under view of head showing gills, nostrils, mouth covered by nasal curtain; D—close-up of curtain; E—head of similar species, Myliobatis aquila.

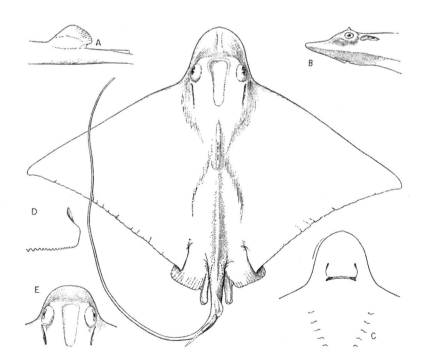

143

Similar species:

- Longnose eagle ray (*Myliobatis longirostris*) lives from southern Baja California southward.

- Striped eagle ray (*Pteromylaeus asperrimus*) is found from Bahia Almejas, Southern Baja California, to at least Panama.

Cow-Nosed Rays

What has been a family, Rhinopteridae, with one genus, *Rhinoptera*, has been folded into the Myliobatidae family. Cow-nosed rays all have the familiar winged shape of many kinds of large rays, but their bovine nose sets them apart from all others. All have the pavementlike teeth of bottom feeders that dine on crustaceans. A cow-nosed ray has a single dorsal fin near the base of a long, whiplike tail bearing one or two stings.

They appear to probe for food by fluttering along the seafloor, sensing prey by detecting weak electrical fields or the bubbling of clam siphons. Sometimes a cow-nosed ray will move its pectorals like fans, stirring up sediment, inhaling it through the mouth and rejecting it through the gill slits. Using this technique, it may dig a foot or more into the seafloor in search of crustaceans and bivalves, scooping up shelled creatures, grinding up the shells in strong teeth, discarding the shell fragments, and consuming the soft parts.

Cow-nosed rays frequently assemble by the thousands, swimming through the sea apparently in a great aggregation. They may be moving en masse to a hunting area.

Atlantic Cow-Nosed Ray *(Rhinoptera bonasus)*

Specimens of this ray vary in terms of stings. Some had one, others two, and some had only scars where their stings had been. Why they had lost them is not known, but stings from this and other species of ray have been found imbedded in the heads, jaws, and mouths of many species of sharks, especially hammerheads.

Large schools may appear at various places along its range.

In North Carolina waters, the chief diet of these rays consists of oysters and clams; those found in New England add lobsters to their diet. Their foraging was reported in New York waters in 1815: "A shoal of Cow-noses roots up the salt water flats as completely as a drove of hogs would do."

R. brasiliensis, similar to Atlantic species in size and shape, is found along the western coast of South America.

Maximum known size: 7 feet wide.

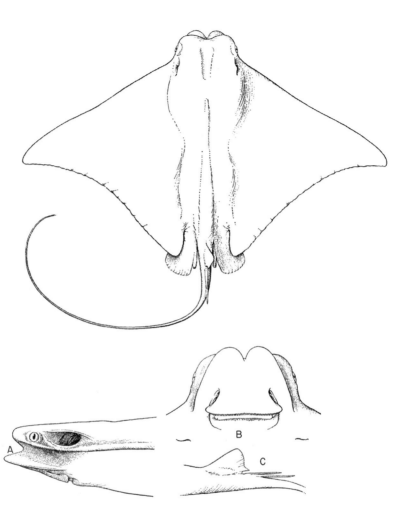

Atlantic cow-nosed ray. A—side view of head; B—under view of head, showing gills, nostrils, mouth covered by nasal curtain; C—tail showing stingers.

Distribution: Along the coast of the western Atlantic, from southern New England to Brazil.

Danger to humans: No reports of attack, but see flap-nose ray.

Flap-Nose Ray (*Rhinoptera javanica*)

The flap-nose resembles other cow-nose rays. This is one of the few species about which mating habits are known. Courtship and mating involves several males and one female. Observers report that the female is usually atop the male and that she may mate with several males within a short time.

Maximum known size: 5 feet wide.

Distribution: Pacific waters, especially bays, estuaries, and reefs, from Japan to Indonesia.

Danger to humans: A fatal attack by this ray species was reported in 1936, when "a fisherman from Bataan succumbed to a wound inflicted in the region of the stomach by the spine of this ray." The attack occurred when a large number swept into Manila Bay, a frequent occurrence during their breeding season.

Family Urolophidae (round stingrays)

Stingarees, as these rays are known in Australia, are small but feisty. They have been seen suddenly swimming in reverse to deploy their stingers; some species have two stingers. Females sometimes wield their stingers to ward off overly aggressive males. The teeth of males are longer than the females' teeth, apparently to give males a better biting hold on a female during mating.

Round Stingray (Urolophus halleri)

California divers are wary around this stingray, which has been blamed for numerous attacks.

A study of more than 4,000 round stingrays in California waters showed that 45 percent had lost their sheaths and venom glands. The researcher, Earl S. Herald, curator of the Steinhart Aquarium of the California Academy of Sciences, found that the larger and older the stingray, "the greater is the possibility of its having lost the venom glands and protective sheath." He saw this as an explanation for why some people stabbed by stingray spines were not poisoned. Another study, however, found that stings that looked clean could still contain venom-producing tissue. So the mystery of selective venom poisoning remained.

Only about five inches long at birth, the round stingray begins a life of voracious eating. One of its favorite foraging techniques is to bite off bivalves' siphons that stick out of the sand.

Maximum known size: 22 inches long.

Distribution: Northern California to Panama.

Yellow Stingray (Urolophus jamaicensis)

Usually found in shallow waters with muddy or sandy bottoms, this little round ray gets its species name from its prevalence in Jamaican waters.

A great white shark bares the jaws that have earned it notoriety as the most feared shark in the world.

(PHOTO BY JAMES D. WATT/MO YUNG PRODUCTIONS, COURTESY NORBERT WU)

A tiger shark bites with a rolling motion, its big, saw-edged teeth chopping large prey.

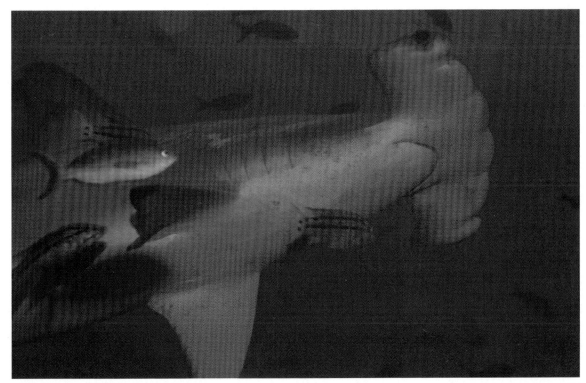

A hammerhead's eyes are at the ends of its elongated head. This expands its field of vision.

(PHOTO BY GRAEME TEAGUE)

Hammerheads, which live in all temperate and tropical seas, are often seen in large schools.

(PHOTO BY GRAEME TEAGUE)

The shortfin mako is the fastest shark in the world. Pound for pound it is also among the strongest.

A megamouth shark in deep sea off southern California. The species was first discovered in 1976.

A sand tiger shark swims near a World War II shipwreck.

Blue sharks like this one regularly migrate across the Atlantic; one blue averaged 44 miles a day.

(PHOTO BY BOB CRANSTON)

The Galapagos shark, found around
Pacific Islands, is considered dangerous
to swimmers.

(PHOTO BY GRAEME TEAGUE)

The oceanic whitetip shark, which is dangerous
and aggressive, is found only in the open ocean.
It has been blamed for attacks on survivors of
ship and aircraft disasters.

(PHOTO JAMES WATT/MO YUNG PRODUCTIONS, COURTESY NORBERT WU)

(Above and below:) The cookie-cutter shark—named for its eating technique—sucks in a cylinder of flesh, rotates its body, and scoops out a bite with razor-sharp teeth, leaving a wound two inches wide.

(PHOTO BY NORBERT WU)

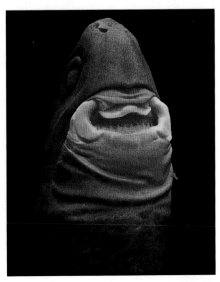

(PHOTO BY NORBERT WU)

A zebra shark, also called the monkey-mouthed shark, prowls the bottom searching for prey.

The whale shark is the largest fish in the world.

A horn shark, named after the bumps on its skull, shows its colors in its seafloor habitat.

(PHOTO BY BOB CRANSTON)

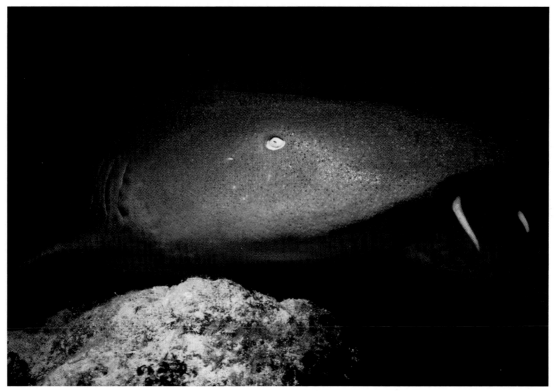

The bottom-dwelling nurse shark pumps water over its gills by opening and closing its mouth.

(PHOTO BY JAY IRELAND AND GEORGIENNE BRADLEY)

A swell shark can inflate its stomach with water and air when disturbed, frightening off predators.

A gray reef shark, here alone, can often be seen in the Pacific in schools of twenty to one hundred.

The elephant chimaera, or elephant fish, swimming here off New Zealand, has a flexible snout.

(PHOTO BY NORBERT WU)

This typical skate uses fleshy, moveable fins to "walk" across the bottom in search of prey.

The electric ray produces an electric shock of 120 volts to defend itself and to stun prey.

A giant devil ray, which
can grow to twenty-two
feet across, "flies"
through the Pacific.

(PHOTO BY NORBERT WU)

The sawfish uses its saw for burrowing and stunning fish.

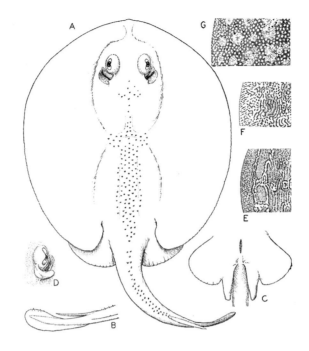

Yellow stingray. A—upper view of female; B—tail with stinger; C—under view of male claspers; D—embryo's eye and spiracle; E, F, and G—pattern variations of three specimens.

Fishermen particularly dread it because it gets into their nets and stabs them when they reach in to get the fish out.

Its snout is pointed, its tail is not as long as its disk-shaped body. Its upper side bears a dark reticulated pattern with yellow spots.

Round rays form large populations in Florida waters. A census of round rays, reported in 1998 by the Reef Environmental Education Foundation counted 1,178 off the Florida east coast and the Florida Keys, with the major concentration around Key Largo.

Mating occurs when a male swims under a female, swings upside down, and inserts a single clasper. Other males sometimes swim by and nudge the mating pair.

Maximum known size: 13 inches wide, 26 inches long.

Distribution: Common in the Caribbean and among the Florida Keys, and along both coasts of southern Florida. Reported as far north as North Carolina.

Family Mobulidae (devil rays)

Devil rays are so called because of their cephalic fins, which, when rolled and projected forward, have the appearance of horns. Members of this family are found in the warm temperature zones of all oceans, and the

Mediterranean. They all have similar habits. They leap; sometimes, several at a time. They live near the surface, seemingly having abandoned the bottom-dwelling life of other rays. They all apparently take in water for respiration through their mouths instead of through their spiracles, which are relatively small.

The family has two genera, *Mobula* (nine species) and *Manta* (now one species; formerly three species). *Mobula* species members have teeth in both jaws and mouths on the lower surface of the head. A member of *Manta birostris* has teeth in the lower jaw only, and its mouth is at the end of the head and extends across.

One or two young are born at a time, sometimes as the mother makes a great leap from the sea. A newborn giant devil ray (*Manta birostris*) may weigh more than twenty pounds.

Giant Devil Ray *(Manta birostris)*

These giants often travel in groups, and several of them have been seen leaping together, sometimes as high as five feet above the surface, possibly to rid their huge bodies of hordes of parasites. Sometimes they somersault, breaking surface headfirst, then revolving on edge in a spectacular cartwheel, with one pectoral fin emerging while the other is descending back into the sea.

A giant—twenty-two feet in breadth—towed a twenty-five-foot motorboat more than ten miles, with the boat's anchor dragging on the bottom part of the time. After five hours it was still alive, though four harpoons and several rifle bullets were imbedded in its body.

They have been seen feeding in large groups while accompanied by dolphins, seabirds, sharks, and other ray species, all apparently hoping to get some of the food—crustaceans, small fish, plankton—stirred up by the devil rays.

A large population of devil rays has become a tourist attraction around the main island complex in the state of Yap, Federated States of Micronesia. Researchers, taking advantage of the population's persistent appearance, have made extensive video records of these rays. Many are recognizable through their color patterns. The rays seem to use the channels around Yap for courtship and for "cleaning" by cooperative fishes. (See Companions of the Shark, page 166.)

Also known as: Manta, manta ray, Hayhay-lua (Hawaii).

Maximum known size: 22 feet wide.

Distribution: Worldwide in warm temperature zones of all oceans, and the Mediterranean. In American waters, the manta ray has been reported from Brazil to the Carolinas, and occasionally to New England and Georges Bank; along the American West Coast, the manta has been captured as far north as Redondo Beach, California.

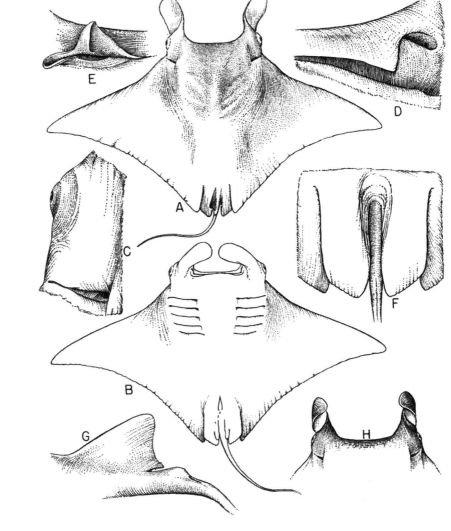

*Giant devil ray.
A—upper view;
B—under view;
C—left eye and spiracle;
D—nostril and nasal
curtain; E—curtain
rolled up to show
internal fold;
F—female's pelvic fins;
G—dorsal fin and base
of tail; H—head
showing cephalic fins
coiled in swimming
position. See also color
insert.*

Danger to humans: Because of their size, these giants can crush a boat—or a person in a boat.

Ox Ray (*Mobula diabola*)

Smallest of the Mobulidae family, *M. diabola* is known principally in Australia.

Also known as: Smaller devil ray, diamond fish.
Maximum known size: 2 feet wide.
Distribution: Australian waters.

Lesser Devil Ray *(Mobula hypostoma)*

Russell J. Coles, in one of his many observations of rays along the North Carolina coast, told of once seeing several lesser devil rays (he called "mantas") pursuing a school of minnows and "rushing right up on the sand . . . until their bodies were nearly half out of the water; but in an instant they were off and scattered out to sea." Coles said that the mantas kept their cephalic fins rolled until they neared the minnows. Then the fins "open, and, meeting below the mouth, form a funnel, through which the 'minnows' are carried into the mouth. On the instant that this rush is over these fins again close up tightly."

This ray also feeds on crustaceans, small fish, and plankton. When captured, it sometimes makes a bell-like sound, but it is not known whether it makes any sound under the water.

The cephalic fins that stick out from the lesser devil ray's head like stumpy arms are said to close instantly around anything that touches the front of its head. A school of these rays once reportedly affixed themselves to the posts of a fence that ran out into shallow water. Occasionally, they may grasp an anchor line in this way, possibly trying to clean off parasites. The grasp of the cephalic fins is weak, so there is no possibility of a lesser devil ray fatally holding on to a swimmer.

Coles, reporting on devil rays mating, said that the male "was above with back just showing above the water and his wing-like pectorals curved upward . . . while the female was oriented so as to plainly show the white side uppermost, with pectorals standing up." Copulation, he said, "was not accomplished by a vertical motion, but by a graceful, serpentine lateral curvature of the spine, as the male alternately advanced one of his *mixopterygia* [claspers] as he withdrew the other." The union was not continuous. Occasionally the two separated, swam around or leaped from the sea, and then resumed mating.

M. hypostoma does not have a tail sting. The much larger (sixteen to seventeen feet) *M. mobula*, which does have a sting, is found chiefly in the Mediterranean, and in the eastern Atlantic from Ireland to Spain, Portugal, the Azores, the Canaries, and tropical West Africa.

Also known as: Manta.
Maximum known size: 4 feet.
Distribution: Western Atlantic from North Carolina to Argentina; Caribbean; Gulf of Mexico.

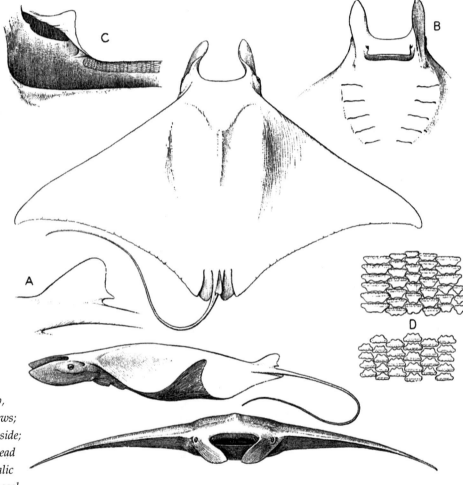

Lesser devil ray: top, side, and frontal views; A—dorsal fin from side; B—under view of head showing gills, cephalic fins, nostrils with nasal curtail covering mouth; C—corner of mouth, right nasal curtain rolled up to nostril and outer tooth band; D—upper (top) and lower teeth.

Japanese Devil Fish *(Mobula japonica)*

Observers have seen these rays leap out of the sea, rising at times as high as twice their width. Sometimes they somersault back and plunge beneath the surface. They feed principally on or near the bottom on crustaceans and small fishes, sometimes swimming near the surface to feed on plankton.

M. japonica has a tail spine.

Also known as: Pygmy devil ray.

Maximum known size: 3½ feet.

Distribution: Eastern tropical Pacific; east coast of Africa; northern New Zealand and north to waters off Japan.

Order Torpediniformes
Family Torpedinidae (electric rays)

Electric rays appear on Etruscan vases, Roman mosaics, and Egyptian murals. Our word "narcotic" comes from the Greek word for the electric ray, *narke*. The Greeks believed that the "numbfish" could bewitch both its prey and the fisherman angling for it. Because Socrates similarly bewitched his listeners with spellbinding oratory, he was compared by his colleagues to the numbfish.

The fascination of the electric ray has persisted through the years, and only in relatively recent times has its electrical-generating ability been understood. The electric organs consist of two groups of highly specialized cells, one organ on each side of the disklike body. These organs consist of muscle tissue in which the ordinary electric-generating ability, found in any muscle, is greatly increased.

Each organ is made up of many columns, running vertically through the body and arranged like large honeycombs. Each column is made up of 140 to more than 1,000 disks, often arranged like the cells of a honeycomb. Each disk is filled with a jellylike substance. The small disks produce the same effect as do the electrical plates in batteries, and, in fact, resemble the original voltaic pile—disks of silver and zinc separated by moistened cloth—that historically led to the development of the battery. Four large nerve trunks lead from a special "electrical lobe" in the electric ray's brain to the electric organs. The nerve trunks branch out to form a complex network of fine filaments that connect with each of the small disks. Thus, the electric ray seems to have voluntary control over its unique organs, which it uses in defense and in stunning prey. (There is also some evidence that the release of electricity is a reflex action when a ray is touched.)

The ray's electricity can produce a spark, make a bulb glow, deflect a compass needle, and, when connected to a telephone, carry audible sound. Repeated use of the powerhouse obviously tires the ray, which must use up energy to produce its electricity. Successive bursts of electricity become more and more feeble, and some time is required for the electric ray to build up strength after it has emitted several shocks. The maximum recorded voltage emitted by an electric ray (*Torpedo nobiliana*) was 220 volts. (The maximum of 550 volts was recorded for the so-called electric eel [*Electrophorus electricus*] found in South America. The electric catfish [*Malapterurus*] of North Africa rivers can produce a voltage of about 220.)

Greeks and Romans, believing in the therapeutic value of the shocks, applied electric rays to the bodies of victims of gout, chronic headaches, and diseases of the spleen. To get rid of superfluous hair, many Greeks applied the brains of the numbfish, mixed with alum. Some also believed that the best way to assure an easy delivery for a woman in labor was to put a numbfish in the same room with her.

In modern times, experimenters have puzzled over the electrically aided hunting techniques of electric rays. Research on one species, the Pacific electric ray (*Torpedo californica*) showed that it produced two types of electrical pulses and used a variety of strategies to capture prey, sometimes twice its own size. Chris Lowe, Dick Bray, and Don Nelson, working off southern California, found that the ray generated steady pulses of electricity when seemingly examining a potential threat. Then, when sensing prey, it swiftly sent out more intense surges.

The researchers observed that the ray had at least three ways to get its prey. By transmitting a powerful blast of electrical energy it could stun a passing fish. Or, hidden beneath bottom sand or mud, it lunges out, emitting energy at full blast. And it was seen swimming slowly over a fish, giving it a jolt, then wrapping the prey in its pectoral fins and, with a twisting maneuver, getting the fish into its mouth. The ray's nocturnal "stalk and shock" tactics have earned it the nickname "night shocker."

Other experiments have shown that the little skate (*Raja erinacea*) and the winter skate (*R. ocellata*) have weak electrogenic organs in the stalks of their tails. The electric discharges they generate usually measure from a few millivolts to a volt or two, not enough to be used for stunning prey. Some researchers have suggested that the weak pulses "jam" the electrogenic locating organs of a frequent predator, the angel shark.

Pacific Electric Ray (*Torpedo californica*)

Similar in shape and characteristics to *T. nobiliana*.
Maximum known size: 4½ feet wide.
Distribution: British Columbia to Bahia de Sebastian Vizcaino, central Baja California.

Electric Ray *(Torpedo nobiliana)*

Torpedo in its scientific name comes from the same Latin word which gives us "torpid." These rays spend much of their time on the bottom, partially buried in the sand and mud, where their dark coloring aids concealment.

Electric rays seem to stun their prey on contact. A two-pound eel, a one-pound flounder, and a salmon weighing nearly five pounds were all found in the stomach of one of these rays, and none of the victims had a mark on its body.

To determine how *T. nobiliana* uses its electric organ to stun prey, Dr. D. P. Wilson of the Plymouth Aquarium in England connected electrodes to a dead nine-inch horse mackerel. As the fish was pulled through an aquarium tank past a *T. nobiliana*, it pounced on the fish. As the ray enfolded the mackerel with its pectorals, the electrodes detected a strong shock. If the mackerel had been alive, presumably this shock would have been sufficient to render it helpless while the ray ate it.

A newborn *T. nobiliana* can generate electricity the moment it leaves its mother's womb, though in the process of birth apparently the mother receives no shocks.

The electrical shock is strong enough to stun a fisherman who handles an electric ray or a bather who steps on one. A fisherman in Provincetown, Massachusetts, reported that he has often received potent shocks "which have thrown me upon the ground as if I had been knocked down with an ax." Spear fishermen have received painful shocks after spearing one and then trying to pull out the metal shaft.

Also known as: Torpedo ray, torpedo, numbfish, crampfish, *Abubunsamu* (an African word for "breaker of hands").

Maximum known size: 6 feet wide, about 200 pounds.

Distribution: Both sides of the Atlantic, from Scotland to the Azores and tropical West Africa on the east; from Nova Scotia to North Carolina on the west. Also around the Florida Keys, in the waters of Cuba, and in the Mediterranean.

Danger to humans: Can stun but not paralyze.

Family Narcinidae (short-nose electric rays)

A family of three genera and four species, these are rounded rays with short, thick tails. Some live in deep waters beyond the rays' typical habitat close to shore. One genus, *Typhlonarke*, consists of blind rays. Two species in this family are found in Baja California waters: *Diplobatis ommata* and *Narcine entemedor*.

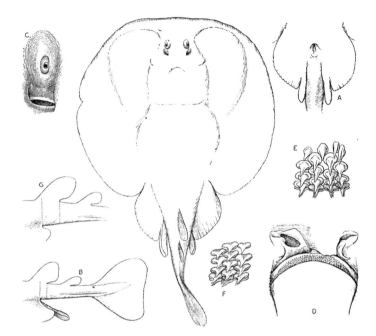

Male electric ray. A—pelvic fins showing cloaca; B—side view of tail, with clasper visible; C—eye and spiracle; D—nostrils and mouth; E—upper teeth from center of jaw; F—upper teeth near mouth; G—side view of female tail. See also color insert.

Japanese Numbfish *(Narke japonica)*

This electric ray produces a relatively weak current, measured at thirty to eighty volts. A sluggish bottom dweller, it has been found in water up to seventy-five feet deep.

Maximum known size: 16 inches.

Distribution: Pacific, from Japan to the South China Sea.

Blind Torpedo Ray *(Typhlonarke aysoni)*

This eyeless ray makes its way along the sea bottom with modified ventral fins that, in a weird way, resemble stumpy legs. The fins project at right angles to the body and their tips are covered with a thick skin. The fins may be an adaptation for moving over the ocean bed. The blind torpedo ray feeds on small fish, shrimp, and crabs.

Maximum known size: 4 feet wide.

Distribution: New Zealand waters.

Family Potamotrygonidae (river stingrays)

River stingrays have been found in rivers throughout the world, but information about them has been scant until recently. They are mostly found in South American rivers flowing to the Atlantic or Caribbean, and in rivers in western Africa. The largest known populations are in the Amazon River and its tributaries, as well as in lakes, rivers, and streams that are in the Amazon's vast realm.

Little is known about them, but researchers have reported that they are bottom feeders. About twenty species have been recorded in the Amazon region. People who have been stung say that the sting is extremely painful and that the wound easily becomes infected. They are considered such a menace that they are banned from being imported into several states, including Arizona, California, Georgia, and Texas.

The rays adapted to freshwater through the aid of a salt-secreting rectal gland. Scientists also believe that their adaptation is aided by their suppression of the concentration of urea in body fluids. They eat small fish, insects, and crustaceans.

Dr. Daniel R. Brooks, of the University of Toronto, using the evolutionary relationships between parasites and their hosts, has speculated how Potamotrygonidae evolved into permanent residents of fresh water.

Because these rays are found in rivers that empty into the Atlantic, biologists assumed that their ancestor was an Atlantic marine stingray that adapted to fresh water and dispersed from the Amazon Basin, spreading throughout South America during the past 3 to 5 million years. But, as Brooks wrote in an abstract of his research, "since the parasites of freshwater stingrays are more closely related to those found in Pacific stingrays, and because adaptation to fresh water appears to have occurred only once, the ancestor of Potamotrygonids would have lived in the Pacific Ocean. The transition to fresh water would have occurred at least 20 million years ago, when the Amazon River flowed west into the Pacific Ocean."

Known species include *Potamotrygon hystrix*, *Paratrygon aiereba*, and *Plesiotrygon iwamae*.

Order Pristiniformes, Family Pristidae (sawfish)

Sawfish have flat, narrow, elongated snouts that look like saws with wide-spaced teeth. These teeth—sixteen to thirty-two on each side of the "blade," depending on the species—are specialized dermal denticles. But, unlike the teeth found in the mouths of sharks, the saw teeth on the sawfish's snout are deeply and firmly embedded in their cartilaginous sockets (see color insert). This may be an evolutionary development, for the fossils of some prehistoric sawfish do not have sockets for the saw teeth, which were then apparently only attached to the skin.

Sawfish propel themselves with sharklike movement of their powerful tails, the aft part of their bodies, and their caudal fin. Their bodies, however, have the basic structure of a ray, including gill slits on the underside. (Saw sharks, which are classified with sharks, have the basic structure of a shark, even though their "saw" snout is anatomically similar to the sawfish's snout.)

Reports of fatal sawfish attacks appear sporadically, particularly in Panama City Bay, Panama (where several fatal attacks have been reported), India, and along Mexico's Yucatán coast.

Speculation has been going on for centuries about the manner in which the sawfish uses its weapon. The sixteenth-century naturalist, Olaus Magnus, Archbishop of Uppsala in Sweden, reported that the sawfish "will swim under the ships, and cut them, that the water may come in, and he may feed upon the men when the ship is drowned." And the eighteenth-century English naturalist, John Lathan, told of "a battle between several Sawfishes and whale, when all of them attacking the whale at once, soon became victorious."

Modern research has shown that sawfish use their saws to stun or slash prey. A sawfish sometimes rises up to attack a school of small fish from below, slashing with its saw to kill fishes or daze them for consumption later. Sawfish seem to spend most of their time feeding on the bottom. They use their saws to poke in the mud and sand, and they often wear down the tips of their saw teeth at this task. Researchers are skeptical about reports that sawfish "saw" chunks of flesh from the bodies of large fish.

Many young are born at one time. In one female fifteen and a half feet long, twenty-three young were found. The pup's needle-sharp saw teeth are encased in a membrane; the "saw" is as flexible as leather at birth. Soon after birth, the sheath is sloughed off and the saw snout hardens.

Smalltooth Sawfish (Pristis pectinatus)

Studies of this sawfish in captivity helped researchers understand the use of the snout "saw." C. M. Breder, at the Lerner Marine Laboratory on Bimini Island in the Bahamas, fed a sawfish small fish or pieces of larger fish. When food was placed on the bottom, the sawfish swam over it and, like a skate, picked it up with its slitlike mouth, which is on its bottom side, aft of the "saw." When food floated on the surface or fell down through the water, the sawfish struck at it sidewise and impaled it on one of its saw teeth. Then it swam to the bottom, scraped the food off the tooth by rubbing it along the bottom, then swiftly swam over it to devour it.

Within three weeks, Breder reported, the sawfish began to change its behavior. No longer did it attempt to impale the fish on the way down.

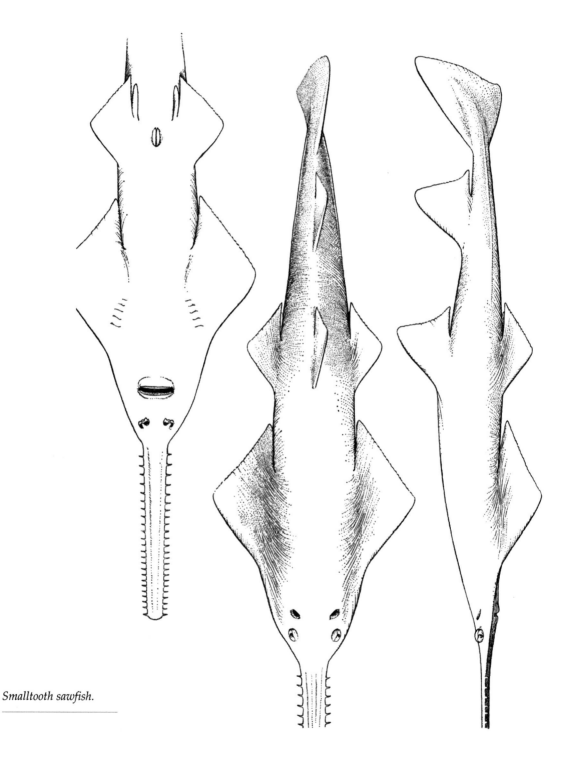

Smalltooth sawfish.

"Evidently in the intervening period," Breder wrote, "it had learned the impalement was unnecessary and there was no danger of the fish swimming away. An hour's delay in feeding was all that was necessary to revive its original energetic attacks on food objects."

P. pectinatus has been reported in numerous rivers throughout its range. Freshwater sightings in the United States include these rivers: Mississippi, Red of Arkansas, Indian and St. Johns in Florida, and rivers along the coast of North Carolina.

A similar species, *P. clavata*, is found in Australia.

Maximum known size: 20 feet.

Distribution: Along both coasts of Florida and northward to North Carolina (with reports as far north as New Jersey); along the coast of the Gulf of Mexico; from mid-Brazil northward along the South American coast; in the Caribbean–West Indian region.

Danger to humans: Avoid contact. Although encounters between sawfish and divers are rare, sawfish of every species have a reputation as a dangerous animal.

Southern Sawfish *(Pristis perotteti)*

A sawfish of estuaries and freshwater habitats, it seems to be as comfortable in salt and brackish water as in the water of rivers and lakes, including Lake Nicaragua. Specimens have been taken 450 miles up the Amazon.

A seventeen-foot sawfish caught off the Texas coast weighed 1,300 pounds, and a West Indian specimen of unrecorded length had an estimated weight of 5,300 pounds.

Maximum known size: 21 feet.

Distribution: In tropical waters on both sides of the Atlantic and Gulf of Mexico.

Green Sawfish (*Pristis zijsron*)

An Australian species known to reach a length of twenty-four feet and described as dangerous when cornered.

Family Rhinobatidae (guitarfish)

The guitarfish gets its name from the look produced by the shape of its head and moderately flattened body—combined, head and body give it the general appearance of a guitar. In France, they see the fish as a violin (*violon de mer*), and in Australia the fish are called fiddler rays and banjo sharks. In India, they are called plowfish, because as they burrow along the bottom in search of prey, they leave furrows on the ocean floor.

The largest guitarfish (*Rhynchobatus djiddensis*)—ten feet long, weighing 500 pounds—have been found in the Indian and Pacific Oceans. Most guitarfish are believed to reach a maximum of six feet, but little is known about their development.

Guitarfish swim along the bottom or lie half buried in sand or mud. An Australian reports that guitarfish there "can be easily approached and picked up by the tail." Swimming, they use their muscular tail for locomotion and their pectoral fins for up and down and sideways navigation. The underside, containing the gills, is flattened like a skate or a ray.

Embryos in the female's uterus are nourished by yolk stored in a yolk sac. There is no placental connection to the mother. Young are born at the completion of a gestation period of unknown length.

About thirty-odd known species of guitarfish live in the coastal waters of most warm seas in the world. They are rarely seen around islands.

Spotted Guitarfish *(Rhinobatos lentiginosus)*

One of the most commonly found guitarfishes in the Atlantic, *R. lentiginosus* is little known. There are not even reliable records on its full adult size. It may grow to several feet in length, but the largest recorded specimen was thirty inches long.

The spotted guitarfish has a thorny snout and is ashy gray to olive or chocolate brown above, with its upper surface "freckled" with small dots; its lower surface is usually yellow or yellowish white. This guitarfish feeds mostly on sand-dwelling crustaceans. Females are known to have given birth to as many as six young at a time.

Maximum known size: Estimated at 5 or 6 feet.

Distribution: Western Atlantic coastal waters from Yucatán to Cape Lookout, North Carolina.

Southern Guitarfish *(Rhinobatos percellens)*

Close to *R. lentiginosus* in appearance, the Southern guitarfish has been found in waters more than 350 feet deep.

Maximum known size: Unknown. Specimens are about 3 feet long.

Distribution: Coastal waters of the western Atlantic from the Caribbean to northern Argentina; reported off tropical West Africa, including the mouth of the Zaire River.

Spotted guitarfish. A—female; B—upper surface of female's snout, showing tubercles; C—male; D—side view of male's tail; E—under view of female's snout.

Shovelnose Guitarfish (*Rhinobatos productus*)

Normally fish of the shallows, the shovelnose guitarfish has nevertheless been found in deep water.

Maximum known size: 5½ feet.
Distribution: Northern California to Gulf of California.
Other Pacific Coast guitarfish:

- Thornback (*Platyrhinoidis triseriata*). About 3 feet; found from Tomales Bay, northern California to Bahia Magdalena, southern Baja California, usually as far as the surf line.

- Banded guitarfish (*Zapteryx exasperata*). Heart-shaped, about 3 feet long; found from Jalama Beach, central California, to Panama, frequently in tidepools. Also known in Brazil.

Subclass Holocephali, Order Chimaeriformes

Chimaeras—named after a mythological Greek creature with a lion's head, a goat's body, and a serpent's tail—have also been called ghost sharks, spookfish, and ratfish. Like sharks, they have cartilaginous skeletons and denticle scales. All the Chimaeroids are oviparous, laying large egg cases, some as long as sixteen and a half inches. Incubation lasts from nine to twelve months. Males have the typical claspers of selachians, but with variations. Some have a "trifid," or three-pronged clasper, and all have a third clasperlike organ on their foreheads. Unique among known fish, the forehead clasper is believed to be used in some way in mating, but its definite purpose is an ichthyological mystery.

They have tongues, like a shark but unlike skates or rays. Their brains and stomachs are like sharks and so is their swimming technique—propulsion by undulating their lower bodies. But they swim slowly and feebly.

Chimaeras also have the covered gill openings of bony fishes, making them seem like some odd link between cartilaginous selachians and bony teleosts. But studies of their fossils and embryology indicate that they are not ancestors of sharks, but creatures that diverged from some early shark stem.

Chimaeras rarely grow to more than six feet in length, and some species are smaller. They are bottom feeders, seeking small fishes and invertebrates.

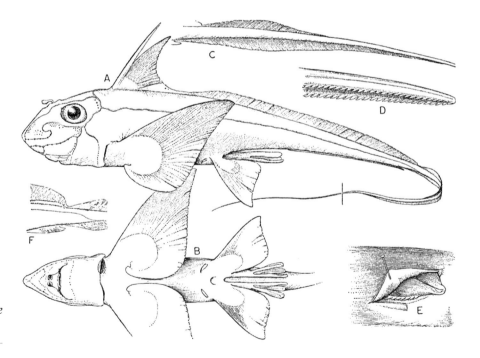

Male Cuban chimaera (Chimaera cubana). *A—side view; B—view from below; C—long caudal fin; D—spine shown on dorsal spine; E—rasp-like tentaculum, a holding structure used in copulation.*

162

Family Callorynchidae, elephant chimaeras

Chimaeras are usually classified into about twenty-eight species in three families. The Callorynchidae family includes the elephant chimaeras, or elephant fish—known in Australia as the Southern Beauty. All members of this family have flexible noses that resemble an elephant's trunk.

Their fringed egg capsules, smooth on one side and furlike on the other, may be as long as sixteen inches

Elephant Fish (*Callorhynchus callohynchus*)

Although most often taken at depths of 30 to 180 feet, it has been found at 600 feet and deeper off New Zealand. It has been found in rivers in South Africa and Tasmania. See color insert for illustration.

Maximum size: Unknown.

Distribution: Southern coast of South America from Uruguay and northern Argentina to Patagonia, Tierra del Fuego, Chile, and Peru; New Zealand, southern Australian waters; South Africa, from Algoa Bay on the east around Cape of Good Hope to Walfish Bay.

Family Chimaeridae (ratfish)

These are short-nosed, long-tailed chimaeras. The species in this family have venomous spines in front of their first dorsal fins.

Atlantic Ratfish (*Chimaera monstrosa*)

This is one of six of similar species found in the Caribbean, the Mediterranean, and Pacific waters.

Maximum size: Unknown.

Distribution: Northeastern Atlantic northward from the Azores and Morocco; South African waters; the Mediterranean; Norway and Iceland.

Ratfish (*Hydrolagus colliei*)

A Pacific chimaera usually found in deep water; but divers have reported seeing it in shallow water at night, with eyes shining like those of a cat.

Maximum size: Unknown.

Distribution: Alaska to California.

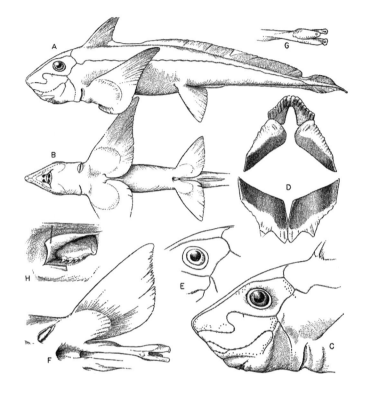

Deep-water chimaera (A and B views of female); C—side view of head of male shows mucous canals (E—in close-up); D—upper (top) and lower dental plates; F—under view of male's tentaculum, used in copulation; G—dorsal view of clasper; H—tenaculum of clasper exposed.

Deep-Water Chimaera *(Hydrolagus affinis)*

Found at depths between 960 and 7,740 feet, this is a fish that resembles other species found from South Africa to Japan. But because it lives at such depths, its habits are unknown.

In the latter part of the nineteenth century, these chimaera were plentiful off Nova Scotia and in the Gulf of Maine. Fishermen went deep for halibut then. As the deep-water halibut fishery declined, so did the taking of deep-water chimaera.

Maximum size: 49 inches.

Distribution: In deep waters of both the western and eastern Atlantic.

Purple Chimaera *(Hydrolagus purpurescens)*

This species is known from one specimen that was dredged up off the Hawaiian island of Kauai between 5,700 and 6,400 feet. It was described as "uniform purplish or plum colored," in contrast to other chimaeras, which are generally silvery gray.

Maximum size: 2½ feet.

Distribution: Unknown.

Family Rhinochimaeridae (long-nosed chimaeras)

Long, pointed snouts give these chimaera their common name; the snout is also acknowledged in the family's scientific name.

This is a worldwide family, with representatives in the Atlantic, off South Africa and Japan, and in the Bay of Bengal. Some have been taken from 6,000-foot depths.

Long-nosed chimaera (Harriotta raleighana)

Because specimens of this species and their egg cases have been trawled from half a mile to a mile and a half down, the long-nosed chimaera is assumed to be a deep-water fish.

Maximum size: 3 feet.

Distribution: In deep waters of both the western and eastern Atlantic, including the Azores and waters off Scotland.

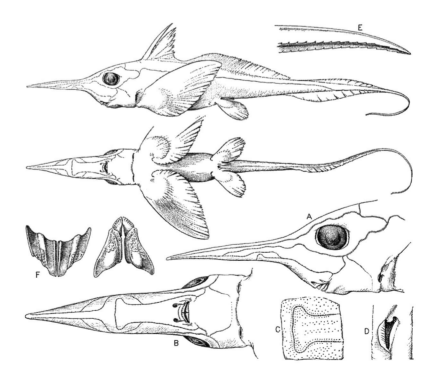

Long-nosed chimaera. A—side view of head shows mucous canals; B—under view of head; C—section of skin showing mucous pores around loop of a mucous canal; D—gill opening, with edge partially rolled forward; E—side view of dorsal spine; F—dorsal plate (upper at right; lower at left).

Companions of the Shark

Pilot fishes, cleaner fishes, and remoras—all bony fishes unrelated to selachians—have formed close associations with many sharks. Pilot fishes are so called because they often swim before a shark and seem to be guiding it. Cleaner fishes do just that, cleansing sharks and rays of parasites. Remoras, or sucker fish, attach themselves to sharks and to some large rays. These companions of the shark are never molested. The coexistence of the shark and its smaller companions is called commensalism—literally, eating from the same table. Their relationship is also symbiotic, for each creature gets something from the relationship: relief from parasites for the shark, food for the associates.

The parasites certainly do molest the shark, but never fatally, for killing the host would be lethal for the parasites as well. They include half-inch copepods that use adhesive pads to stick to sharks' fins and feed on skin secretions. Other copepods have claws that dig into a shark's tough skin and feed on blood and surface secretions. A third kind is a form of barnacle that attaches to the dorsal fins of dogfish as larvae, a root growing into the shark and living off nutrients found there. Sharks leaping from the water may be trying to rid themselves of these parasites.

A particularly repulsive copepod lives in the eye of the Greenland shark. About an inch long, it anchors on the surface of the eye and lives there throughout the shark's life. Sometimes so many of these copepods crowd into the eye that the Greenland shark's eyesight is impaired.

Some isopod crustaceans that inhabit the shark's gills, mouth, and skin are so big that *they* have parasites. Another type of parasite is so large that Australian Aborigines call it "the shark's wife."

Sharks also suffer from tapeworms. The typical tapeworm, while living in the shark's gut, periodically breaks off a segment of its foot-long body. This starts a complex life cycle: the shark excretes the segment; when it is consumed by a free-swimming copepod, eggs within the segment hatch; the copepod is then eaten by a bony fish; a shark then eats the fish, and the cycle resumes in the shark's gut.

Pilot Fish (Naucrates ductor)

Herman Melville described the immunity that pilot fish enjoy as they swim around ferocious sharks, hunting for other fish to eat:

> . . . They have nothing of harm to dread
> But liquidly glide on his ghostly flank
> Or before his Gorgonian head;
> Or lurk in the port of serrated teeth. . . .
> An asylum in jaws of the Fates. . . .

Only in poetic fancies do pilot fish swim into the jaws of sharks. The zebra-striped pilot fish's behavior—darting ahead of a shark as it approaches prey—inspired stories about how the tiny pilot leads the great shark around, as a Seeing Eye dog leads a blind man.

The shark needs no pilot to guide it, but the pilot fish certainly uses, if not needs, the shark. Besides getting morsels of food from the shark's biting and chewing of prey, the pilot fish gains protection from other sharks, for it appears that no shark harms any pilot fish.

Several pilot fish swim in front of sharks (particularly whitetip sharks), often within inches of a shark's jaws, feeding on crumbs of food. They seem to ride a small pressure wave set up by the big fish. Others swim along, maintaining an almost constant position near the shark's pectoral fins. Occasionally, they may dart away from their shark to get morsels of food, but, as a scientist remarked about this behavior, they "hurry back again like children afraid of losing their nurse."

When a large shark is hooked and is being hauled out of the water, its pilot fish excitedly swim around the ascending body, almost as if they are fretting about the loss of their protective companion. Then they skitter off and immediately seek another shark.

Cleaner Fishes

Many fishes earn a living by cleaning parasites and dead skin tissue from other, larger fishes. Such interspecies behavior is particularly true between sharks and several species of wrasses, known as the "cleaner wrasses" (*Labroides* spp.). These tropical, brightly colored fishes have been seen eating parasites lodging in the gills and mouths of sharks and large rays. Wrasses of the genus *Bodianus* have also been observed cleaning sharks. There seems to be a species-to-species relationship among the wrasses, with some specializing in sharks and others in rays.

Some grooming wrasses that live in reefs set up "cleaner stations," caves or crevices where sharks and rays come to be groomed. They may be wanting to get rid of their parasites, but they also seem to enjoy the sensation of grooming: "Fish wanting to be groomed (host fish) will often adopt a specific posture that communicates its desire and enables the cleaner to better inspect for ectoparasites," Scott W. Michael writes in *Reef Sharks and Rays of the World*. "Sharks and rays expand their gill slits, distend their jaws, slow their swimming rates, and adopt specific postures to help the parasite-feeding fish accomplish its work."

Remora *(Echeneis naucrates)*

Using a modified dorsal fin that works like a suction cup, remoras attach themselves to sharks. Young remoras, perhaps to stay out of the way of

*Galapagos shark with
an attached remora.*

aggressive oldsters, sometimes attach themselves inside the mouth, spiracles, and gill slits of sharks. Remoras, like cleaner fishes, help to rid sharks of parasites. They also eat bits of food ignored by the shark, along with plankton, which they consume as the host swims through the sea. Remoras feed on the placentalike tissue that enshrouds newborn sharks—remoras have been seen attached around a female's cloaca, apparently in anticipation of birth. Remoras are not parasites; they do not suck blood or injure the shark.

A remora can latch on while the shark is moving by the use of tiny barbs on the disk. The barbs act as hooks while the remora gets in position to use its suction mechanism. The remora's first dorsal fin has modified to form an oval plate on the top of its head. The surface of the plate is ridged, like the sole of a boot. When the remora wants to attach itself to a shark, it swims upward until the disk comes in contact with the shark. Then, by muscular action, it raises the ridges and rim of the disk, creating a partial vacuum.

Experiments have shown that the disk's sucking power is about fifteen pounds per square inch. Since a larger remora's disk covers an area of more than eight square inches, it can theoretically hold on with a grip that could lift 100 pounds.

The remora was called the "ship-holder" by ancient Greeks. The genus name *Echeneis* means "those that hold back ships," and remora comes from a Latin word meaning "a delay." The historian Pliny said that the Emperor Caligula was fatally delayed on his voyage to Antium by remoras that held his ship despite 400 oarsmen's efforts to free it. Mark Antony's defeat at Actium was blamed on remoras that kept his ship fast when Antony ordered it into battle. We also have it on the word of Ben Jonson that a remora can "stay a ship that's under sail."

Remoras of this and other species have been found attached to manta rays, sunfish, sea turtles, whales—and certainly to ships. Mantas are often accompanied by remoras attached under their wide pectorals or in their mouths.

Christopher Columbus reported seeing natives in the New World using a strange fish that was tethered on a line and sent out to attach itself to a sea turtle, which was then hauled in on the tether. The natives were using a remora to fish with. In some parts of Australia and China, in Zanzibar and Mozambique, the technique is still used by native fishermen. In Madagascar, native sorcerers place dried pieces of the remora's disk about the neck of an unfaithful wife so that she will return to her husband—and stick to him.

When the shark feeds, the remora may detach itself by relaxing its disk muscles. It then swims off for the crumbs. When it finishes eating, the remora reattaches itself to the shark and awaits its next meal. Remoras will sometimes swim independently after prey that is simultaneously being attacked by the host shark. Four or five remoras may attach themselves to a single big shark—and even more onto whale sharks.

Also known as: Sucker fish.

Maximum known size: 3 feet.

Distribution: Tropical and semitropical seas.

A great white shark attacks a cage off Australia.

CHAPTER 5

When a Shark Attacks

We live on a watery planet with sharks in every sea, and we often venture into those seas. But shark attacks on people are extremely rare. Each year, throughout the world, there are probably seventy to a hundred shark attacks. Five to fifteen are fatal. The chances of being attacked by a shark, it is often said, are about as great as being struck by lightning. The annual risk of death from lightning in the United States is, in fact, thirty times greater than that from shark attack. In 1986, lightning killed 166 people in South Africa—and a shark killed one person.

Alligators are also killers, but "man-eating sharks" get more publicity; *Jaws* conjured up an image of a shark, not an alligator. In a comparison of shark and alligator attacks in the United States, researchers of the International Shark Attack File noted that between 1948 and 1995, alligators killed eight people whereas sharks killed six.

For every 1,000 people who drown in the United States each year, one person is attacked by a shark. And, unlike victims of drowning, people survive shark attacks. Snakes, bees, wasps, and dogs cause far more deaths than sharks do. So does driving to and from the beach.

Australia's coasts teem with sharks. At one Australian beach, a statistical analysis showed that for each bather attacked by a shark, about 30 million bathers had suffered no more than sunburn. Of the swimmers who have enjoyed Florida waters in modern times, about one out of every 5 million bathers has been attacked in any way by a shark.

But statistics cannot still the fear evoked by the sight of a dark dorsal fin. And statistics have a way of quickly changing. Surges of attacks occur for no discernible reason. In California, the surge began in 1989, with four attacks in 1989, five in 1990, three in 1991, two in 1992, and three in 1993. Surfers were frequent victims, and the white shark (usually called the great white shark) was the shark most frequently blamed. Between 1982 and 1987 there had been twenty shark attacks in California and Hawaii. Between 1987 and 1993 there were thirty-three—most of them on surfers. Attacks also increased in Florida: twenty-two attacks in 1994; twenty-eight between January and October 1995. The suspected attackers were not great whites but blacktip sharks three or four feet long.

Another drastic statistical shift came in 1997 when the number of unprovoked shark attacks throughout the world soared from thirty-six to fifty-six. The record high was seventy-two in 1995, when twenty-five attacks occurred in Florida. Researchers attributed the sharp rise to the fact that hurricane-driven winds brought larger waves to Florida's east coast, and the waves brought more surfers, along with more encounters with sharks.

Matthew Callahan, in an International Shark Attack File report, said that in 1997 the United States had the largest number of attacks: thirty-four. Australia had five attacks, Brazil four, the Bahamas and South Africa three each, and Japan and New Guinea had two each. Mexico, Fiji, North Africa, Reunion Island in the Indian Ocean, and Vanuatu in the South Pacific each reported an attack.

Callahan said that the number reflected the availability of sharks and the amount of time people spent in the water. He said that the reason for the increase was unclear, but may have been partly related to warmer temperatures seen in 1997.

"The United States has a high rate of tourism and beach activity, and a high level of aquatic activities. On top of that, the United States has a large amount of coastline," he said. Despite the large number of attacks in the United States, the fatality rate was much lower than in any other country, Callahan said.

Nearly half of all the attacks in 1997 involved surfers, windsurfers, and rafters, according to the study. Other victims were swimmers, waders, and divers. The study said that the number of attacks last year in Florida nearly doubled to twenty-five from thirteen in 1996.

We do not know exactly how many victims are claimed by the shark. Many people who disappear at sea undoubtedly are unrecorded shark victims. The sea is a dangerous place, and more and more people are swimming, diving, and boating in this dangerous place. Many of them will suffer or even die. But the deaths and injuries will be caused by drowning, cardiac arrest, dehydration, jellyfish stings, and sunburn. Many, too, will be slashed—but by the edges of sea shells and broken beer bottles, not shark bites.

A phenomenal increase in surfers has led to an increase in shark attacks off favored surfer beaches in California, Florida, Oregon, and Australia. In the early 1950s, when surfing was beginning to become popular around Santa Cruz—California's "Surf City"—there were perhaps 1,500 surfers. Today, along the entire West Coast, there are an estimated 500,000. Also, the surfers' habits happen to coincide with the sharks' habits: Both favor dusk and dawn, the surfers for surfing, the sharks for eating. And surfers often hunt for the perfect wave in areas where sharks hunt for food. To a shark, a surfer in a shiny black wetsuit may look like an elephant seal or sea lion—the favored prey of white sharks.

Surfers also may look like a school of mullet, shark researcher George Burgess told *Surfer Magazine*. "Here in Florida," he said, "the soles of the feet and palms of the hands tend to be much lighter than the rest of the surfer's tanned skin. Black-tip sharks, who are very good at distinguishing contrast, naturally perceive the flashing white as fish bellies."

Speaking about the increasing number of attacks, Burgess said in 1995, "The water does not belong to human beings. When you're entering the ocean, you're entering the wilderness. It's not jumping in your pool in your backyard."

Sharks are not the only dangerous animals in the sea. There are barracudas, moray eels, octopuses, sharp-spined sea urchins, and the poisonous creatures lurking in certain coral reefs. Stingrays, toadfish, catfish, and jellyfish can inflict painful injury on swimmers and waders. The Portuguese man-of-war's tentacles—sometimes as long as fifty feet—have specialized cells that produce painful stings and welts when touched by an unwary swimmer.

But it is the shark that swimmers fear the most. The fear surges from deep in the human psyche. For a long time, however, the fear of being eaten alive was a potential reality only for big-game hunters and seafarers. Not until the twentieth century did shark attacks become a subject that interested the American public.

Shark Attack Skeptics

In a paper written in April 1916, three of the most renowned shark experts in the United States all but dismissed the possibility of a shark attack on a "living man." As a postscript, one of the authorities added, "Cases of shark bite do now and then occur, but there is a great difference between being attacked by a shark and being bitten by one, and the cases of shark bite are usually found to have been due to someone incautiously approaching a shark impounded or tangled in a net, or gasping on the shore. And, under such circumstances, almost any creature will bite."

Recalling an unclaimed $500 reward that had been posted for proof of a shark attack north of Cape Hatteras, he concluded, "That this reward was never claimed shows that there is practically no danger of any attack from a shark about our coasts."

Shortly after this was written, during the summer of 1916, in a period of twelve days, sharks killed four people and attacked a fifth along the New Jersey coast. The attacks inspired a panic that closed beaches and resorts. (These events became nearly half a century later the basis for the book and movie *Jaws*.)

Not until the 1916 attacks did people in the United States believe that sharks went after swimmers. In fact, even after two fatal attacks that year, the experts still did not concede the existence of dangerous sharks in northern Atlantic waters.

One theory held that heavy cannonading in the North Sea had driven sharks across the Atlantic to more tranquil seas. Another theory suggested that sharks were feeding on swimmers because they had been deprived of their usual diet of refuse from passenger liners, whose sailings were being curtailed by German U-boats. The European war also spawned the idea that sharks had been feasting so well on war dead floating down rivers into the sea that they had undergone a change of dietary habits.

In October 1916, the shark experts reappeared to write: "It must be admitted that deaths from shark bite within a short radius of New York City would seem to be one of those unaccountable happenings that take place from time to time to the confounding of savants and the justification of the wildest tradition."

The attacks of 1916 inspired the idea of a "Shark Year," some kind of extraordinary migration that drew an unusual number of sharks to the New Jersey coast. Some confirmation of the theory came from Edwin Thorne, a member of the Board of Managers of the Zoological Society, who, between the years 1911 and 1927, spent a total of 302 days looking for sharks in Long Island's Great South Bay. During those years, he sighted 1,799 sharks and killed 305 of them. In 1916 alone, he saw 277 sharks and killed 102—in no other year did he see or kill as many.

Nearly all the sharks killed by Thorne were female brown sharks that had entered Great South Bay to give birth to their young. An increase in the number of brown sharks in New York waters would have had no direct connection with the New Jersey attacks. But the increase did raise the question of whether a population explosion in indigenous sharks some- how had brought about the appearance of the white shark.

By the 1930s, the 1916 attacks had faded into newspaper clippings and once more the experts claimed that sharks were not dangerous animals.

William Beebe, the famed underwater explorer, scoffed at stories of shark attacks. Beebe, in his bathysphere at the bottom of the ocean, had peered through the thick windows and had seen sharks. He had observed them close at hand while in a bathing suit and diving helmet, in fairly shallow water. None had menaced him. Once, Beebe said, he had asked the head of the pearl-diving industry in Ceylon if sharks bit men.

"Why, yes," the head pearl diver replied. "We lose many men. They go down, disappear, and we see blood coming to the top of the water."

"Now, tell me," Beebe said, "as one man of science to another, did you ever know a shark to bite a man?"

The way Beebe told the story, the head diver grinned sheepishly and answered: "No, but the tourists like to hear such stories, so we tell them what they want to know."

Attacks upon swimmers were attributed to "large fishes." That was the label used in 1924, for instance, when a man was attacked by "a large fish" while standing near the shore of Folly Island, South Carolina. More than 100 stitches were needed to close the wounds in his left leg. Two months after the attack, he went back to the hospital, complaining about intense pains in his left knee. The knee was operated upon, and a remnant of a tooth was removed. The tooth, then identified as a barracuda's, was examined years later and shown to be a shark's. Despite the evidence, the belief persisted that sharks did not attack bathers. Even a confirmed attack did not dispel the belief. That attack—the first known fatal shark attack in New England waters—occurred on July 25, 1936, about 150 yards off Hollywood Beach, just above Mattapoisett Harbor in Buzzards Bay, Massachusetts. The victim was a sixteen-year-old boy. A companion saw a shark suddenly seize his left leg and pull him under. The companion got him into a boat and to shore, where he died.

Skepticism about shark attacks persisted up to the advent of World War II. When the war began, neither sailors nor ocean-spanning pilots were prepared for what awaited them if they were cast into shark-infested waters. Survivors of a British warship torpedoed in the South Atlantic in December 1941, for example, reported attacks on life rafts by a pack of sharks. How many drowned—and how many were devoured by sharks—will never be known. Nor will it be known how many people were killed by sharks in other wartime disasters.

U.S. survival manuals published at the start of the war dismissed the shark as "slow-moving, cowardly, and easily frightened off by splashing." The shark was described as "a wary fish, suspicious of noise, movement, unfamiliar forms. This trait alone would restrain a shark from attacking a swimming person." Men in the water were advised to hit sharks on the nose, stab them, or "grab a pectoral fin as he goes by, and ride with him as long as you can hold your breath."

Dr. George A. Llano, an Air Force research specialist who was himself a life raft survivor, made a study of airmen who went down at sea during the war. Of 2,500 reports, only 38 mentioned contacts with sharks. But, as Llano remarked, "When sharks are successful, they leave no evidence, and the number of missing airmen who may have succumbed to them cannot be estimated. . . .

"Men have spent hours in the water among sharks without being touched, and in view of the evidence some of the escapes seem little short of miraculous. The one feature all accounts illustrate is the fact that, though clothing cannot be depended on to prevent attack, sharks are more apt to bite a bare than a clothed body."

The Sharks of the *Indianapolis*

In the movie *Jaws*, Quint tells a horror story about the World War II sinking of the cruiser *Indianapolis* and the attack on survivors by packs of sharks. The story is true.

After delivering components of the Hiroshima atomic bomb to Tinian Island in July 1945, the *Indianapolis* sailed to Guam, then continued toward Leyte in the Philippines. On July 28, the cruiser was torpedoed by a Japanese submarine and quickly sunk. About 850 men survived the sinking and floated in the water or on life rafts. More than 50 injured men died during the night.

The sharks came at dawn, attacking the clusters of men suspended in the water in their life jackets. One survivor counted twenty-five attacks, another counted eighty-eight.

Sharks kept coming, sometimes in packs, sometimes as solitary marauders, day after day. By the time rescuers arrived four days after the sinking, only 318 men survived. More than 500 men had vanished during the ordeal, and sharks had got most of them.

After the war, interest in shark attacks paralleled the boom in swimming, surfing, and recreational boating. Then in 1974 came the publication of *Jaws* by Peter Benchley and the showing the following year of the movie of the same name. For the first time, moviegoers could *see* shark attacks, if only by a mechanical monster. *Jaws* launched a new and enduring wave of loathing toward sharks, any sharks—big or small, harmless or potentially dangerous.

Coincidentally with *Jaws* came an increase in research on sharks and shark attacks, much of which has been woven into the work of the International Shark Attack File, the most reliable source of information on a subject persistently mishandled by much of the media.

The International Shark Attack File

The United States Navy has traditionally had more than a passing interest in shark attacks. Memories of the *Indianapolis* and other documented attacks during World War II inspired the Office of Naval Research to fund a search for a shark repellent and an increase in shark-related research programs. A conference, sponsored by the American Institute of Biological Sciences, drew scientists from thirty-four nations to New Orleans in 1958. Concerned about the lack of dependable information on shark behavior and the scarcity of facts about shark attacks, the scientists formed a working group, which created the Shark Research Panel (SRP). Its members were Perry W. Gilbert (chairman), Sidney R. Galler, John R. Olive, Leonard P. Schultz, Stewart Springer, and later Albert L. Tester and H. David Baldridge. The panel initiated formation of the Shark Attack File, the first such attempt to comprehensively document attacks on a global, historical basis. In 1963 Schultz made the first attempt to examine the files by drawing up a list of shark attacks for the world (coauthored by Marilyn H. Malin). It appeared in *Sharks and Survival*, the first of two Gilbert-edited volumes emanating from the Navy's support of shark research.

From 1959 to 1971, information on shark attacks throughout the world were collected by the Smithsonian Institution, Cornell University, and the Mote Marine Laboratory of Sarasota, Florida. Searching through old medical journals, ships' logs, hospital and physicians' records, and newspaper files from all over the world, the panel analyzed 790 shark attacks deemed well enough documented to warrant study. Even decades after that first breakthrough study, the facts, reduced to statistics, still hold up and are worth noting:

- Of the 790 attacks, 599 were unprovoked. Of individuals attacked, 400 died and 390 recovered. (Many records are incomplete; the total number of persons attacked is not known.)

- Most attacks (75.4 percent) in Australian, North American, and African waters occurred in summer months. But in equatorial waters, attacks occurred equally in all months. This means that the so-called "shark-attack season" is nothing more than the human swimming season, whenever that happens to be.

- Most individual attacks (62.2 percent) occurred within 300 feet of shore.

- Most victims (63.3 percent) were swimming or floating on the surface when attacked.

- Few attacks occurred at night, but proportionately more nighttime swimmers are attacked than daylight swimmers. Nighttime is feeding time for many species of shark. (In the tropics, knowledgeable natives usually will not enter the water at night, though they may swim unconcernedly during the day, even when sharks are present.) See **Attacks: When, Where, What** (page 204) for additional details.

U.S. Navy support of the file ceased in 1968, but the file continued and grew. Researchers began placing the information onto IBM-type punch cards. Out of this pioneer computer work came 1,165 case histories of attacks on individuals, 151 on boats, and 100 during air and sea disasters. The SRP also coordinated more than 100 studies of shark biology and behavior and tested more than 200 chemical compounds, biological products, and devices in a search for shark deterrents.

When members of the SRP received word of a shark attack anywhere in the world, they attempted to get documentation from reliable witnesses, doctors, hospitals, police departments, scientists, and others. A two-page form requesting information concerning the details of the attack was sent to anyone willing to supply documentation.

The Shark Attack File was originally kept by Leonard P. Schultz in the Division of Fishes of the Smithsonian Institution, with a duplicate working file maintained by the chairman of the Shark Research Panel, Perry W. Gilbert at Cornell University. Sometimes a physician in the area would be asked to help, or one of the many ichthyologists cooperating with the panel went to the scene. If the victim survived, he or she was asked to fill out a detailed questionnaire. Whether the victim lived or died, witnesses, policemen, hospital attendants, his physician, and his relatives were interviewed.

The questionnaire and the interviews sought such information as the depth, the temperature, and the condition of the water; the time of the attack and what the weather was like; the color of the victim's clothing or bathing suit, and the color of his or her skin; the kind of shark and who identified it; the nature and treatment of the wounds; and how both the victim and the shark behaved before, during, and after the attack.

The panel divided attacks into two broad categories: provoked and unprovoked. Provoked attacks included incidents involving fishermen being bitten while hauling sharks into a boat or trying to untangle sharks from nets. The panel also looked at air and sea disasters, categorizing attacks on victims or survivors as unprovoked.

Another category that showed up early in the research was designated as a "boat attack"—when sharks made deliberate physical contact with a boat, life raft, water ski, or accessory equipment. In 1960, for example, there were twelve such incidents, none of them fatal.

In 1996, off New South Wales, Australia, a mako shark bit off the bow of a twenty-one-foot boat, dumping three men and a woman into the sea. The shark did not attack the swimmers. And in 1993 a white shark lunged at a kayak off the coast of Sonoma County, California, hurling the occupant into the sea amid four other kayakers. As in the Australian incident, the shark did not attack her or the other kayakers, who managed to get her and her kayak to shore.

At Mote Marine Laboratory, 1,165 reported attacks and case histories were analyzed in a 1973 report, *Shark Attack Against Man: A Program of Data*

Reduction and Analysis, by H. David Baldridge, a retired U.S. Navy officer. Using a computerized study that sought common factors in the attacks, the report examined data from attacks as far back as 1580, with the emphasis on modern attacks. (The 1580 attack involved a sailor who was killed by a large shark when he fell overboard on a voyage from Portugal to India—see page 215.) More than two thirds of the reports are from attacks that occurred after 1940—except for World War II, a period for which records are spotty, as Llano's research had shown.

After Navy support of the Shark Attack File ended in 1968, it began wandering, first to the Mote Marine Laboratory in Florida and then to the University of Rhode Island, where it was maintained and enlarged under the direction of John McAniff of the National Undersea Safety Program. Funding again dried up, and once more the file had to find a new home. In 1988 the records, by then known as the International Shark Attack File (ISAF), were transferred to the Florida Museum of Natural History, under the auspices of the American Elasmobranch Society, an international society of scientists who study sharks, skates, rays, and chimaeras. The keeper of the ISAF is George H. Burgess, with Matthew Callahan.

"We continue to document attack records from the somewhat incomplete 1968–1988 period as well as investigate new ones," says Burgess, who often is sought out by the media for comment on attacks. Data from Baldridge's long-lost computer punch cards have been entered into a computer database. Other databases have been contributed, through Elasmobranch Society members' contacts, by attack monitors in California, Hawaii, Australia, and South Africa.

"We welcome the unsolicited documentation of any attack from all time periods," Burgess says. "Newly acquired data will be added as it appears, and periodic analyses of the database will be performed to determine trends in local and worldwide attacks. We currently are working on a revision of Baldridge's synthetic analysis of worldwide attacks. The database is also made available to qualified biologists and physicians who wish to address specific questions regarding shark attack."

Inquiries from the media and general public are answered by the ISAF staff, but actual access to the files is otherwise limited to scientists. Because the ISAF contains much information that is confidential, such as medical and autopsy reports, graphic medical photos, and personal interviews, access is carefully guarded. A panel of AES shark researchers must approve each request for information about a given incident. Approval is given on a case-by-case basis.

From the data first assembled by the Shark Research Panel in the 1950s and from work that continued into the 1990s, some general ideas have appeared. In *Shark Attack,* for example, Baldridge noted that many sharks took one or two bites from a victim and then swam away. This led to speculation that some sharks were not "man-eaters" but "man-biters." There are few documented attacks that end with the shark consuming its victim. But it happens. In 1985 in Australia, a woman snorkeling in seven feet of water was grabbed by a white shark, which bit her in half and swam off, then returned and seized the rest of the woman's body. In another Australian incident in June 1993, a scuba diver and his bride were on their honeymoon near Byron Bay, 400 miles north of Sydney. A white shark appeared, attacked the man, and swam off with him in its jaws. A short time later fishermen caught a sixteen-foot white shark, which rammed their boat, spat out human remains, and swam away.

Worldwide, according to those who maintain the International Shark Attack File, there are probably 70 to 100 shark attacks annually, of which about 5 to 15 are fatal. They say "probably" because not all shark attacks are reported. "Our information from Third World countries is especially poor, and in other areas efforts are sometimes made to keep attacks quiet for fear of bad publicity," said the 1997 report on file findings. "Historically, the death rate was much higher than today, but the advent of readily available emergency services and improved medical treatment has greatly reduced the chances of mortality. Actual numbers of shark attacks certainly are going up each year because of increasing numbers of bathers in the water, but there is no indication that there is any change in the per capita rate of attack."

ISAF records show that the steady rise in attacks is directly related to world population growth and the increasing use of the seas for recreation and commercial purposes. The records show what appears to be a drop in the number of attacks in the 1970s and 1980s. But this reflects the relatively inactive state of the ISAF during those decades. The ISAF particularly welcomes reliable information from that era. (See **Where to Give Attack Information,** page 206.)

Divers Amid Sharks

Spearfishing increases the chances of shark encounters. Researchers advise spearfishers that trailing fish juices and swimming erratically while pursuing fish attract hungry sharks. Generally, spearfishing on an outgoing tide, which may attract sharks from offshore to the fishing site, is less safe than fishing on an incoming tide, when there are usually fewer sharks inshore from the site.

An abalone diver, interviewed for a 1997 Discovery Channel documentary on sharks, said that the presence of white sharks was a peril he had to face. "The first key to white shark safety," the diver said, "is spotting him before he spots you, or at the same time he spots you. The minute he loses the element of surprise, we feel like that's a big factor, and the key thing again is to stay on the bottom, stay low to the rocks—climb into a hole if there's one near by. Don't go anywhere. The guy who swims to the surface is going to get bit for sure."

He considers springtime to be relatively safe because for years he had never seen a shark at that time of year. For the unpredictable white shark, however, there is always a first time. And one day in spring the abalone diver saw a flash about thirty-five or forty feet away. *That was a white shark,* he thought. Then, *No, that wasn't a white shark. Whitey's not out here this time of year.* "And then I looked down and picked an abalone, and I looked up and he was coming straight at me. This thing was huge.

"It was like laying [*sic*] on the street and having a station wagon drive over you. . . . But it didn't come back, and I waited for about five minutes, and it didn't come back, and it didn't come back. I worked my way back to the boat, just hugging the bottom real close. I still didn't see it, still didn't see it." When he reached the boat, he "made the fastest free ascent in the history of mankind. . . . And I pretty much walked on water the little distance I had to go, and then climbed up the ladder. I remember taking the regulator out of my mouth when I hit the deck. It was full of white foam, and I realized my mouth had gotten completely dry, and I kind of was just slobbering this white foam.

"I'm afraid of white sharks. I guess I'm not afraid enough to stop what I'm doing. I'm cautious. But I feel like we've achieved some kind of working relationship. We've achieved kind of a harmony where I can continue to work the areas that I'm working. The shark's looking for specific circumstances, and as long as I stay out of those situations, I'm going to be safe."

In September 1995, another California abalone diver, working out of a kayak, survived an attack that ended with four teeth embedded in his calf. He was in about thirty feet of water and hauling himself into the kayak when a shark grabbed his left leg. His diving partner helped to pull him away from the shark and into the kayak. As Fire Chief Jerry Hartman of Shelter Cove said, "In the tug of war, the fish let go."

But in a 1998 attack by a nurse shark in Florida waters, the fish refused to let go. The attack on the teenage swimmer began when he grabbed the tail of a small nurse shark, which turned around and bit the victim's chest. The teenager, with the shark still locked onto him, was taken to a hospital emergency room. A surgeon split the shark's spine to kill it and get it to release its hold. The boy's wound was not serious.

The basic rule that stems from these experiences: Don't panic. Well documented attacks on free-diving abalone divers and surfers indicate that a panicky, water-stirring flight may provoke a shark and escalate the strike into a fatal attack.

In August 1996, a California diver free-diving for abalone in what divers call the Red Triangle—the area between Bodega Rock, the Farallon Islands, and Santa Cruz—was bitten in the chest, shoulder, and arm by what he identified as a ten-foot white shark. Between 1960 and 1996, sharks in the Tomales Point area wounded at least six people. But the 1996 attack was the first recorded in eleven years. The diver said that while swimming about eight feet below the surface he saw the shark ten feet below him, traveling in the same direction. Suddenly the shark whirled and darted up to attack him, biting him in the chest. The diver tried to drive off the shark but "its mouth was too big." The shark changed its grip on him and then released him. The bleeding diver swam about twenty yards to his boat. The shark did not renew the attack.

Less than two months later, at Dillon Beach, within sight of Bird Rock, a surfer was attacked by what he described as an eighteen-foot white shark. The surfer was in ten feet of water about 100 yards from shore when he "felt a nudge" and a shark grabbed his leg, flipping him and his surfboard over. The shark released him, and the surfer made it to shore on his board. His wounds were not serious.

A remarkably detailed account of an attack was given by another victim, Marco Flagg, a thirty-one-year-old diver. He was diving in a wet suit in the afternoon of June 30, 1995, outside Bluefish Cove, at Point Lobos State Park, Monterey, California. The water, he reported, was "flat calm." He had logged approximately 300 dives throughout Californian waters as well as in the Caribbean, the Pacific, the Mediterranean, the Arctic Ocean off Greenland and off Cape Horn, South Africa.

Propelled by a diver scooter, he was about fifty feet down when "I looked to my right and saw the massive pectoral fin attached to the end of a torpedo-shaped body of a large fish. . . . Somewhat stunned, I quickly thought that the animal matched the shape and size of a white shark. . . . Maybe 15 to 20 seconds after the first sighting (I had already turned the scooter around), I looked to my left and below and saw the massive, wide open, near-circular, teeth-lined mouth of an animal coming at me. The mouth appeared to have a diameter of certainly more than two feet but most likely not more than three feet. I thought, 'Oh, shit,' and shortly (one second) thereafter felt a severe but dull pressure on my body. I do not recall being shaken by the animal nor taking any significant evasive or defensive action. Instead, I appeared to be free from its hold after maybe two seconds. . . ."

Flagg managed to reach the inflatable boat from which he had begun his dive. He jettisoned the scooter and got into the boat. His diving partner joined him and they headed for shore. "I had a dull pain in my gut," Flagg later reported, "but thought that there was probably no big loss of blood, as I was still conscious." He had a wound nearly two inches in diameter on his left forearm, a cut requiring eight stitches on his left leg, and a cut on his lower abdomen requiring two stitches. A large scratch was also found on the aluminum housing of a dive computer he was carrying. This, probably along with his air tank, may have absorbed enough of the shark's force to save Flagg's life.

"From a single incident," he said, "it is impossible to tell what factors were involved in the shark choosing to attack me. My simple suspicion is that it was hungry and that I happened to run across its path."

See **Wind Surfer Attacks**, page 185.

Attacks in California

Attacks on humans in northern California and Oregon have notably increased since 1959, according to information gathered by Steinhart Aquarium and the National Marines Fisheries Service. The increase paralleled a surge in California's white shark population. Research indicates that attacks will continue and even rise, keeping pace with increases in white sharks' seal prey and the number of people venturing into the water.

Attacks rarely occur in southern California, where seal populations are low. Perhaps also significant, say researchers, is the fact that southern California abalone divers are allowed to use scuba, while northern abalone divers cannot; breathhold-diving keeps them around the surface and thus increases their chances of their being attacked. Between 1926 and 1996 there were sixty-seven white shark attacks in California—sixty-five in northern and central California. (Other sources, which use data about attacks on ships and unsubstantiated accounts, puts the number of attacks closer to 120.) During that time there were also eleven attacks in Oregon, one in Washington, and two in Guadalupe Island, Baja, California. (This is probably low because Baja statistics are unreliable.) Six confirmed California attacks were fatal, as was one in Oregon. Here is what the victims were doing when they were attacked:

Swimming	9	Snorkel diving	7
Free diving	23	Scuba diving	12
Surfing	26	Kayaking	4

Wind surfers form the latest group of water users who are potential prey to sharks. A wind surfer, for example, was one of the shark attack statistics in 1995. He was attacked off Davenport, California, in September of that year. He had just completed an outside jibe and was not yet planing, when, without warning, the shark bit and held on to the back of his board. He jumped off and swam away, then moments later when the shark let go, swam back to his rig, and sailed in. There were teeth marks on both rails of the board, on one side between his rear and front straps, and on the other side near the fin—indicating a mouth span of about two feet; this would make the shark almost certainly a white shark twelve to fifteen feet long.

Numerous white sharks have been seen off the Farallon Islands, which lie close to shore and form the northern tip of the Red Triangle—the other tips are Bodega Rock and Santa Cruz—because so many attacks have occurred within its bounds. The Red Triangle attracts white sharks because the area is full of their favorite prey, seals. Divers and other visitors to Año Nuevo, the Farallones, or Guadalupe Island always see seals with fresh or healing shark wounds.

Seals have highly developed hind flippers and smaller, underdeveloped foreflippers. Sea lions have longer flippers and can rotate their hind flippers, making them more maneuverable. The difference in anatomy attracts white sharks to seals, for sea lions tend to be more adept at escaping from white sharks.

Researchers in the Farallon Islands noticed that white sharks usually attack a seal by rising from below and biting the seal in the head. While the seal bleeds to death, the shark releases the carcass, which floats to the surface. White sharks attack a sea lion with a hard strike while the sea lion swims on the surface. The strike often propels the shark out of the water with the sea lion captive in its jaws. The bite does not kill the sea lion. Instead, it founders on the surface until the shark returns, makes the final kill, and begins feeding. A "bite and spit" strategy has been observed in many attacks on people. This leads to the theory that the primary strike is the only contact—as if the shark finds a human being unpalatable. And, as one researcher put it, "We are mostly muscle, where the pinniped body has a great deal of fat. It is theorized that the shark somehow senses this and abandons us as a potential meal because our bodies are not as energy-rich as the pinnipeds."

The Red Triangle has been notorious since the 1960s. In January 1964, for example, a shark—almost certainly a white—swam into the midst of six divers, singled out one, and ripped at his legs. He survived. (In a study of 334 shark attacks, 40 percent of the victims suffered wounds to the calf or knee and 33 percent to the thigh. Arms and legs are the most likely target for a shark; in this same study, 78 percent of the wounds were to hands, arms, legs, and feet.)

One day in 1994, Andrew Carter, a well-known South African professional surfer, felt something land on him as he surfed about 200 yards off East London, a surfer's paradise south of Durban. He looked over his left shoulder. "I saw a big, black, shiny head. Its teeth were embedded in my thigh and my board. We were gripped in its mouth like a big sandwich."

Carter rolled off his board. The white shark bit down on the board, taking a chunk out of it, and dived.

Another surfer, John Borne, saw what happened and yelled, "Shark attack!" He saw a third surfer, Bruce Corby, coming toward him and asked him if he had seen what had just happened. "John, I've just lost my leg," Corby said, according to the London *Sunday Telegraph*'s account of the attack.

Carter survived, with 400 stitches in his torn buttock and thigh. Corby died, the first person to be killed by a white shark since the country passed a law making the white shark a protected species. (See chapter 8.)

Wind Surfer Attacks

For a long time, wind surfers believed that no one in their sport had ever been attacked by a shark. They stopped believing that in 1982 when Scott Shoemaker was attacked while windsurfing in Hawaii. According to an account in Windsurfing Magazine, *he "was sailing at full speed, well away from the shore, when a sudden impact caused his board to spin out, leaving him dangling from his booms with a [four- to five-foot] reef shark attached to one thigh. He let go of the boom, pushed the shark off with his hand and crawled onto his board to await the next attack. When none came, he mustered his nerve, jumped in the water, rearranged his rig, water-started and sailed to shore." Friends rushed him to a hospital, where 120 stitches sewed up his leg wounds.*

Longtime surfer and avid wind surfer Mike Schecter related another attack story to Elise MacGregor, who told it in Windsurfing Magazine: *". . . When Schecter was surfing with his buddies down in Acapulco, a decidedly irate shark, swimming at an alarming speed, made his way toward the group. Everyone quickly paddled for the beach, but the shark popped up right beneath one fellow's board, chomping and snapping. Following a dramatic struggle, the surfer managed to catch a wave into the beach, followed by the shark, who unsuccessfully chased him onto the sand. Frustrated, the shark turned away and headed down the coast, leaving the surfers with a premonition of bad things to come. Sure enough, a Canadian tourist was reportedly eaten later that day."*

Hawaiian wind surfer Roddy Lewis was attacked, by a ten- to twelve-foot tiger shark while enjoying Maui's Wailuaiki Bay in the spring of 1993. As he paddled out for another sail, he looked at the murky water and thought, This is perfect water for sharks. *Moments later a shark grabbed his leg and tried to pull him under. Lewis beat his fists on the side of the shark's head and drove it off. He then somehow caught a wave and got to shore. He and his leg survived.*

Year of the Shark

Just as the Red Triangle has entered the lexicon of the surfers and divers, so has the idea of the "Year of the Shark," a belief that a surge in white shark populations occurs in certain years, for unknown reasons. The year 1959 was called California's Year of the Shark. It began on May 7, when a swimmer was killed by a shark near San Francisco's Golden Gate Bridge. On June 14, Robert Pamperin, was diving for abalone about fifty yards off La Jolla with another diver, Tom Lehrer. Suddenly, Pamperin rose high out of the water. His face plate had been torn off. He screamed once.

"I was swimming about fifteen feet from Bob," Lehrer said later. "I heard him calling, 'Help me! Help me!'

"I swam over to him. He was thrashing in the water, and I could tell he was fighting something underneath . . ."

In the next instant, Pamperin went under. Lehrer peered underwater through his face plate. The water, though bloodied, was remarkably clear, and he saw his friend's body in the jaws of a shark.

"It had a white belly and I could see its jaws and jagged teeth," Lehrer said. "I wasn't able to do anything more. So I swam to shore to warn the other swimmers."

Before 1959 ended, there were three more attacks in California: a spearfisherman whose left leg was slashed by a hammerhead shark 300 yards from where Pamperin had been devoured; a swimmer whose left arm was raked from wrist to elbow by a shark off Malibu; and a diver who lived to tell how a shark bit down on one of his rubber fins, "shook me like a dog shakes a bone," and then released him, unharmed.

How many other victims had there been in the Year of the Shark? Captain Charles Hardy, chief of San Diego lifeguards, remarked after Pamperin's death that three persons had disappeared in the area during the previous three months, and that their bodies had never been found. And eight days after Pamperin was killed, a shark was caught off Catalina Island, about sixty miles north of La Jolla. In its belly was a man's watch, too badly deteriorated to be identified. Pamperin had not worn a watch. Whose watch was it? Had a man lost it at sea and, as it fell to the bottom, had its gleam lured a curious shark? Or had a man been wearing it?

Attacks in Hawaii

In February 1992, surfer Bryan Adona disappeared after heading out on his board at Leftovers, a surfers' spot near Waimea Bay, on the north shore of Oahu. His board was found the next day, bearing the teeth marks of what appeared to be a tiger shark. A few months before, Martha Morell, swimming near her home on Maui, was attacked and killed by a twelve-foot tiger shark about 100 yards offshore.

On October 22, 1992, surfer Rick Gruzinsky, in the waves off the north shore of Oahu, Hawaii, felt a jolt under his surfboard. Out of the sea came a shark, which twisted its head and clamped down on the surfboard, biting with a typical twisting motion. While Gruzinsky held onto one end of the board, the shark bit off the other. Gruzinsky, untouched, lived to tell the tale. Two weeks later, off the island's west shore, a shark bit a surfer in the leg. He bled to death. In December another shark off the north shore bit a chunk out of a surfer's board. There was also a fatal shark attack in 1992 in the waters of Maui.

Attacks have been going on for a long time in Hawaii. Between 1779 and 1996, there have been 101 confirmed shark attacks in the Hawaiian

Islands, forty-three of them fatal. Attacks have increased since 1950, with fourteen attacks in the 1950s, twenty-four in the 1980s, and fourteen between 1990 and 1997. A study that focused on eighty-three attacks between 1828 and 1997 showed a wide distribution of attacks both in geography and time:

Island	Total Attacks	Fatal	Most Recent Fatal Attack
Oahu	34	11	1994
Maui	20	3	1991
Hawaii	12	7	1991
Kauai	12	3	1986
Molokai	5	0	

A study of the attacks showed that victims had been engaged in the following activities (numbers in parentheses indicate victims who died):

Activity	Count	Died		Activity	Count	Died
Swimming/snorkeling	23	(8)		Body surfing	3	(1)
Spearfishing while snorkeling	6	(1)		Inner tube (with lobsters)	1	
Scuba diving	4	(3)		Wading	1	
Spearfishing with scuba	2	(2)		Fell/swept into sea from land	16	(16)
Hard-hat diving	1			Fell off boat or capsized	4	(3)
Surfing	16	(2)		Fishing/crabbing	13	(4)
Body boarding	5	(2)		Activity unknown	5	(1)
Windsurfing	1					

After the 1992 attacks, the Hawaii Institute of Marine Biology at the University of Hawaii began the first systematic study of tiger shark behavior. Researchers put sonic transmitters in the sharks and tracked them. Early results contradicted folklore that tigers had a coastal territory, much as dogs do. They range for great distances, and their attacks on humans are extraordinarily rare. Shark expert Kim Holland, who headed the study, noted that in 1994 there had been two people bitten by sharks off Hawaii. Both survived. "When you think how many thousands of people there are in the water every day, 365 days a year, that's really incredible," he told a newspaper reporter. "These animals aren't just biting anything that is the right size in the right place. If they were, we would have dozens of attacks a week. They must be very, very conservative in what they do."

Attacks Along U.S. East Coast

Most attacks along the U.S. East Coast (north of Florida) have not been fatal. Many attacks have been blamed on blacktip sharks and spinner sharks, 6- to 9-foot species that normally live on a diet of fish and probably bite humans only by mistake.

The number of attacks, confirmed and unconfirmed, reported for each state is:

Georgia	6	New Jersey	28
South Carolina	31	New York	12
North Carolina	4	Connecticut	2
Virginia	5	Massachusetts	7
Delaware	4		

Florida Attacks

Florida, with its 1,277 miles of coastline, is home to at least forty species of sharks, many of them dangerous. So a large number of recorded attacks—305 up to 1996—is no surprise.

In November 1998, Florida recorded its first fatal attack in ten years when a nine-year-old boy was killed near shore at Vero Beach by what officials called "a large shark." The torso and legs were all that remained when rescuers found him in shallow water. His death was the first recorded fatal shallow-water attack on any U.S. shoreline since 1978. Two weeks earlier, a thirteen-year-old boy was surfing a few miles from Vero Beach when a shark bit the boy's right leg, then immediately released him. The wound required thirty stitches. The species of shark was unknown in both attacks.

In at least 50 percent of recent attacks, the victim has been a surfer. One attack on a surfer was in three feet of water off Boca Raton, Florida. He survived. Fatal attacks in Florida average less than one a year.

1980s:	98 attacks	1992:	12
1990:	11	1994:	22
1991:	16	1995 (Jan.–Oct.):	28

Gulf Coast Attacks

Researchers report 30 attacks in the water of the Gulf states:

Alabama	2	Louisiana	2
Mississippi	2	Texas	24

South Africa Attacks

From 1963 to 1997, there were, on average, three shark attacks each year. Fewer than 10 percent were fatal. Then, in the summer of 1998, there came eight attacks, with one fatality: a bodysurfer who was mauled by a white shark off Gonubie Point, south of Durban.

Among the victims who survived was South Africa's boogie-boarding champion, twenty-two-year-old Neal Stephenson. But he lost his right foot and was badly mauled in an attack in Plettenberg Bay. Stephenson was surfing on his boogie board with a friend near a school of dolphins when a shark seized his leg. The friend got him ashore.

The spate of attacks began when two surfers were attacked within two hours off beaches about thirty miles apart. Descriptions of the sharks indicated that one surfer was attacked by a ragged tooth (*Eugomphodus taurus*), known in America as the sand tiger shark, and the other by a great white. Both surfers survived.

Prior to the puzzling series of attacks in 1998, South Africa had prided itself on the effectiveness of antishark nets.

Studies of attacks in South Africa showed that more sharks struck swimmers and surfers in the late afternoon than at any other time of the day, even though most people were in the water in the late morning and early afternoon. "This," said a digest of the studies, "is presumably related to the nocturnal activities of many sharks that venture inshore to feed. Shark attacks have often taken place in very murky waters when the rivers come down in flood. Zambezi sharks find these situations extremely attractive and they have been responsible for many attacks in water no more than waist deep. While the number of incidents in KwaZulu-Natal has been reduced by the use of shark nets, the number in the Eastern and Western Cape has increased."

Surfers and spearfishermen are more likely to be attacked than swimmers. "This is not surprising," said the report, "as wetsuits enable the wearers to spend long periods in the sea and, furthermore, they venture further offshore than swimmers. Sharks are attracted by the blood and irregular vibrations of a struggling fish after it has been shot, and there are several cases of a spearfisherman being bitten while finning to the surface immediately after he has shot a fish. There has only been a single attack on a scuba diver in South Africa, in which the victim was fatally injured while swimming at the surface before descent.

"Many of the injuries inflicted on humans by sharks have been minor, and it is probably incorrect to conclude that every incident is the result of a shark trying to eat its victim. Many sharks—especially the great white, tiger and Zambezi (bull)—are aggressive species."

The Natal Shark Board, which supervises much of the research into shark attacks in South Africa, attributes a decrease in fatal injuries to the development of a treatment procedure and techniques that shark-savvy emergency medics use to stabilize victims on the way to the hospital.

Why Do Sharks Attack?

After some twenty years of studying sharks, Dr. Samuel Gruber, professor of marine science at the Rosenstiel School of Marine and Atmospheric Science at the University of Miami, once asked how anyone can predict anything about "something as wild and immune from investigation as an attacking white shark?" We "simply cannot know what is in the mind of an animal," he added.

Research, however, is adding to our knowledge about the way sharks hunt and attack. Sharks, for example, can detect and will swim toward extremely weak electrical fields that surround their prey. This was demonstrated by A. J. Kalmijn, who showed that sharks would attack an electrical source that produced a field similar to that produced by a fish. Gruber suggested that a shark snapping at a nonfish was responding to a stimulus and was making a "reflexive bite." That is the kind of bite a shark might make in an attack on an object from which is emanating a stray galvanic field, such as a metallic boat or oceanographic gear. Some sharks have a reputation as "boat biters," a habit that researchers have attributed to responses to the boat's electrical field.

Gruber estimated that "somewhat less than half of all attacks (excluding open-ocean and some other 'special' situations) are motivated by feeding or predation." Another researcher, Donald R. Nelson, a professor of biology at California State University, Long Beach, calls pelagic sharks "apex predators exquisitely tuned to their special sensory worlds." After studying shark behavior in natural surroundings, Nelson identified four general attack situations:

1. *Unprovoked:* A person in the water, who has not stimulated the shark, is nevertheless attacked (usually by a large shark). The assumption is that the person was regarded as prey and the shark took the opportunity to feed.

2. *Unprovoked with "distress stimuli":* One or more people in the water— typically, victims of an aircraft or ship disaster—are thrashing about. Perhaps there is blood in the water. Responding to "strong feeding stimuli," Gruber wrote, even small sharks "may attempt to bite pieces from the victim. The presence of abnormally intense feeding stimuli may cause a group of sharks to transcend their usual predatory behavior patterns and enter a state known as a feeding frenzy."

3. *Provoked with physical contact:* Typically, divers grabbing the tail of a shark and taking a ride. Most such "hobbyhorses" are nurse sharks. One study of attacks on divers showed that nurse sharks were responsible for eighteen attacks, compared to eleven involving white sharks. In many cases, the so-called "harmless" nurse shark took a "defensive bite" and rapidly swam away.

4. *Provoked without physical contact:* The victim and shark meet unexpectedly. Cornered or perhaps defending territory, a shark makes an aggressive gesture that the person fails to recognize. The shark then strikes and speeds away.

Researchers believe that there are three major kinds of unprovoked shark attacks: **hit and run, bump and bite,** and **sneak.** Most shark attacks on people involve only a single bite that occurs during a hit and run. The bump and bite and the sneak attack are more dangerous because during them the shark may bite the victim several times.

Researchers have shown that the shark uses several senses to identify its potential prey. First the shark hears and feels the vibrations of sound waves created by motion, probably interpreting the splashes of swimmers and divers as the movement of an injured fish or seal. The chemical odors all living things emit, even underwater, also alert the shark that a potential meal is nearby. The shark is also drawn to prey by what it sees. Contrasts and bright colors seem to attract it.

The shark concludes its exploration of a human in the water through physical contact, often in the most common kind of attack, the hit and run.

Sometimes, a shark will exhibit "threat posture" before an attack, pushing its pectoral fins downward, arching its back, and raising its snout.

Hit and Run This is the most common kind of attack, typically in the surf zone, with swimmers and surfers the usual targets. The victim and shark meet unexpectedly. Cornered or perhaps defending territory, a shark makes an aggressive gesture, which the person fails to recognize. Then the shark strikes and speeds away. The attack is rarely fatal.

The victim seldom sees the attacker, but sometimes a shark will precede an attack by changing its normal smooth swimming to a jerky, rigid, unusual pattern. In a hit and run, the shark inflicts a single bite or slash wound and does not return. Most of the time, these probably are cases of mistaken identity that occur in murky water when the shark may confuse a person with a seal or sea lion. A feeding shark must make quick decisions and rapid movements to capture its traditional food items. Adding to the conditions for an attack are what researchers call "provocative human appearance"—splashing, shiny jewelry, brightly colored swimsuits, tanning that produces contrasting skin-swimsuit colors, and tanning that makes tempting little targets of the white soles of the feet.

Attacking Species of Sharks
1554–1997

Genus	Species	Common Name	Unprovoked Attack	Provoked	Air-Sea Disaster	Boat Attack	No Assignment	Total
Carcharodon	carcharias	white	231	4	0	52	24	311
Galeocerdo	cuvier	tiger	67	3	1	8	25	104
Carcharhinus	leucas	bull	57	6	0	0	6	69
Carcharias	taurus	sand tiger	31	14	0	6	2	53
Carcharhinus	spp.	requiem	28	11	0	1	2	42
Carcharhinus	limbatus	blacktip	20	2	0	0	0	22
Sphyrna	spp.	hammerhead	17	4	1	5	4	31
Prionace	glauca	blue	14	10	3	3	0	30
Carcharhinus	melanopterus	blacktip reef	13	1	0	0	0	14
Isurus	oxyrinchus	shortfin mako	12	10	0	15	1	38
Carcharhinus	amblyrhynchos	grey reef	9	1	0	0	0	10
Carcharhinus	brachyurus	bronze whaler	9	1	0	1	0	11
Negaprion	brevirostris	lemon	9	7	0	5	0	21
Carcharhinus	perezi	Caribbean reef	7	9	0	0	0	16
Carcharhinus	brevipinna	spinner	5	1	0	0	0	6
Carcharhinus	plumbeus	sandbar	5	1	1	0	0	7
Ginglymostoma	cirratum	nurse	5	16	0	0	2	23
Carcharhinus	longimanus	oceanic whitetip	4	1	0	0	0	5
Orectolobus	barbatus	wobbegong	4	12	0	0	7	23
Carcharhinus	obscurus	dusky	3	1	0	1	0	5
Triakis	semifasciata	leopard	3	0	0	0	1	4
Carcharhinus	falciformis	silky	2	1	0	0	1	4
Notorhynchus	cepedianus	sevengill	2	2	0	0	0	4
Carcharhinus	galapagensis	Galapagos	1	0	0	0	0	1

Genus	Species	Common Name	Unprovoked Attack	Provoked	Air-Sea Disaster	Boat Attack	No Assignment	Total
Carcharhinus	gangeticus	Ganges	1	0	0	0	0	1
Galeorhinus	galeus	tope	1	0	0	0	0	1
Isistius	brasiliensis	cookiecutter	1	0	0	0	0	1
Isurus	spp.	mako	1	0	0	0	0	1
Lamna	nasus	porbeagle	1	0	0	1	1	3
Sphyrna	lewini	scalloped hammerhead	1	0	0	0	1	2
Squalus	acanthias	spiny dogfish	1	0	0	0	0	1
Triaenodon	obesus	whitetip reef	1	1	0	0	0	2
Alopias	spp.	thresher	0	1	0	4	0	5
Carcharhinus	albimarginatus	silvertip	0	1	0	0	0	1
Carcharhinus	altimus	bignose	0	1	0	0	0	1
Carcharias	ferox	bigeye sand tiger	0	2	0	0	0	2
Cetorhinus	maximus	basking	0	0	0	2	0	2
Heterodontus	francisci	horn	0	1	0	0	0	1
Hexanchus	griseus	sixgill	0	0	0	0	1	1
Rhincodon	typus	whale	0	0	0	1	1	1
Somniosus	microcephalus	Greenland	0	0	0	0	1	1
Sphyrna	zygaena	smooth hammerhead	0	0	0	0	1	1
TOTALS	42 species		566	125	6	105	80	882

Positive identification of attacking sharks is very difficult since victims rarely make adequate observations of the attacker during the "heat" of the interaction. Tooth remains are seldom found, and diagnostic characters for many carcharhinid sharks are difficult to discern even by trained professionals. Realistically, almost any shark in the right size range, six feet (1.8 meters) or greater, is a potential threat to humans. Source: International Shark Attack File.

"We suspect that, upon biting, the shark quickly realizes that the human is a foreign object, or that it is too large, and immediately releases the victim and does not return," says a report based on International Shark Attack File data. "Some of these attacks could also be related to social behaviors unrelated to feeding, such as dominance behaviors seen in many land animals."

Hit and run victims usually suffer relatively small cuts and scratches, often on the leg below the knee.

Bump and Bite This is a more serious kind of attack. A brief bump against the object brings the shark's electroreceptors into action. After determining that the object is alive, the shark may then bite it. The shark initially circles the victim before bumping. The assumption is that the person does not provoke the shark but is merely was regarded as prey, which the shark takes the opportunity to feed upon.

Sneak A strike that occurs without warning. The shark simply lunges, usually from below the victim, and bites, usually repeatedly.

Bump and bite and sneak attacks, while less common than hit and run attacks, produce more serious injuries and most fatalities. These types of attacks usually involve divers or swimmers in relatively deep waters, but they also can occur in shallows near shore in some areas of the world. During both bump and bite and sneak attacks, sharks commonly make repeat assaults on the victim, who usually suffers many serious bites. Injuries are usually severe, and the attack is frequently fatal. Researchers believe that the shark is driven by hunger or by a perception of threat by the human being. This is not a matter of mistaken identity. Sneak attacks and bump and bite attacks are also made on the survivors of shipwrecks or downed aircraft.

One theory holds that some attacks, particularly on people with surfboards, involve mistaken identity: The shark thinks the surfer is a seal. In a test of this theory, John McCosker of the Steinhart Museum in San Francisco placed a mannequin on a surfboard off Dangerous Reef in Australia and chummed the water around it with animal blood. Lured by the blood, a great white shark saw the surfboard and attacked—although there was neither blood nor meat on the board or on the wet-suited dummy. In another test, sixty feet below the surface, a dummy in a scuba suit was not attacked until McCosker attached a fish to it, in the way that divers sometimes tie a speared fish to a line about the waist. That did attract a shark. "I think you're much better off underwater than at the surface," McCosker told an interviewer. "In fact, I'm convinced you're better off, and I think the experiment proves it."

White sharks, shortfin makos, tiger sharks, and lemon sharks all have been implicated in attacks on small sportfishing and commercial fishing boats, particularly when the sharks were hooked. A few boats have been demolished by whites and makos. Boats with leaky, dirty bilges trailing fish juices may be inviting a white shark attack. Contrasting bottom colors and bright, spinning propellers may also lure curious large sharks. But they usually are content to lurk under fishing boats and steal fishes that are hooked. Any large and dangerous sharks should be shot or otherwise subdued before being boarded on a boat.

In several Australian shark attacks, a single victim seemed to have been selected from several bathers. That victim was wounded or killed and the rescuers untouched. This led to the theory that the rescuers of an attack victim were somehow themselves immune from attack. But this theory was demolished by research showing that of sixty-eight individuals who have gone to the aid of a victim of shark attack, twelve, or 17.7 percent, have been attacked.

But if you place yourself in a dangerous situation, you do not necessarily invite a shark to attack you. This was once underlined by the famed shark expert, E. W. Gudger, who wrote, "At Key West, I have seen boys diving for pennies off the old Mallary Line dock, while 200 yards away, a dead horse drifting out with the tide was surrounded by four or five 10-foot Tiger sharks bucking and surging, trying to tear it apart so that they could eat it. The point is plain—the Tigers preferred dead horse to live boy."

What Sharks Are Attackers?

Of the some thirty fatal attacks worldwide each year, an estimated one third to half are made by white sharks, often referred to as the great white shark (see page 196). Studies of attacks along the northern California coast, for example, show that between 1926 and 1993 there were sixty-nine attacks by white sharks; seven were fatal. Other sharks notorious for attacking people are the tiger shark, and the bull shark (also known as the cub shark, ground shark, or requiem shark). All are large sharks, found in seas throughout the world. They eat large prey, such as marine mammals and sea turtles, and can thus show interest in a prospective meal the size of a human swimmer or surfer.

Other species implicated in attacks are the great hammerhead, the shortfin mako, the oceanic whitetip, the gray reef shark, the Caribbean reef shark, the Galapagos shark of Pacific islands, and bull shark populations living in rivers. (The bull shark is also found in Lake Nicaragua, and is perennially blamed for attacks.) Researchers in Florida, which reports twenty to thirty hit and run attacks a year, add to the dangerous shark list the blacktip, the spinner, and the blacknose. Oceanic whitetips, large predators found in deep tropical waters throughout the world, do not live near land. They are often the sharks responsible for deaths among survivors of air and sea disasters.

The gray nurse shark, known in North America as the sand tiger shark, has been blamed for many attacks in Australia. Some authorities, warning that almost any large shark six feet or more long is a potential

White Shark Attacks

Of the shark attacks that occur throughout the world each year, about thirty are fatal, and an estimated half to a third of those fatal attacks are made by white sharks. In a typical year, white sharks are also responsible for two or three non-fatal attacks on swimmers, surfers, and divers.

Attacks by white sharks between 1980 and 1990:

California

10/17/80	Moonstone Beach
12/19/81	Monterey*
2/7/82	Stillwater Cove
7/24/82	Point Buchon
8/29/82	Morro Bay
9/19/82	Bear Harbor
9/15/84	Pigeon Point*
9/30/84	Tomales Bay
12/6/86	Carmel
8/15/87	Tunis Beach
4/24/88	Morro Bay
8/11/88	Crescent City
1/12/90	Montara
8/9/90	Jenner
8/28/90	Trinidad Head
7/1/91	Año Nuevo Island

Oregon

10/27/80	Douglas County
8/20/83	Tillamook County
9/30/84	Tillamook County
10/23/89	Cannon Beach

South Africa

1/3/80	Ballito
6/29/82	Ntlonyana*
9/20/83	False Bay
1/4/85	False Bay
1/17/85	Eldridge Natal
10/24/85	East London
9/3/86	Dyer Island
12/22/86	Saou Beach*
1/28/87	Cape Province
9/13/87	Province
10/12/87	Cape Town
9/17/89	Smitswinkel Bay
11/26/89	Smitswinkel Bay*
6/24/90	Mossel Bay

Chile

1/5/80	Miranda Los Vilos*
3/4/81	Coquimbo
12/15/88	Valparaiso*

South Australia

12/24/83	South Neptune Island
3/5/85	Durdin Peake Bay

Mexico

9/11/84	Isla de Guadalupe

*fatal attack.

threat to humans, also list the lemon shark and the blue shark. The whale shark, usually a gentle, easy-going creature, has attacked people who bothered it; its huge size makes any interaction with humans highly dangerous. Some species, such as the bottom-feeding nurse shark, are extremely sluggish and do not have sharp teeth, but they will attack when disturbed. For more about these sharks, look them up in chapter 3. See list of attacking species, pages 192–193.

What Attracts Sharks?

- **Sounds.** Certain types of irregular sounds, such as those made by a swimmer in trouble or an injured fish, definitely attract sharks. Sound, rather than sight or smell, seems to be a shark's primary cue for moving toward a target, even from a long distance. Anything unusual, such as the impact of an aircraft plunging into the sea or the mass of sounds transmitted through the sea when a ship sinks, appears to attract sharks, and may trigger attacks.

- **Colors.** Sharks seem to be able to distinguish light colors from dark. Sharks of at least some species may be able to tell one color from another. Yellow, white, and silver seem to attract sharks. Many divers maintain that clothing, fins, and tanks should be painted in dull colors to avoid shark attacks. One group of experimenters, noticing the sharks' preference for a certain shade, dubbed the standard life jacket color "yum-yum yellow."

- **Movement.** Certain irregular movements, such as those made by a swimmer in trouble or a wounded fish or seal, seem to attract sharks. Diving from a boat at sea or even in a harbor may invite shark attack. There are several records of divers who were attacked the moment they entered the water. Similarly dangerous is the sport of being towed in the water by a moving ship. When a person is being towed he or she may look like a fish to a shark.

- **Blood.** Even greatly diluted and in small quantities, fresh blood, from any animal, definitely attracts sharks. So does vomit, offal, garbage, and carrion. In one case, a scuba diver was swimming near the bottom when his nose began bleeding. Some of the blood was draining into his mouth exiting in a stream of blood-tainted bubbles. A small shark, apparently aiming for the source of the alluring blood, twice struck at the diver's head and face, then darted away. The diver was only slightly injured. Even the trace of blood from a woman who is menstruating is believed enough to lure a shark.

Shark Avoidance Rules

If you want to avoid sharks, follow these rules, based primarily on the findings of George W. Burgess, director of the International Shark File:

- Always stay in groups, since sharks are more likely to attack a solitary individual.

- Do not wander too far from shore. This isolates you and puts you far away from help.

- Avoid being in the water during darkness or twilight hours when sharks are most active and can see you while you cannot see them.

- If you sight a large shark, leave the water as soon as possible, swimming smoothly to avoid exciting the shark. If diving, keep submerged and watch the shark until you can quickly surface and get out of the water.

- Do not enter the water if bleeding from an open wound or if menstruating.

- Do not wear shiny jewelry; the reflected light resembles the sheen of fish scales.

- If you wear a black wetsuit, remember that it may make you look like a seal and increases the probability of attack by white sharks. Surfboards that contrast with the water surface from below may be more attractive to sharks, as well.

- If you are spearfishing, do not carry speared fish on your person, or on a stringer or tether; get the fish out of the water as soon as possible.

- Avoid waters near sewage discharges (feces and urine may be shark attractants) or waters being used by sport or commercial fishermen, especially if there are signs of bait fishes or feeding activity. Diving seabirds are good indicators of such action.

- If fishes begin to behave erratically or congregate in unusual numbers, leave the water.

- Do not believe that sightings of porpoises indicate the absence of sharks. Both often eat the same prey.

- Use extra caution when waters are murky.

- Remember that uneven tanning and bright colored bathing suits can attract sharks. They can see contrast particularly well.

- Don't splash around while wading; try not to splash while swimming.

- Do not swim with dogs. Their erratic movements may attract sharks.

- Be careful in waters between sandbars or near steep drop-offs. These are favorite hangouts for sharks.

- Get out of the water if sharks are seen—or if sharks are known to frequent the area. (As noted above, in California, white shark attacks have repeatedly occurred in the same small areas favored by these sharks.)

• Do not harass a shark, no matter how small. (The youngest shark to bite a human was an unborn sand tiger shark pup who bit a marine biologist who was examining the uterus of the dead mother.)

Where Are Most Attacks?

Researchers try in vain to pinpoint the most likely places for shark attacks. Florida, Hawaii, Australia, and South Africa have large numbers (see previous pages for these numbers). But note that other regions also produce alarming statistics. When worldwide lists are drawn up, English-speaking places suspiciously prevail. Baldridge noted this in his 1974 study, which showed, for example, only six attacks along the Atlantic coast of Africa.

Shark attack records seem to appear predominantly not in places where sharks attack but in places where there are observers who write in English. In the *Indian Medical Gazette* of April 1, 1881, for example, a British surgeon routinely reported that "more than 20 persons have been severely bitten by sharks this year. Almost all were fatal." There are no comparable indigenous records. Similarly, reports of shark attacks in Philippine waters are few, unless records in English are consulted. The log of the USS *Dale*, for another example, recorded a fatal attack in Canacao Bay in 1917 and records of the U.S. Naval Hospital in Canacao graphically describe how nearly the entire abdominal cavity of the sailor had been torn away.

During later years—particularly during World War II and the Cold War, when the U.S. armed forces maintained bases in the Philippines—record keeping there improved, and reports on attacks were passed on to the International Shark Research Panel. Elsewhere, reporting has depended, almost totally, upon English-speaking, or at least Westernized, record keepers. The result has been a consistently distorted panorama of worldwide shark attacks.

Stopping the Shark: The Net

The quest for dependable defenses against shark attacks began with efforts to protect beaches full of bathers. In 1934, after four fatal attacks in the waters off Sydney, Australia set up a Shark Menace Advisory Committee, which recommended a "systemic and continuous meshing programme" be inaugurated along Sydney's beaches. Critics called the meshing "a stupid, futile waste of money," and not until 1937 were the first antishark nets set up outside the breakers athwart the probable paths of sharks. From December 1, 1939 to December 1, 1940, the nets snagged 751 sharks, and

A shark is caught in a gill net off New Zealand.

Sydney beaches became safe from sharks. Elsewhere, along unprotected beaches, at least one swimmer a year was killed by a shark.

Of all the places in the world where shark and people share the seashore, the most dangerous place has been a stretch along the Indian Ocean known as the Natal Coast. From Isipingo Beach south of Durban, South Africa, to Umhlanga Rocks, sharks have always been a menace to bathers. In the 1940s and early 1950s there were twenty-one attacks, seven of them fatal.

Following the Australian strategy, in 1952 South African government officials ordered the placing of seven large-meshed gill nets, each about 440 feet long, along Durban beaches. In the first year, 552 sharks were caught in the nets and Durban became a safe place for bathers.

But attacks continued, particularly at resorts south of Durban. Between December 1957 and Easter 1958, sharks killed five people. Panicky swimmers virtually abandoned the beaches, and the coastal tourist industry was threatened with ruin. Fearing financial disaster, several coastal towns tried erecting wire-and-net barriers in the surf zone. But the waves soon destroyed them. A South African Navy frigate dropped depth bombs off the beaches and killed at least eight sharks and countless fish. The frigate-produced bouillabaisse reportedly lured more sharks to the area.

In 1964 shark nets were installed at some of the larger vacation resorts to the north and south of Durban. The Natal Provincial Administration created the Natal Anti-Shark Measures Board (now called the Natal Sharks Board), charging it "with the duty of approving, controlling, and initiating measures for safeguarding bathers against shark attacks." By March 1966 there were fifteen beaches with protective nets.

The net defense has continued to grow; more than forty bathing beaches are now protected by nearly thirty miles of nets. Typically, the nets are laid in two rows, parallel to bathing beaches, about 1,500 feet offshore. Each year, about 1,400 sharks are entrapped in the nets—along with dolphins, sea turtles, and seabirds. Some 250 sharks that are still alive are tagged and released by crews on ski boats, who usually inspect the nets every weekday.

Sharks can get over, under, and around the nets. But they seem to work, reducing attacks around Natal to almost zero; the two or three attacks a year along the South African coast are almost always elsewhere along the coast. No one quite knows why. Dr. David H. Davies, director of the council of the South African Association for Marine Biological Research and an early investigator of the nets, was baffled by the apparent effectiveness of the nets as a shark barrier.

"There is no really satisfactory explanation for the success," Davies said. The nets "do not form a continuous wall, and at all times sharks are able to penetrate the area between the beach and the nets by swimming between separate nets or round the ends. Sharks have been found to have been gilled on either side of the nets when traveling both toward and away from the beaches. The only reasonable explanation for the success of the set-net system seems to be related to the already established fact that it is possible to reduce a shark population by systematic netting. This has been shown in commercial shark fisheries in various parts of the world. . . ."

Kill the Sharks

If nets kill sharks, why bother to erect nets? Why not simply kill the sharks? Hawaii has twice tried this strategy.

Between 1886 and 1958, there had been sixteen known shark attacks in Hawaiian waters, five of them fatal. In 1958, after a shark killed a fifteen-year-old boy, Hawaii went on a shark-killing rampage. Two days after the boy was killed, a research vessel sent to the attack site near Lanikai killed three tiger sharks, along with two smaller sharks.

People chipped in to start a "shark control" fund to finance the catching and killing of sharks. A merchant offered a $20 bounty for any shark caught in Oahu's inshore waters. A jewelry company said it would pay 25 cents for each shark tooth a hunter brought in.

The fund-financed shark ship killed sixty-three sharks in forty-eight hours. During the yearlong campaign, 697 sharks and 641 unborn pups were captured and destroyed. On each trip around Oahu, the ship found fewer sharks.

Shark killing continued for some time, as a public service and also as a sport. Gradually, the hunting eased off, and the shark populations apparently built up again. No one seemed to notice the buildup until 1992, when Hawaii was stunned by four confirmed shark attacks—one fatal—and a probable attack on a surfer who disappeared.

Hawaii's Department of Land and Natural Resources ordered a task force to begin "a shark population control program," which was supposed to involve education, research, and hunting. What mostly happened was hunting. Volunteers eagerly killed dozens of sharks, most of them tiger sharks, the sharks most often blamed for attacks on human beings in the Hawaiian Islands. The task force officially killed ten tiger sharks; vigilantes killed at least twenty-two more. Eventually, there were fifty-eight known kills.

"We don't know if they were 58 out of a population of 59 or 58 out of a population of 58,000," said Dr. Kim Holland, a shark expert with the Department of Land and Natural Resources. There was so much shark blood flowing that some native Hawaiians were appalled, for, to them, the Tiger shark is *Aumakua*, a god.

Searching for a Shark Chaser

The quest for a shark repellent confounded researchers for both the U.S. Navy and the Royal Navy during World War II, when tales of "shark-infested waters" terrified servicemen and their relatives and sweethearts. Politicians had to do something, and so they ordered research that would at least solve the morale problem. President Roosevelt wanted the mothers of America to worry less about their boys. Prime Minister Winston Churchill, former Lord of the Admiralty, asked in Parliament whether the government was doing all it could to find a shark repellent, replied, "You may rest assured that the British Government is entirely opposed to sharks."

Scientists, responding to frantic U.S. Navy requests for a shark repellent, during World War II experimented with seventy-eight substances, including several poison gases. They finally selected copper acetate, whose odor resembled the stench of dead or dying sharks. In experiments, sharks struck again and again at baited lines, identical with the others except for the repellent, which was suspended in a bag directly above the bait. (Shark fishermen long have known that the smell of decomposing fish drives off sharks.)

The repellent appeared to be an astounding success and, dubbed "Shark Chaser," it was rushed into production. Cakes attached to life jackets contained copper acetate mixed with a nigrosine-type dye, which released a blue-black cloud. Servicemen were instructed to open the envelope and swish the cake around them when threatened by sharks. The repellent would diffuse in the sea and surround the swimmer with a cloud of dye and copper acetate.

How effective it was will probably never be known. Thousands of men were set adrift in seas all over the world during the war, and undoubtedly the repellent provided them at least with an important psychological weapon against sharks. "Beyond question, the greatest value of the Shark Chaser was the mental relief and sense of security it afforded the men who had it on hand," observed George Llano, the Air Force researcher who studied wartime survival at sea.

Before the invention of Shark Chaser, some rescued airmen claimed sharks could be driven off by sea-marker dye, a brilliant yellow preparation used to stain the water to facilitate rescue; others complained that sharks were attracted by the dye. Many men put their faith in water-purifying tablets, the theory being that the chlorine in the tablet repelled sharks. At least twice during the war, the survival manuals themselves were used to shoo away sharks. In both incidents, downed airmen tore up the manuals and saw sharks leave the water around the life raft and swim off to examine and presumably eat the pieces of paper.

Shark Chaser went on sale to civilians in the 1960s, in packets for divers and in liquid or packet form to protect commercial fishermen's nets from sharks. Packets were also still issued to U.S. servicemen and attached to the life jackets of astronauts and carried in the equipment of U-2 spy plane pilots.

In tests, Shark Chaser was dubiously effective. Bob Dyer, a champion Australian shark fisherman, for example, put Shark Chaser in waters bloodied by whales killed by professional whalers. Some of the sharks were repelled, but others ate the packets during feeding frenzies. "We have excellent movies of the shark swimming through U.S. Navy shark chasers," reported James R. Stewart, a diving officer at the Scripps Institution of Oceanography. "Most of us have considered it a great psychological crutch but that is all. After all, it has 'shark repellent' reprinted right on the packet. However, I have yet to meet a shark who could read."

In research at the Lerner Marine Laboratory, a lure (usually fresh blood in a porous container) was suspended from a line on a long bamboo pole and presented to sharks in the experimental pens for ten minutes. The sharks "readily" approached a lure "through a cloud of copper acetate," a report said, but, when Shark Chaser was used, "the sharks repeatedly avoided the lure. . . . This suggests that possibly the 'Shark Chaser' dye is more repellent to sharks than is the copper acetate. . . . The value of copper acetate as a shark repellent is open to serious question."

A U.S. Navy diving manual warned that "shark repellents are use-less" when sharks "are hunting in packs and food or blood is present." The British Shallow Water Diving Unit at Nassau reported: "The use by us of shark repellent [copper acetate] did not prove anything. It does not seem reasonable to suppose that a shark in the fury of an attack would pause or retreat from its headlong rush for food because it did not care for the smell of the repellent. Again, if the repellent were effective if would be only so down tide."

Dr. Albert Tester, a University of Hawaii zoologist, summing up reports on shark repellents, said, "I do not think at the present time that we have a sure-fire repellent of any kind." Tester, in his own quest for a repellent, sought the role of smell in shark predation. He collected human sweat and added it to shark food extract. In tank tests with several species of sharks, most sharks were repulsed by the sweat-scented food. He concluded that "it seems safe to assume that shark attack on humans is not motivated by the smell of human sweat."

Shark researchers in South Africa have taken another path toward a repellent: a personal antishark electric device. The Shark POD (Protective Oceanic Device) takes advantage of a shark organ, Lorenzini's ampullae, which can sense minute electrical fields generated by marine animals, helping the shark to home in on prey. The POD, designed specifically for scuba divers, consists of three components linked by cables: a unit strapped to the dive cylinder, an electrode attached to one of the diver's fins, and a switch on a shoulder strap.

The POD encloses the diver in an electrical field that is too weak to annoy any humans but strong enough to repel sharks. In tests, sharks stayed about three to twenty feet away from the POD. Designers of the POD sought the creation of an electric field that would repel white, tiger, and bull sharks.

The Natal Sharks Board plans to patent the use of the POD to shark-proof surfboards and paddle skis. Another version of the POD is being developed to replace some shark nets in relatively sheltered waters. "We are working on an adapted system that would involve running a cable through sheltered coves, marinas and harbors where there are shark problems and could be used instead of nets," says Sheldon Dudley, marine biologist at the Sharks Board. "But it won't be feasible in the immediate future to remove nets like those in South Africa and Australia because the cables can't withstand heavy surf conditions."

Attacks: When, Where, What

Early findings by the Shark Research Panel have stood the test of time. The following information comes from some of those findings, which led to all subsequent research into shark attacks.

When

The peak period for bathing is during the daylight hours, from 8:00 A.M. to 7:00 P.M., and this corresponds with the period of the day when most shark attacks occurred. Records show that most attacks occur between 11 o'clock in the morning and 6 o'clock in the afternoon—findings based on 159 instances in which the time of attack was carefully recorded.

> Midnight to 6 A.M: 3.1 percent of the attacks
> 6 A.M. to noon: 22 percent
> Noon to 6 P.M: 66.7 percent
> 6 P.M. to midnight: 8.2 percent

Where

Attacks usually occur close to shore. Of 217 attacks, 62.2 percent were within 300 feet of shore.

Within 100 feet:	38.2 percent
100 to 200 feet:	16.6 percent
200 to 300 feet:	7.4 percent
300 to ¼ of mile:	8.3 percent
¼ mile to 2 miles:	10.6 percent
Open sea:	18.9 percent

Later research has showed that most attacks continue to occur in waters near shore, "typically inshore of a sandbar or between sandbars where sharks feed and can become trapped at low tide." Another likely attack site is an area that sharply drops off from shore. Such areas attract fish, including the sharks that feed on them.

What

Based on 306 cases, here is what people were doing when they were attacked:

Swimming on the surface: 57.2 percent.
Wading or standing in knee-deep to chin-deep water: 20.8 percent.
Swimming or standing close to where fish were swimming or being caught: 10.3 percent.
Resting, floating, or clinging to a float: 6.4 percent.
Spearfishing or diving and carrying fish: 5.3 percent.

Where to Give Attack Information

If you know about an attack, forward documentation or contact the File at the following address:
International Shark Attack File, American Elasmobranch Society
Florida Museum of Natural History, University of Florida
Gainesville, FL 32611
Telephone: (352) 392-1721
Fax: 352-846-0287
Email: gburgess@flmnh.ufl.edu

Researchers also want documentation about past attacks, particularly from the 1968 to 1988 period.

CHAPTER 6

Tales of
the Shark

Superstition about sharks dates to ancient times, when they were honored as powerful gods that lived in the ocean depths. Pacific legends said that *mano-kanaka*, or shark men, took on human form and ranged the islands, pulling pranks, causing confusion, and brewing other mischief. In Vietnam the whale shark is known as *Ca Ong* or "Sir Fish." On sand dunes along the Vietnamese coast are small altars, erected by fishermen to pray for the protection of Sir Fish, an aristocratic god.

Stars that the Greeks saw as Orion's Belt were to the Warrau Indians of South America the missing leg of Nohi-Abassi, a man who had got rid of his mother-in-law by inducing a murderous shark to devour her. Nohi-Abassi's leg was cut off by his sister-in-law, apparently playing the role of a shark, and Nohi-Abassi died. His leg went to one part of the heavens, the rest of him to another.

The discovery of a previously unknown shark—the megamouth—in 1976 inspired new stories about seemingly mythical monsters in the sea. For centuries, sharks have been the most popular subjects of monster tales. In the Pacific especially, legends about sharks are legion. In some legends the shark is a vengeful god; in others, the shark is a cunning devil. In Hawaii and in the Solomon Islands, where the shark god still is known as *takw manacca*, people made human sacrifices. In the Solomons, ritual murder for the shark god continued into the early 1900s. And in some iso-lated communities, the ritual may still secretly endure.

On many a Pacific island, it was only natural to believe that the shark god desired human sacrifice, for again and again he would snatch a man, woman, or child. As worship became more ritualized, and the ultimate homage of human sacrifice became theology, a chief or high priest went among his people at fateful times. An acolyte accompanied him, carrying a noose similar to a shark snare. At a signal from his leader, the acolyte hurled the noose at a crowd. The person—whether man, woman, or child—around whom the noose fell was immediately seized and strangled. The body was ritualistically cut into pieces and flung into the sea for the ravenous shark gods.

In ancient Hawaii, Hawaiian kings hurled human beings to royal sharks: The kings were also said to have sponsored gladiatorial contests between starved sharks and native gladiators. The warrior's only weapon was a shark-toothed dagger, a short length of wood shaped like a stout broomstick, gripped in his hand. Protruding from the stick was a shark's tooth, which stuck out between two fingers of the man's fist. He tried to get under the shark and slit its belly—a seemingly impossible feat, consid-ering the toughness of the shark's hide.

The gladiatorial combat took place in a shark pen, a circle of lava stones, enclosing about a four-acre area at the edge of a bay in what is now the U.S. Navy base at Pearl Harbor. The circle of rocks had an opening on its seaward side so that water could flow into it. Fish—and human bait—were thrown into the pen to lure sharks through the passage. When a contest was to take place, the passage was closed so that neither opponent could escape. Some of the stones that formed the shark pen were still in place when con-struction of the naval base began in the early 1900s.

In the Solomons, deified sharks lived in sacred caverns built for them near shore. In front of these caverns were erected great stone altars upon which were placed the bodies of chosen victims. After mystical ceremonies, the bodies were then given to the sharks. Some sharks in the Solomons were regarded as incarnations of dead ancestors. These were good sharks, which would help their relatives. Alien sharks, who ventured into the islands on evil missions, were thought to be malevolent. But fishermen could sup-posedly drive these evil sharks away by brandishing before them small wooden statues representing the native sharks.

Mythological sharks often guided lost fishermen to land and even saved swimmers from other sharks. A goddess in the form of a stingray saved people lost at sea by loading them on her broad back and landing them on shore.

Missionary William Ellis wrote of shark worship he had witnessed in the Society Islands in the early nineteenth century. He said that islanders dei-fied the blue shark but killed and ate other species. "Rather than destroy the Great Blue sharks," the missionary said, "they would endeavor to propitiate their favor by prayers and offerings. Temples were erected in which priests officiated, and offerings were presented to the deified sharks, while fishermen and others, who were much at sea, sought their favor."

The coming of Christianity lessened shark worship among the Pacific islands, but the new religion did not completely stamp out devotion to the shark. On Samoa, for instance, the man-eating white shark was looked upon as an emissary of Moso, the god of the land. To protect his coconut or breadfruit trees, a Samoan would fashion from coconut fiber an image of the shark, and suspend the idol in the tree. Similar images were placed in gardens to protect them. If a thief stole from a shark-guarded tree or garden, he risked being devoured by a white shark the next time he went fishing. The story is told on Samoa about a native, newly converted to Christianity, who showed his contempt of this superstition by mockingly thrusting an arm into the mouth of one of the shark idols. Shortly thereafter, so the story goes on, the native went on a fishing trip and was seized by a shark that bit off his arms.

A Catholic priest, the Reverend A. J. Laplante, witnessed shark charming in the Fiji Islands during the decade he spent as a missionary there between 1928 and 1938. Twice a year, when the natives made a drive for tribal feasts, or when they wanted to make their swimming areas safe from sharks, shark-kissing ceremonies would be held. According to Father Laplante, "The night before the drive, the man who wants the shark fishing done goes to the house of the chief, who is also the sorcerer or medicine man. There they enact a ceremony which survives from their oldest superstitions and beliefs.

"This ceremony always includes the presentation of *kava*—a mildly narcotic beverage made from juice extracted from finely ground root—and the sacrifice of an animal. The *kava* is drunk and some of it is sprinkled on the important main post of the house, where the spirit lives, and the animal is strangled, cooked and eaten.

"The next day, the natives drive the sharks into a large net, the shark-kissers wade out, seize the man-eaters, kiss them on their up-turned bellies and fling them on the bank. I don't know how they do it, but, among the natives, it is taken for granted that once a shark is kissed—upside down—that is the end of it."

(Modern researchers have found that many sharks of many species become immobile when they are turned over; stroking the belly also seems to help prolong the comalike state.)

Pearl divers off the coast of Sri Lanka have long relied upon shark charmers to protect them from sharks. Sir J. Emerson Tennent, who studied the customs of what was then Ceylon, reported in 1861 that the "mystic ceremony of the shark charmer" was "an indispensable preliminary" to every pearl hunt. "His power," Sir Tennent noted, "is believed to be hereditary; nor is it supposed that the value of his incantations is at all dependent upon the religious faith professed by the operator, for the present head of the family happens to be a Roman Catholic. At the time of our visit, this mysterious functionary was ill and unable to attend. But he sent an accredited substitute, who assured me that, although he himself was ignorant of the grand and mystic secret, the mere fact of his presence, as a representative of the higher authority, would be recognized and respected by the sharks."

The blending of sharks and sorcery is complex, and neighboring islands sometimes show vastly different attitudes toward the shark. In the Tabar Islands of the Bismarck Archipelago off New Guinea, sharks are caught, but in the nearby Tanga Islands there is a long-standing taboo against the hunting of the shark, which is believed to be a dangerous wizard. There are reasonable grounds for this superstition, because shark hunters caught their prey by snaring them from canoes. Snared sharks frequently towed away their would-be captors' canoes and neither canoes nor canoeists were ever seen again.

In New Zealand, among the Maori, shark fishing was once a religious ceremony supervised by a priest who stood atop a rock on shore and directed as many as a thousand men who set out to sea in big canoes on two specified days of the year. They hunted, on these appointed days, only one kind of shark—*kapeta*, apparently a species of dogfish. Other species of sharks could be caught any time.

Woven into the rich tapestry of Hawaiian legends are many tales of sharks—tales still told by venerable *kanakas*, repeating the words heard from the lips of their fathers' fathers, who lived when myths shrouded the islands. In those old times, a chief might will his bones to friends or personal servants so that they could fashion shark hooks from them. In some areas, the bones of great fishermen or brave chiefs were particularly prized for making hooks for the catching of the fabled shark.

Here is a story as told to Mary Kawena of Pupukea Ahupua'a-O'ahu. It was posted on a new medium for spreading stories—the Internet.

A Tale of *Pu'uloa*

"*Pu'uloa* is the old name of what is now Pearl Harbor on the island of Oahu. Legend says that sharks living there long ago were ruled by a queen called *Ka'ahu*, once a lovely girl who lived with her family beside a little stream that flowed into Pu'uloa. Often, says the legend, Ka'ahu and her brother went down to the harbor to swim, happy as fish. A shark god liked to watch them jump and swim. They should be sharks, he thought, and live in Pu'uloa. So he changed their form.

"That night, when the children did not return for dinner, their parents searched for them. The mother heard her husband calling. 'There are sharks in our stream!' he said. 'Young sharks.' The wife came quickly to stand beside the stream. The two young sharks swam close. 'They are not afraid,'

SHARKS ON THE INTERNET

The latest place to find the shark is on the Internet. Here are some of the best sites:

The American Elasmobranch Society
http://www.elasmo.org/

Mote Marine Laboratory
http://www.mote.org/

Mote's Center for Shark Research
http://www.mote.org/~rhueter/shark_research.phtml

Newsletter of the shark specialist group of the International Union for Conservation of Nature and Natural Resources (IUCN)
http://www.flmnh.ufl.edu/fish/research/IUCN/breakingnews.htm (latest shark news)

The International Shark Attack File
http://www.flmnh.ufl.edu/fish/research/ISAF/shark.htm

Elasmobranch Research at the Monterey Bay Aquarium
http://www.mbay.net/~mollet/Index.html

The Shark Foundation
http://www.shark.ch/home.shtml

The Pelagic Shark Research Foundation
http://www.pelagic.org/

Fiona's Shark Links
http://www.oceanstar.com/shark

she said, 'and see! They are opening their mouths for food. They're hungry!' She turned to her husband. 'These are our children!' she exclaimed. 'They have been changed to sharks and come to us, as always, for their food.'

"The man looked long as the two swam close, rubbing the bank and opening their mouths hungrily. Then he brought food. He gave each a drink of 'awa (alcohol) then peeled bananas for them. When they had eaten enough, they swam away. Next day they came again for food. All the relatives of those children heard how they were changed. 'Shark sister and shark brother,' they called the two. They saved food for them, hung about their necks and played with them in Pu'uloa.

"The day came when the two had grown so big they could no longer swim up the shallow stream for food. Their relatives understood and carried 'awa and bananas to them in Pu'uloa. Years went by. Ka'ahu became the queen of the sharks and her brother, Striking Tail, was also honored by the other sharks. The parents of those children died but brothers, sisters and other relatives still loved and fed the sharks...."

Later, in a fit of jealousy over a beautiful lei given to a young girl, Ka'ahu ordered the girl killed. In remorse, she ordered her shark never to kill again. And people understood that they were safe in Pu'uloa. In return for the sharks' protection, people protected them.

When old Hawaiians heard that the U.S. Navy planned to build a base at Pu'uloa, they remembered that Ka'ahu's son had had his home in a cave beneath the place where the huge dry dock would be built. "Choose another place for your dry dock," they warned. "The spirit who guards the cave will not like men to build above it."

But the warnings went unheeded, and construction of the dry dock began. When it was nearly finished, it suddenly collapsed. But no one was killed. "Ka'ahu loved people," the Hawaiians said, "and wanted no one killed at Pu'uloa."

Shark Man Tales

Kamo-hoa-lii, so another tale goes, fell in love with a maiden, Kalei, whom he saw swimming in the sea. Kamo-hoa-lii transformed himself into a man, married Kalei, and fathered a child. Kamo-hoa-lii then returned to the sea as a shark. The child, Nanaue, looked like any other child—except that on his back he bore the mark of his shark father, the mouth of a shark. Although Kamo-hoa-lii had warned that the child must never be fed the flesh of an animal, the taboo was broken, and Nanaue thus learned the magic of making himself into a shark. As a shark, he devoured many islanders. Finally, he was caught and his body, in the form of a great shark, was taken to a hill in Kain-alu.

"And even today," the old storytellers say, "the hill they took Nanaue to is called Puumano, the Shark Hill.... The people took bamboos from the sacred grove of Kain-alu and made sharp knives from the bamboo splits, and they cut pieces from the body of the shark man. But the gods were angry, and they took the sharpness from the bamboos in the sacred grove, and to this day the bamboos of Kain-alu are not strong and they cannot cut."

Another old tale of a shark man reemerged in 1956 when the Bishop Museum in Honolulu acquired an ancient relic known as *Kapaaheo*, the "Shark Stone." According to the legend of *Kapaaheo*, maidens of the Big Island—the Island of Hawaii—went swimming in a cove that sheltered them from the sea. Many times a swimmer would disappear and never be seen again. Coincidentally, a mysterious stranger was always nearby when a maiden vanished. Fishermen near the cove were suspicious of the stranger, but they could not prove that he had anything to do with the disappearances.

One day, armed with their spears, they went swimming with the girls. When a shark attacked the group, the fishermen stabbed it several times, and the shark fled. A short while later, the mysterious stranger was found on the shore, dying of spear wounds. And when he died, his body turned into *Kapaaheo*, a large stone shaped like a shark.

When the museum announced that it was going to ship *Kapaaheo* from the Big Island to Honolulu on Oahu, Heloke Mookini, a seventy-one-year-old islander, had a dream in which his mother visited him and told him of *Kapaaheo*, and asked him to help with its removal.

"So I went to the stone," Heloke later recounted, "and saw three bulldozers that were damaged from trying to lift the stone on a sled. I hit the Shark Stone with a rock, and the sound was like a dull thud. I knew the stone was unhappy. So I told it that to go to the Bishop Museum and be with all its old friends of Hawaii would be the best thing."

Heloke said he tapped the stone again, and "the sound was now like a clear ringing sound which meant that the stone was happy."

Kapaaheo was no longer stubborn, for, according to a story in the *Honolulu Star-Bulletin*, "The next day a single bulldozer pushed the stone onto a sled without any difficulty."

One of Japan's mythological deities is a god of storm, known as the Shark Man. In fact, the shark is so terrifying in Japanese legends that during World War II, when the Chinese sought a talisman to be painted on war planes raiding the Japanese, they chose the tiger shark. The American pilots who flew these shark-invoking planes were known throughout the world as the "Flying Tigers," but actually they should have been called the "Flying Sharks."

Jonah and the Shark?

A legend from Papua New Guinea tells of the wondrous deliverance of Mutuk, a man who was swallowed by a shark. The details of Mutuk's sojourn in a shark's belly are not as well known as Jonah's stay in "a great fish"—generally thought to be a whale. But the two stories are basically similar.

There is support for the claim that Jonah was swallowed by a shark, not a whale. The Bible says that Jonah was swallowed by a fish, and, though the biological distinction probably was not known to biblical scribes, the whale is a mammal, not a fish. Bishop Erik Pontoppidan of Norway, a prolific writer on real and imaginary creatures of the sea, in 1765 wrote a long and learned paper which proved, to his satisfaction at least, that Jonah had been gulped down by a basking shark. Anatomically, this would be difficult for a basking shark, whose diet is restricted to plankton and whose gullet would have trouble passing a prophet. For this reason, supporters of the Jonah-shark theory favor the white shark *(Carcharodon carcharias)*, which certainly is a man-eater. But the regurgitation of a living man would be far more miraculous on the part of a white shark than a whale. (The notion that Jonah was swallowed by a whale may have been inspired by the fact that Joppa, whence Jonah was going when the sailors tossed him overboard, was an ancient whaling port.)

Indians and Sharks

Sharks found their way into the myths of many American Indian cultures. The Tlingit of southern Alaska divided tribes into *tus*, or "shark," lodges. The chief of one of the tribes was called *Ha yeak*, a Tlingit term for the hollow left in shallow water by a swiftly swimming shark. To the Tlingit, the skate was known as "the canoe of the land otter." Shark crests marked the carved emblems of tribal clans, and the sticks the Indians used in playing a gambling game, vaguely similar to dice, were named after several animals, including the *tus*. Apparently through intratribal trade, tribes far from the sea knew about sharks. Laurence M. Klauber, an outstanding herpetologist and an authority on the rattlesnake, was surprised to discover that some tribes, unfamiliar with the sea, called rattlesnakes "little sharks of the woods."

In South and Central America, images of sharks appear on ancient pottery, and figurines depicting swimmers being devoured by sharks have been unearthed by archeologists. They also have found stingray barbs that were probably used as sacrificial knives on altars where human victims were offered to the gods. Along the Honduran coast, even today Indian children play an old, old game in which the child who is "it" dives into the water and tags other children by pinching or biting them. The game is called "playing at shark."

Sailors' Stories

In the days of sail, many ports of call were reputed to be the homes of sharks known by name. Two of the most infamous were Port Royal Jack at the entrance to the harbor of Kingston, Jamaica, and Shanghai Bill in Bridgetown Harbor, Barbados, West Indies. Shanghai Bill was said to have eaten many a sailor, but it was a shaggy dog that did him in. Bill, it seems, seized in his great jaws one day a big brown sheepdog that had fallen into Bridgetown Harbor. The dog's hair got caught in Bill's teeth, and he choked to death. This may be the world's first shaggy dog story.

Sharks did follow sailing ships because a steady diet of galley garbage flowed in the ships' wakes. Sharks that picked up the scent of such an easy meal followed a ship for weeks. Sharks even bit off the brass rotators of the "patent logs" that ships trailed behind them to register their speed.

One of the earliest English-language references to shark attacks occurs in a 1580 *Fugger News-Letter*, which gives this eyewitness account of how a seaman virtually fell into the jaws of a shark, somewhere between Portugal and India:

> When a man fell from our ship into the sea during a strong wind, so that we could not wait for him or come to his rescue in any other fashion, we threw out to him on a rope a wooden block, especially prepared for that purpose, and this he finally managed to grasp and thought he could save himself thereby. But when our crew drew this block with the man toward the ship and had him within half the carrying distance of a musket shot, there appeared from below the surface of the sea a large monster called Tiburon; it rushed on the man and tore him to pieces before our very eyes. That surely was a grievous death.

This attack, incidentally, is the first reported in the International Shark Attack File, which now contains nearly 2,800 accounts.

Ships' logs recount many similar tragedies, but there were some close races which the mariners won. The captain of the *Ayrshire* fell overboard during a cruise in 1850. His valiant Newfoundland dog leaped into the sea to save him. A shark headed for them, but, according to the log, both the captain and the dog were saved. The captain was unscathed. The dog's tail was bitten off.

Many a sailor who died aboard ship and whose body was buried at sea found his tomb in the belly of a shark. The superstition grew that sharks somehow knew when a man was about to die, and the appearance of sharks in the wake of a ship came to be considered an omen of death. One skipper who sailed out of San Francisco added to the legend. He often carried the bodies of Chinese who died in the United States, and, according to ancient custom, had to be buried in China. The skipper wrote that on voyages when he carried corpses his ship was followed by a pack of sharks that could detect the corpses even though they lay in lead-lined coffins deep in the hold.

Ships Named *Shark*

The sailors' dread of sharks has not spawned a superstition against naming ships *Shark*. Six United States Navy ships have been called *Shark*. The first, a 198-ton schooner of twelve guns, was launched in 1821 and had for her first commanding officer a young lieutenant named Matthew Calbraith Perry, who three decades later, as Commodore Perry, would lead the first American mission to Japan. The Confederate *Shark* was captured by a Union ship off Galveston, Texas, on July 4, 1861. Her name was retained until she was formally taken over by the U.S. Navy on September 5, 1863 and renamed *George W. Rodgers*.

The Navy took over a thirty-ton motor yacht on May 24, 1917, and placed her in commission as the *Shark.* She served through World War I as a patrol craft and ended her Navy career on November 16, 1919. The other Navy ships named *Shark* were submarines. The first earned one battle star in World War II and was sunk with no survivors to causes unknown. The next *Shark* was on her third war patrol in October 1944 when she was lost with all souls. The most recent *Shark*, a nuclear-propelled attack submarine, was completed in 1961 and decommissioned in 1990.

Watson and the Shark

Sharks appear in several British coats of arms, the most famous being that of Sir Brook Watson, who in 1749, at the age of fourteen, lost his right leg below the knee to a shark. An orphan who was a member of a ship's crew, he was attacked while swimming in Havana Harbor. Years later, when he became a baronet, Watson created a coat of arms that "may contain an allusion to an awful event in his life, and be a memorial of his gratitude to Heaven for his signal preservation on that occasion." The coat of arms includes a demitriton grasping a trident and repelling a shark in the act of seizing its prey. Also in the coat of arms are "a human leg erect and erased below the knee," along with a Neptune "repelling a shark in the act of seizing its prey proper."

Fellow crewmen saved Watson, and he never forgot them. Fitted for a wooden leg, he went to Boston and then to Nova Scotia, where he helped British Americans who were fleeing the Revolution. He next sailed to London, where he became a merchant prince. Turning to politics—and using his shark-gnawed leg as a conversation piece—he was elected to Parliament. He later became the Lord Mayor London. In 1778 he asked John Singleton Copley to reconstruct the event that had shaped his destiny.

Watson's recollection of the attack was magnificently portrayed by Copley in *Watson and the Shark*, which was exhibited at the Royal Academy in 1778. Copley's painting—hailed by a critic as a work that "stands alone in its age"—shows a boatload of seamen rushing to help the boy in blood-streaked water. The painting was a sensation, a time-freezing work that makes a masterpiece of a moment. Looking at it, the viewer sees a story that has not ended, a painting that does not disclose whether the lad will live or die.

The seemingly spontaneous poses in the painting appear to have been based on historical precedents, according to a guide published by the National Gallery of Art, which possesses the painting. The harpooner's pose, for example, resembles Raphael's altarpiece in which the Archangel Michael uses a spear to drive Satan out of heaven.

Acclaim for the painting led to Copley's appointment to the Royal Academy. He earned a fortune selling engravings of its design. Copley, the greatest American painter of the eighteenth century, journeyed to England just before the American Revolution. He never returned to America—and he did not visit Cuba to create the painting.

Copley used maps and prints to set the scene, but he did little research to portray the shark, which is an inaccurate rendering of what appears to be a combination of a tiger shark and a white shark, both notorious as man-eaters in Havana Harbor.

Shark Detective Stories

Three times sharks have exposed crimes that would never have been detected without them. Each of these true stories is well documented.

Crime No. 1: Truth from the Jaws of a Shark

On July 3, 1799, the *Nancy*, a brig of 125 tons, slipped out of Baltimore and into the Chesapeake, bound south for waters barred to American ships by a British naval blockade. To evade the blockade, her owners had hit upon a scheme to disguise her true identity: get new counterfeit papers and toss the real papers into the sea if challenged.

The *Nancy* sailed first to Curaçao, a Dutch colony in the West Indies, where she obtained fraudulent ownership papers indicating that she was owned by a Dutchman. With these papers, she sailed on. But, on August 28, she was overtaken by a British cutter, *HMS Sparrow*. The cutter's captain, Lieutenant Hugh Wylie, unimpressed by the Dutch papers, put a prize crew aboard the *Nancy* and order it taken to Port Royal, Jamaica, where the case could be settled in the Court of Vice-Admiralty.

Meanwhile, the crew of another British vessel, the *Ferret*, caught what was probably a tiger shark, in whose jaws were found the papers of an American ship called the *Nancy*. By chance, the captain of the *Ferret* invited Lieutenant Wylie aboard for breakfast around the time the shark was captured. Wylie examined the shark-produced papers and immediately perceived the fraudulence of the Dutch papers he had sealed with his own hand when he sent the *Nancy* to Port Royal.

The "Shark Papers," as they came to be called, were introduced into court in time to prove the true ownership of the *Nancy*, and, on November 25, 1799, she and her cargo were condemned as a prize.

When the case ended, the shark's jaws, which measured twenty-two inches at their widest point, were set up on shore in Kingston as a warning to perjurers that the truth can be found, even if it is sunk in the sea. And with the jaws was a sign that said: "Lieutenant Fitton recommends these jaws for a collar for neutrals to swear through."

Crime No. 2: The Witness Was a Shark

In November 1915, the U.S. government brought to trial, in the U.S. District Court for the Southern District of New York, four executives of the Hamburg-American Steamship Company. They were charged with violation of U.S. customs laws. But, in effect, they were being tried to put on record Germany's use of neutral American ports by falsely registered freighters that were used to carry supplies to German U-boats and raiders.

In his opening statement, Assistant U.S. Attorney Robert B. Wood told how a Norwegian ship, the *Gladstone*, had been given a provisional registry as the Costa Rican ship *Marina Quesada* and, on December 16, 1914, had sailed from Newport News, Virginia. Ostensibly, she was headed for Valparaíso, Chile. Actually her mission was to rendezvous with German raiders in international waters.

Early in January 1915, Wood said, the ship's Costa Rican flag was hauled down and a Norwegian flag was run up. The name *Marina Quesada* was painted out, and *Gladstone* was once more painted on her bows and counter. And, as the *Gladstone*, after some minor adventures and misadventures, she anchored in the harbor of Pernambuco (now Recife), Brazil.

"And there," Wood recounted, "the customs authorities demanded the ship's papers, and the Captain, after giving several excuses, put the papers in a leather pouch and got in a small boat and dropped the papers overboard.

"Now, gentlemen, I do not vouch for this story, but one of the witnesses says that the crew of a Brazilian warship lying alongside the *Marina Quesada* killed a shark, and in the belly of the shark they found the ship's papers. At all events, we have not been able to get hold of the papers."

The witness was John Olson, chief engineer of the ship. He told, on the stand, the story of the ship's masquerade and its arrival in Brazil. He said that the captain of the ship had dropped the papers as he entered a small boat that was to carry him to shore. Later, Olson testified, the captain told the first mate about the incident and said: "Did you see the trick I done?"

"Did you see any of the ship's papers again?" Olson was asked on the stand.

A. I seen the handbag; yes sir.

Q. Whereabouts?

A. In a news office in Pernambuco.

Q. Did you ever see any of the papers?

A. No, sir.

Q. Did you leave the ship there?

A. Yes, sir.

At this point in Olson's testimony, according to the *New York Times* account of the trial, Olson seemed about to say more. But, "to his evident great disappointment," the *Times* reported, "Olson was not allowed to tell of the ship's papers being found on the inside of a shark."

Thus, the mystery of the shark of Recife was never cleared up, at least publicly. The only record is in the transcript of the trial, which includes the scant remarks in Wood's opening statementl. But, even with the shark as only a phantom witness, the story of the *Gladstone–Marina Quesada* was put into the record, along with many details of the German government's flagrant violations of U.S. neutrality—and the four Hamburg-American executives were found guilty.

Crime No. 3: The Shark Arm Mystery

On April 18, 1935, an Australian fisherman named Albert Hobson hauled up a fishing line he had set the day before about a mile off Coogee, a popular Sydney bathing beach. He had caught two sharks. A small shark apparently had taken the bait during the night. Then, not too long before Hobson arrived in his boat, a fourteen-foot tiger shark had nearly devoured the smaller one, whose remains were still on the hook. The tiger, still alive, had entangled itself in Hobson's line.

Hobson and his brother Charles managed to get the big shark ashore. With the help of spectators who had watched the capture from the beach, the two brothers dragged the shark across a stretch of sand to the Coogee Aquarium. By the time it was placed in the aquarium pool, the shark looked more dead than alive. For twenty-four hours it lay in the pool, apparently lifeless. Oxygen was pumped into the pool. This seemed to help. By April 20, two days after its capture, the shark was eating all the fish thrown to it. But on April 24, the shark stopped eating and hardly moved.

Next day, while fourteen persons stood at the pool watching the listless shark, it suddenly came to life. It lashed the water with its tail, rushed to the shallow end of the pool and whirled about in eccentric circles. One of the spectators who was standing about ten feet from the shark, saw a brown, foul-smelling scum erupt around the shark. And he saw, emerging out of the cloud and slowly rising to the surface, the remains of a rat...the body of a seabird...and a human arm, with a rope tied around its wrist.

The arm was taken to the city morgue, where Dr. Arthur Palmer, the government medical officer, examined it. The arm—the left arm of a muscular man—was intact and remarkably well preserved. On its forearm was a tattoo of two boxers confronting each other, one in blue trunks, the other in red. A six-inch rope was tightly knotted about its wrist. The knot was a seaman's knot, a clove hitch.

Dr. Palmer called in Dr. V. M. Coppleson, a Sydney surgeon, for consultation. Coppleson, who had been making a detailed study of sharkbite wounds, saw immediately that the arm had not been ripped from the man's body by a shark. It had been cleanly severed at the shoulder by a knife. No surgeon had done it, for the usual procedures in surgical amputation had not been followed.

A medical student could have severed the arm from a cadaver and, either the arm had somehow been dropped in the sea, or a prankster with a grisly sense of humor had thrown it into the aquarium pool. Both possibilities were quickly ruled out. Spectators at the pool recounted their story of seeing the shark regurgitate the arm; inquiries at medical schools established that no cadavers or portions of cadavers were missing.

The shark was killed. A few fish bones and part of a small shark were found, but there were no other human remains, not even a shred of clothing. So the arm was the only clue to the man's identity.

A Sydney police fingerprint expert peeled off the wrinkled skin of the hand, treated chemically to remove its wrinkles, and got a set of fingerprints. They matched the prints of James Smith, a former amateur boxer who ran a billiard parlor in Rozelle, a Sydney suburb. Smith's prints were on file in Sydney because he had been arrested three years earlier for illegal betting. Smith was known to be a friend of several criminals, but he himself was not considered to be a criminal by the Sydney police.

William Prior, superintendent of the Criminal Investigation Branch of the New South Wales police force, knew he was looking for a murderer, but he could not prove that a murder had been committed. Smith had disappeared, but the arm was not enough evidence to warrant an inquest. The coroner could not assume that Smith was dead until other parts of his body were found. Prior asked Gilbert P. Whitley, shark expert of the Australian Museum in Sydney, to gather all possible scientific data on the food and physiology of digestion of sharks, particularly tiger sharks.

While Whitley gathered information about sharks, Prior's detectives began looking for a killer. The detectives soon discovered that Smith, a pool-hall operator, had been involved in some seemingly shady business deals with Reginald William Holmes, a wealthy Sydney boat builder. When questioned by the police, Holmes admitted knowing Smith and giving him money for business purposes. Smith had last been seen in the company of Patrick Brady, who shared a cottage with Smith in the fishing town of Cronulla. The landlord reported that after they left the cottage, a trunk, a mattress, some rope, and sash cords were missing. (These articles were never seen again.) He also stated that he had found a can of evil-smelling liquid in the cottage, which he thought was blood.

Police found Brady and charged him with the murder of Smith. Four days later the police received a startling phone call: Reginald Holmes was racing his boat around Sydney Harbor with a bullet in his head. When they caught up with Holmes, he was babbling incoherently—"Jimmy Smith is dead. I'm nearly dead, and there is only one other left." Holmes did not die. An X ray showed that a .32 caliber bullet had flattened itself against the unusually thick frontal bone of his skull. In the hospital, Holmes told police that Brady had told him, "I had a row with Smith and I have done him in . . . . If you tell the police I've done this, I'll murder you, too."

Several days later, Holmes was released from the hospital. On June 12, police found Holmes dead in his car, a bullet in his chest.

Now the police had two murders, and the Crown had two shaky cases. It was almost impossible to make the charge against Brady stick: There was no body; there was no known date of death; there were no clues as to how Smith was murdered. Brady was tried for Smith's murder and acquitted when a judge directed a jury to find him innocent because of insufficient evidence. Two men were later tried for Holmes' murder. The first trial ended in a hung jury, the second with a jury verdict of acquittal.

Brady insisted on his innocence until he died in 1965.

Invoking a shark as part of one's fate—*Scuto Divino*, "under God's protection," says the motto on Watson's arms—places one inside the myths of the shark, a realm of savage mystery and myth. Rare is the use of the shark to induce sympathy for a cause or a country. Yet there are those who do indeed conjure up the shark as a talisman of fate or strength. Sharks appear on postage stamps of French Somaliland, Ifni, Eritrea, Tristan da Cunha, Gibraltar, Spanish Guinea, and Kenya. And when the Solomon Islands became independent in 1978, its new green and blue flag was emblazoned with frigate birds, a crocodile, and a shark. Later, however, in official descriptions of the flag, the Solomon Islands did not mention the creatures. It was as if the shark were there but invisible, as corporeal as a myth.

CHAPTER 7

Seeking the Shark

"At last he showed, broadside, limned dark against the blood-stained water . . . gaping, his terrible jaws spread, his wide, weary tail churning the water. He was overcome but not beaten. He had the diabolical eye of a creature that would kill as he was being killed." Hauled into the boat, "the mako lurched out with snapping jaws, half way up to the gunwale, to sink his teeth on the side of the boat . . . .

"I never loved sharks, but at that moment I repented of my lust to kill these death-dealing engines of the deep. . . . He was the ninetieth mako for me and that should be enough. He weighed 510 pounds and was the second largest I had caught. . . . New Zealand's premier sporting fish, as game as he was beautiful, as ferocious as he was enduring."

With accounts like that, Zane Grey, author of *Riders of the Purple Sage* and other western novels of the 1920s and 1930s, helped to popularize sharks—particularly the mako—as game fish. Of the mako, he wrote, "It is really unfitting to call him a shark at all," a remark that underscored the sport fishermen's prejudice against sharks in Zane Grey's time. But mako became the first shark ranked as a game fish; other species were added in later years. Fishes that once were called "the poor man's marlin" were to become the objects of tournaments with a top prize of $50,000 or more.

Ernest Hemingway was also an avid shark fisherman. In 1936 he caught a record mako, weighing 786, off Bimini, the Bahamas. Nearly two decades later, in *The Old Man and the Sea,* he wrote of a mako:

> He was a very big Mako shark built to swim as fast as the fastest fish in the sea and everything was beautiful about him except his jaws. His back was as blue as a sword fish's and his belly was silver and his hide was smooth and handsome. He was built as a sword fish except for his huge jaws which were shut tight now as he swam fast, just under the water with his high dorsal fin knifing through the water without wavering. Inside the closed double lip of his jaws all of his eight rows of teeth were slanted inwards. They were not the ordinary pyramid-shaped teeth of most sharks. They were shaped like a man' s finger when they are crisped like claws. They were nearly as long as the fingers of the old man and they had razor-sharp cutting edges on both sides. This was a fish built to feed on all the fish in the sea. . . .

After the book and movie *Jaws* made the great white shark a world-wide celebrity in the mid-1970s, it far surpassed the mako as the most hunted shark. Fishing for the great white was the oceanic version of big game hunting: a duel between a human being and a savage, man-killing beast. *Carcharodon carcharias*—the white shark, as it is now officially named—has virtually no commercial value, but it has become the ultimate game fish for the sports fishers who have chosen shark as their quarry.

In August 1986 Donnie Braddick, fishing off Montauk, Long Island, with Frank Mundus, a famed shark fisherman, caught what was described as "the largest fish ever taken on rod and reel," a white shark seventeen feet long weighing 3,427 pounds. But, because a whale carcass was used to attract the shark, the catch was disqualified as a world-class record fish by the International Game Fish Association. (See **Official Shark Catch Records**, page 253.)

Mundus was used to such frustrations. In 1964, about ten miles off Montauk, he had harpooned a white shark seventeen and a half feet long and weighing an estimated 4,500 pounds. He said he drove five harpoons into the shark before he could tow it ashore. There, a bulldozer dragged it up the beach and Mundus killed it with a .30 caliber rifle. A record shark, but not a shark that made the official record books.

Mundus, who often has been identified as the model for Quint, the Captain Ahab of *Jaws*, retired from shark fishing in the early 1990s after more than forty years as a charterboat captain. Mundus has never acknowledged his relationship to the fictional Quint, but he has been quoted as saying that he never read *Jaws*.

So great has been the demand for whites on the end of the line that it was given special protected status in 1994 in California, South Africa, and part of Australia. (See chapter 8.) Sports fishing of the white shark continues, legal but regulated, in those areas. Elsewhere, however, whites get no protection. And, as a game fish enthusiast complained in 1997, "Big sharks are growing harder to catch every year, and anglers must be content with even a bantamweight."

But great whites were scarce, compared to other species. (During an 1985–86 tagging operation on the U.S. East Coast, only one white shark was tagged; of 51,379 sharks tagged from 1963 to 1983, only fifty-nine were white sharks.) East Coast sports fishermen had to be satisfied with the most common makos and hammerheads. But there was compensation: A shark might bring in $200 or $300 from a restaurateur who wanted an exotic fish on the menu. In 1980 alone, sports fishermen pulled in 3,210 tons of shark, most of them off Montauk Point on Long Island or off the waters around Cape May, New Jersey. By comparison, commercial fishermen landed 458 tons that year.

Game anglers fish for sharks in tournaments and on ordinary fishing trips. The latter usually catch small coastal sharks that are generally not targeted by commercial fisheries. But commercial and recreational fishermen can affect the shark fishing of each other. Commercial shrimp fishermen in the Gulf of Mexico, for example, catch and discard many small coastal sharks (mostly sharpnose), inadvertently depriving sports fishermen of the sharks. The opposite also happens: game anglers seek blacktip sharks, a species seasonally taken by long-line and drift gill net fishermen for commercial sales. Many southern shark tournament anglers also fish for the same large coastal species taken by commercial fishermen. Tournament anglers in mid-Atlantic states and in southern New England fish for shortfin mako and blue sharks that are caught incidentally by large pelagic longline fisheries. Sharks taken by anglers along the Atlantic and Gulf coasts are often sold to commercial fish buyers.

On the U.S. West Coast, many sports clubs have focused on sharks, any sharks. White sharks were more plentiful in California waters than on the East Coast. California fishermen were catching ten to twenty a year. But the idea of catching any kind of shark caught on. No sharks were immune. One year, about twenty-five yards off Santa Monica, a spear fisherman killed a 1,400-pound basking shark—a huge, lumbering species that has never been mistaken for a man-eater. Another favorite spot for shark killing was Monterey Bay, about sixty miles south of San Francisco. There, twice a year, shark derbies were held. In a typical derby, fishermen would reel in about 150 sharks and rays whose total weight would be around 2,000 pounds.

Shark killing had become a tradition off Moss Landing, California, long before *Jaws*. In 1946, oystermen had hit upon the idea of inviting people to come and kill leopard sharks and large rays that were eating oysters. The hunt became an annual event: a shark "derby" that drew crowds to Moss Landing and put a tourist event on the calendar. Year by year the shark and ray population decreased.

By the early 1990s conservationists were targeting shark slaughters, pointing out that wanton killing of an apex predator threatened delicate marine ecosystems. At an annual shark-fishing tournament in Virginia Beach, Virginia, in 1992, for example, none of the sixty tournament anglers caught a shark over the 300-pound-minimum. In past years, contestants usually hauled in a half dozen sharks over 500 pounds. A study of thirty-four sportfishing tournaments in Florida between 1971 and 1991 showed a decline in the number and size of sharks caught.

About sixty-five shark tournments are staged along the eastern Gulf Coast alone. Ocean-going shark fishermen, particularly those who fish in big-money tournaments from California to Montauk, are not the only seekers of shark. Beach and surf fishermen also cast for shark, as do pier fishermen. In 1964 the largest tiger shark on record was caught from a pier in Cherry Grove, South Carolina.

Many tournaments are encouraging tag-and-return fishing, enforcing restrictions on minimum sizes, and putting observers in boats to insure that the rules are not broken.

In 1991 the Pelagic Shark Research Foundation in California, beginning a campaign against wanton shark killing, aimed at the annual massacre in Moss Landing. The foundation succeeded in getting some conservation rules accepted. They also got the derby pushed back from early July to early August to avoid the most important period of the sharks' breeding cycle. But one group of participants, archers who enjoyed killing with arrows, ignored the rules. The foundation kept up its campaign. What had started as a way to kill oyster-eating sharks was looking like a way to hurt the local ecosystem. In 1995 the sponsors of the annual hunt withdrew their support. Although individual archers continue to kill sharks and rays in the area, there no longer is a shark derby in Moss Landing.

In Australia, divers had made a sport out of killing the gray nurse shark *(Odontaspis arenarius)* with underwater shotguns called powerheads. They killed so many that Australia prohibited the killing of gray nurse sharks. Other species were also gaining protection. Rodney Fox, an Australian sport diver, was almost bitten in half by a white shark. "I can't blame the shark," Fox said years later. He was spearfishing and there was a great deal of blood in the water. "I'm just lucky he only bit me and let go. If he'd bitten down and shaken me in the feeding technique, I wouldn't be here." To close his wounds took 462 stitches. Incredibly, Fox survived intact and has joined efforts of South Australia Game Fishermen's Association to tag rather than kill sharks.

Game fishing continues in the oceans of the world, but no longer is shark killing a blood sport driven by the obsessive compulsion to slaughter an enemy. Under the International Game Fish Association, shark fishing is as much a governed sport as is fishing for any other game fish. And in the sagas of game fishing for shark, no story can top those of Alfred Dean, the champion of champions.

Landing the Great White

Alfred Dean caught the four largest fish ever taken on rod and reel—each a white shark and each weighing more than a ton.

Dean caught his first shark in 1939. It weighed 868 pounds. In the years that followed, Dean's prowess as a shark fisherman increased, and so did the weight of his sharks. His fishing ground was the Great Australian Bight, a huge, crescent-shaped curve along the southern coast of the continent. Great schools of fish sweep through the Bight, and, competing for food among them, are innumerable sharks, including some of the world's largest.

In 1951, Sir Willoughby Norrie, governor of South Australia, caught a 2,225-pound white shark, at that time the largest fish ever landed with rod and reel. Dean was determined to beat Norrie's record, and, in 1952, he did.

Dean's encounter with his first record shark began at 2 o'clock one morning when his hired boat was riding at anchor in the Bight after a futile, all-day search for sharks big enough for Dean's taste. A banging on the hull of the boat awakened him. He rolled out of his bunk with a flashlight, went on deck, and in the flashlight's beam caught the dorsal and tail fins of the biggest shark he had ever seen. The shark was violently nuzzling the boat, drawn by the scent of whale oil dripping from a tank in the stern. (Using whale oil, and an occasional bucketful of steer's blood, Dean had laid down an alluring slick that sharks picked up miles away. This shark had followed the bait trail to the boat.)

All night long the shark banged noisily against the side of Dean's boat; once it grappled the propeller and shook the boat. Soon after dawn, Dean dropped his line off the stern, and the shark took it, racing off 250 yards. The shark writhed and rolled. Once it leaped almost fully out of the water. But, by fighting on the surface instead of sounding, the shark soon tired. It was all over in about forty-five minutes. The shark, a white, weighed 2,333 pounds and was sixteen feet long. The world's record belonged to Alf Dean. Less than a year later, he topped his own record by landing a 2,372-pound white shark.

On April 10, 1955, Dean caught a 1,600-pound shark, lashed it to the side of the boat, and went off looking for a bigger one. Suddenly, a huge shark began to attack the 1,600-pounder. Oblivious to Dean, who clouted it with the handle of a gaff, it kept ripping big chunks out of the dead shark. Finally, the mate aboard the boat threw a set of baited hooks to it. The shark lunged for the line, but somehow managed to hook itself in the tail. Dean fought to land the shark, tail-hooked or not. It was impossible. He cut the line. Again, a set of hooks was cast out, and the shark grabbed for the bait, this time hooking itself in the mouth. Dean struggled for half an hour to set the hooks. They tore out, and the shark disappeared.

The boat had gone about a mile from the spot where the shark first struck. Dean decided to head back to the spot and anchor. As soon as the boat anchored, the same shark—the cut line still hooked in its tail—reappeared. Dean tried again, and this time, after a fight of an hour and a half, he landed a shark weighing 2,536 pounds. Dean had once more broken his own record.

Dean broke his world record a fourth time, in 1959, when he landed a 2,664-pounder. But Dean's biggest fish, like the biggest fish of all fishermen, was the one that got away.

In Australia they began calling Alf Dean's biggest fish Barnacle Lil, for she was a female and she had broken the heart of many a shark fisherman. Dean met her one moonlit night in the Bight, when she banged his boat and tore off a seal carcass that Dean had hung over the stern of his boat to lure sharks. He got a look at her as she lingered near the surface a few yards from the boat and estimated that she was more than twenty feet long and weighed at least 4,000 pounds.

He lowered a new seal lure over the side. Near it he dropped his line, baited with his favorite shark bait, seal liver, skewered on two large hooks. Barnacle Lil charged for the hooks, the lure, the liver, even part of the boat's transom. Through the spray churned up by her explosive lunge, Dean could see that she had the hooks in her mouth. He put his reel in gear and set the hooks. Time after time, she fought the hooks by rocketing to the surface and lifting her body nearly out of the sea. For two more hours she fought. Then, slowly, he began reeling her in.

He got her to the side of the boat. A crewman reached his gloved hands down to the wire leader attached to the end of the line. (Under game fishing rules, in order to claim a record, the fisherman cannot be aided until he brings his fish to gaff. At that time, another person can grasp the leader, but not the line. During a fight, no part of the fishing tackle may be touched by anyone except the fisherman.)

Barnacle Lil was not through. She suddenly found new strength and whirled seaward again, tearing the leader out of the boatman's hands. "Twenty men could not have held it," Dean later said.

Dean's hands were turning to mush. Blisters erupted and broke on his palms. His fingers, chafed raw by the constantly bobbing rod, were stiff with pain. His legs were knotted with cramps. The aching muscles in his back and arms seemed ready to burst. And the fight went on. One hour . . . two hours . . . Three times Dean brought the shark to the boat. Three times the glistening leader cleared the water, and three times Barnacle Lil dashed out to sea with new strength.

As the fight went into its fifth hour, Dean was seized by a new torment, stomach cramps. Still in the bolted-down tractor seat he used for his fishing chair and still fighting the shark, he relieved the cramps somewhat by urinating in a can, a feat he never could figure out how he performed.

After five and a half hours, Dean knew he could hold out no longer. But some tremor in the line, some mysterious signal he felt almost intuitively, told him that Barnacle Lil was tiring. Once more, with aching hands, he began to reel in. He got her to the boat, and the boatman began pulling up the leader. About ten feet of the thirty-foot leader were in the boat when Barnacle Lil made her last, wild try for freedom. She dove, straight down. The leader, snagged on the boat's pipe railing, followed the shark down, tore out seven feet of railing, then snapped. Barnacle Lil was free.

Several big game fishermen had sighted and pursued her before Dean hooked her. Others saw and chased her after his epic encounter. She was never caught.

Dean, who was born in 1904, died in 1991.

Snaring a Shark

One of the oldest devices for catching sharks in Micronesia is the shark snare, a coarse rope of plant fibers. A noose fashioned from the rope was dipped into the sea from a canoe. The fisherman attracted sharks to the area by swinging a rattle, usually hollowed-out coconut shells or large sea shells threaded onto a stick. When the rattle brought a shark near to the canoe, small fishes or bits of meat were swirled in the water to lure the shark's head into the noose. When the noose suddenly was drawn tight, it snared the shark just behind the gill slits. As the shark struggled, it was clubbed to death. The Maoris of New Zealand favored the noose method on mako sharks because they treasured the center teeth, called *ngutukao*, as ear ornaments. The teeth might have been damaged if a hook had been used.

Some snare fishermen found that their hands were the most dependable bait for sharks. While one occupant of a canoe trailed his hand along in the water, another man dropped a noose aft of the enticing hand. The shark swam into the noose in pursuit of the hand. Then, when the shark's body was well into the noose and the jaws near the hand, the noose was tightened and the man withdrew his hand. The hand had to be gently, slowly swished in the water. If the hand moved slowly, so did the shark. If an unwary "bait man" jerked his hand or made a sudden movement, the shark would strike—and snatch off the hand.

Pacific Islanders who use shark rattles believe that when a shark hears the sound, it believes it is hearing the excited cries of seabirds feeding upon a shoal of small fish, and the shark rushes to share in the feast. Divers on Thursday Island, Australia, are afraid to go after crawfish (spiny lobsters) in deep water because they believe that when a crawfish snaps its tail when someone tries to catch it, the sound lures sharks.

Diving with Sharks

Modern shark hunters are confronted by a steady decrease in shark populations in many parts of the world. Ecotourists, seeking ways to enjoy ecosystems without hurting them, often seek scuba and snorkel diving for recreation. To add adventure to their travels, they have begun diving amid sharks. Now "adventure travel" advertisements routinely offer "A Shark Diving Encounter!"

From Australia's Great Barrier Reef and New Zealand and the islands of French Polynesia to Rhode Island, people are seeking thrills by seeking sharks close-up.

Some of the encounters are "cage dives," in which scuba divers crouch in cages while sharks swim around them and nuzzle the steel bars. In the waters off Rhode Island, the sharks are relatively harmless blue sharks. In cages in Australia, the nuzzlers are white sharks.

In San Diego, California, shark divers don steel-mesh suits and climb into cages lowered into a baited area. Customers get a certificate that says, "This diver did step off the back of a boat, without being pushed, into the nearly bottomless Pacific Ocean, swarming with hungry sharks baited up close with blood in the water."

There are also encounters without cages. In a typical "shark feeding tour," divers are taken down forty or fifty feet to a spot where the tour operators know sharks will congregate. A sealed container of dead fish is anchored on the bottom. Divers form a circle around the container. A tour guide opens the container and ten or more reef sharks materialize to eat the easy food. They are so preoccupied with the meal that they do not notice the divers. When the food disappears, so do the sharks.

In the Bahamas, both cage dives and open-water dives are offered. The attracted sharks are silky, Caribbean reef, bull, and tiger sharks. Operators tend to identify all sharks as bulls and tigers because they have more ferocious names—and reputations—than silkies and reef sharks.

"You only live once," says an Australian advertisement for a cage dive in white shark waters. "So why not give it a go?"

Many researchers are concerned about the effects of cage diving on shark populations. Acting on this concern, California's Monterey Bay National Marine Sanctuary has banned shark-cage diving and chumming to attract sharks. According to the federal regulations, "attracting" means any activity that lures or may lure white sharks by using food, bait, chum, dyes, acoustics, or any other means. Monterey encompasses 5,000 square miles and is the largest marine sanctuary in the world.

Shark Medicine

Since Aristotle's time, there has been a belief in the shark as a source of healing potions. Ancient Greeks rubbed the ashes of a shark's tooth on a child's gums to relieve teething pains, boiled shark brains in oil and applied the ointment to an aching tooth to ease pain, and used the liver of the skate as a remedy for earache. They believed that the flesh of an angel shark prevented swelling of the breast, that the brain of the torpedo ray was a good depilatory, and that the liver of a stingray cured scrofula, relieved itching, and cleared up skin diseases.

Fishermen have insisted for years that shark oil is equally good externally as a balm for rheumatism, an ointment for burns, or an antiseptic for cuts—and internally as a cough medicine, a laxative, and an all-around tonic. Modern cosmetic manufacturers have touted shark oil as an ingredient for facial creams. Tiger shark vertebrae are ground into a face powder used by Japanese geisha girls. Shark cartilage has been used as artificial skin for burn victims; shark liver oil is used in Preparation H, the hemorrhoid medication; shark corneas have been used experimentally as artificial human corneas. Shark oil also has been used in the tempering of high-grade steel, the manufacture of margarine, in the currying of leather, the making of soap, as an oil in paints, as a high-quality lubricant, and to clean the delicate works of watches.

During World War II, shark liver oil was the source of about 75 percent of the vitamin A produced in the United States. Never before had fishermen earned so much money so quickly. A San Francisco fishing boat went off on a four-day hunt for one of the best species for oil, soupfin sharks. The boat came back to the wharf with $17,500 worth of shark. One fisherman made $40,000 in five months. Students at the University of Washington skipped classes to fish for shark in Puget Sound. Farm boys who had never been to sea were recruited by shark fishermen and earned as much as $800 for a week's work. Cojimar, Cuba, the setting of *The Old Man and the Sea*, was one of many places on the Gulf of Mexico where small "shark factories" sprang up during the shark oil boom. In the factories, livers were chopped into fist-size chunks and rendered down in big vats. The oil was skimmed off, cooled, canned, and shipped to U.S. dealers for about $4.75 a gallon, depending on its vitamin potency.

U.S. West Coast fishermen, for the most part, threw away all but livers. But Chinese traders usually managed to get the fins, which they sold at premium prices. Profits were made on nearly every part of the shark. Meat was cut into steaks, frozen, and shipped to countries, primarily in South America, where there was no prejudice against eating shark. Less palatable meat was used in poultry and livestock feed preparations. What was left of the shark was ground up for commercial fertilizer.

Fins were cut off and sold to shark fin buyers. Shark teeth were bought by costume jewelers. Jaws of big sharks were dried, preserved, and sold to game fishermen in search of trophies. Shark hides were tanned into leather. (See **The Many Uses of Sharkskin**, page 236.)

Recently it is shark cartilage that is being promoted as a substance that wards off cancer. The claim is based on the medical theory "tumor antiangiogenesis," which holds that since cancerous tumors can only survive when they are nourished by blood vessels, the tumors can be killed by inhibiting the supply of blood vessels. Since cartilage has almost no blood vessels, research focused on the possibility that cartilage might produce a chemical that blocks the angiogenesis factor, and that this blocker might help in the treatment of cancer. After three decades of research, the results are still inconclusive.

Sharks in fact do seem to be immune to cancer. But that immunity may be an illusion. Sharks' skeleton is cartilage, not bone. So, since they do not have any bones, they cannot get cancer of the bone. And, lacking bone marrow or a lymph system, they cannot have those kinds of cancer. A fisheries industry executive, Dr. I. William Lane, made the leap from theory to practice in a book, *Sharks Don't Get Cancer,* published in 1992. Through his patented method for processing shark cartilage, he launched a $50-million-a-year industry.

Shark cartilage is marketed as a powder or as gelatin capsules containing the powder. The source of most cartilage are spiny dogfish and scalloped hammerheads, usually caught in the Pacific. The demand for cartilage is one of the causes for the steady depletion of some shark populations. (See chapter 8.)

Dr. Judah Folkman, the Harvard Medical School researcher who proposed the antiangiogenesis theory, said that Lane's leap of faith from Folkman's research results to ingesting raw cartilage powder is "like going from Kitty Hawk to the moon."

The National Cancer Institute has found no evidence that shark cartilage can prevent cancer. But doctors in Cuba, after treating cancer patients with a commercial product made of shark cartilage, claimed to have observed remarkable results. And the belief has persisted that sharks may offer a treatment for cancer.

The Smithsonian Institution's Registry of Tumors in Lower Animals, has cataloged fewer than twenty-five tumors from sharks or rays. "Most of these are classified as fibrous responses to wounds, parasites, or goiters (enlarged thyroid glands sometimes developed by sharks in captivity), leaving only eight to ten legitimate tumors among all the shark and ray tissues examined," according to Dr. Carl A. Luer, Biomedical Program Manager at Mote Marine Laboratory. Luer, a member of the board of directors of the American Elasmobranch Society, directs research using sharks and skates as laboratory-animal models to investigate mechanisms of cancer inhibition and cellular immune function. Most of the research has been on nurse sharks and clearnose skates.

The low incidence of tumors among the sharks and their relatives led biochemists and immunologists at Mote to explore what mechanisms might explain the unusual disease resistance. "To do this," Luer says, "we . . . designed experiments to see whether tumors could be induced in the sharks and skates by exposing them to potent carcinogenic (cancer-causing) chemicals. This was done by placing the chemicals in their food or surrounding tank water, or by direct injection into their muscles. Then, we monitored subsequent pathways of metabolism or detoxification of the carcinogens in the test animals. While there were similarities and differences in the responses when compared with mammals, no changes in the target tissues or their genetic material ever resulted in cancerous tumor formation in the sharks or skates.

"The chemical exposure studies, encompassing about ten years of research effort, have led us to more recent investigations of the shark immune system. As with mammals, including humans, the immune system of sharks probably plays a vital role in the overall health of these animals. But there are some important differences between the immune arsenals of mammals and sharks.

"The immune system of mammals typically consists of two parts which utilize a variety of immune cells as well as several classes of proteins called immunoglobulins (antibodies). Compared to the mammalian system, which is quite specialized, the shark immune system appears primitive but remarkably effective. Sharks apparently possess immune cells with the same functions as those of mammals, but the shark cells appear to be produced and stimulated differently.

Mote researchers, in cooperation with others at Clemson University, are focusing on the differences between mammals and sharks in the regulation of immune cells. Because some cancer treatments involve stimulating immune cell production, a better understanding of how the immune cells are controlled in sharks may aid human research. "But," Luer cautions, "human health applications from our research are many years in the future, and will rely on continued funding and active collaboration with the drug industry and medical community."

A drug called squalamine (the name comes from the Latin word for "shark," *squalus*) gives scientific credibility to the ancient belief in shark medicine. In 1993 the National Academy of Sciences described the organic chemical as a potent weapon against several kinds of bacteria, fungi, and parasites. Researchers believe that squalamine's potency against bacteria is on about the same level as ampicillin. Squalamine is derived from the tissue of the dogfish shark.

Dr. Michael A. Zasloff, who headed the squalamine research team, first became interested in sharks when he visited the Mount Desert Island Marine Biological Laboratory at Salisbury Cove, Maine, where research focused on dogfish. He was intrigued by the fact that shark pups are never infected by the sea water that their mother circulates through her fallopian tubes during pregnancy. Also, he noted, sharks rarely become infected after surgery. Stomach extracts from sharks killed many kinds of microbes.

Whatever the ultimate result of research into shark medicine, the effects on sharks themselves may prove to be disastrous. To meet the demand for cartilage, sharks have been killed by the tens of thousands. Much of the cartilage harvest takes place in the Pacific port town of Puntarena, Costa Rica. The shark are taken off Cocos Island, site of Cocos Island

National Park, which has a protected area nine miles wide around the island. Several species of shark are caught both within and beyond the nine-mile limit. Shark researchers say the population is collapsing here, as it is in some waters off Nicaragua and Mexico.

Shark Weapons

From Greenland, where knives were made from the teeth of the Greenland shark, to Hawaii, where clubs were studded with the teeth of mako and tiger sharks, every culture touched by sharks has made use of them as weapons. In old Hawaii, mourners struck themselves with a shark-tooth mallet during rites for the dead. Another selachian weapon was the *aero fai*, a stingray stinger. The Maoris of New Zealand call the seven-gilled shark that lives in their waters a *tuatini*. From its teeth they once made a sawlike instrument, the *mira tuatina*, which was said to be used only for cutting human flesh. The Maoris associated sharks with blood, war, and death. They mixed shark oil with red ocher and painted it on their war canoes and the funeral monuments erected in memory of their greatest chiefs. They also used shark oil as a cosmetic, a hair dressing, and for anointing bodies in their elaborate funeral ceremonies.

Shark Cuisine

In *The Ecclesiazusae,* Aristophanes wrote of a communal state ruled by a council of women. Citizens eat in public halls at public expense. To serve every diner a favorite dish, the women offer a single meal that has everything on the Greek menu. The meal is described in what is probably the world's longest word, a word that runs to 77 syllables in Greek, and when translated into Latin contains 179 letters. And right in the middle of it, along with the leek, the oyster, the wine sauce, and the pullet's wings, are the skate and the shark.

Throughout the world since antiquity, sharks have been a staple of diet. In the United States, however, the shark's reputation as an eater of swimmers and divers has not helped its popularity. And who wants to eat something called a dogfish? A member of Parliament once pleaded for standardizing shark nomenclature in British fish markets. He lamented the habit of calling all species of sharks by the same name, dogfish. Spur dogfish, he said, is "sweet and nutritious"; sandy dogfish is "quite good to eat." But some kinds of dogfish, he admitted, "smell like a polecat." About 30 percent of the fish-and-chips shops in southern Britain and 6 percent in the north use "piked dogfish" (*Squalus acanthias*). Dogfish is sometimes marketed in Britain as "rock salmon."

In some countries—and in some American fish markets—shark meat is not identified as such or is marketed under disguised names. Dogfish may become "grayfish" and skates are sold as "rajafish." With the aid of a cookie cutter on the pliable, fleshy wings of skates, selachian counterfeiters can punch out what looks, to an untrained eye, very much like a scallop. Even when dogfish are marketed openly, they may be called Gulf of Maine shark.

Prejudice against the shark has been traced back to the Bible: "These may ye eat of all that are in the waters: Whatsoever hath fins and scales in the waters, in the seas, and in the rivers, them may ye eat. . . . Whatsoever hath no fins nor scales in the waters, that is a detestable thing unto you" (Leviticus 11:9–12). In the opinion of Isaac Ginsburg, zoologist of the U.S. Fish and Wildlife Service, to whom this biblical admonition was submitted for a modern interpretation on ichthyological grounds, sharks are not under the ban. Ginsburg pointed out that sharks have fins and scales, though the scales, in the form of denticles, are technically placoid scales, and differ markedly from the usual scales found on fish. Ginsburg extended his opinion to cover shark liver oil. Whether for religious reasons or not, Israelis do not eat much shark.

Moslems are split on the shark issue. In the Persian and Oman Gulfs, the eating of fish without scales, including both sharks and catfish, is forbidden by the dietary laws followed by the Shiah Mohammedans who predominate in Iran. The Sunni Muslims of the Arabian Peninsula do eat the sharks they catch in the Persian Gulf. In the Philippines, researchers of the Fish and Wildlife Service were surprised to learn that Christian Filipinos rarely eat shark, but Muslim Filipinos do.

Shark fin soup, an epicurean dish of pre-communist China, was forbidden as decadent and bourgeois by the communist leaders of the People's Republic. But when a capitalistic economy bloomed in post–Cold War China, the ban on shark fin soup was lifted.

People in Korea, China, and Japan have been eating shark since earliest recorded times. Probably nowhere on earth are sharks consumed as avidly as in Japan. Lower-grade sharks are made into fish cakes, called *kamaboko*. Shark is also sold both fresh and canned. Smoked shark, marinated in soy sauce, is one of the canned products of the large Japanese shark fisheries industry.

Sharks, skates, and rays are eaten by most nations whose shores are washed by the Indian Ocean. On the west coast of India, sharks and rays are a favorite food of all classes. In the eastern coastal districts of Madras, only the very poor eat sharks and rays. Under a government-sponsored program, shark liver oil has been distributed to hospitals and sold at low prices to the public to increase the vitamin A in the diet of the poor.

Shark meat is tasty and nutritious, if properly prepared. Sharks must be served as fresh as possible, for the meat spoils quickly. And if it is to be salted, it must be salted right away. The meat of some species is so strongly flavored that it must be toned down by icing for twenty-four hours, then soaking for two hours in brine. Shark liver should never be eaten because its high concentrations of vitamins can cause illness.

Two simple shark recipes:

SHARK CHOWDER

2 pounds shark	Few sprigs of parsley
½ pound salt pork	1 quart milk, hot
2 small onions, sliced	Salt and pepper, to taste
1 quart sliced raw potatoes	

Wash the shark thoroughly, cover with cold water, and boil until tender. Flake the fish or cut it into small pieces. Save the water. Cut the salt pork into small pieces and fry until crisp, then remove the pork scraps. In the fat fry the sliced onions, then add the potatoes and a little parsley and cook until done, adding a little water if necessary. When the potatoes are soft, add the hot milk and the flaked fish, salt and pepper, and heat through. Split Boston crackers or pieces of pilot bread may be placed in the chowder, or served with it.

SHARK MARSEILLAISE

2 large onions	1 pinch saffron
2 tablespoons olive oil	Salt and pepper, to taste
4 tomatoes	½ glass water or fish stock
1 clove garlic	2 pounds shark

Chop the onions fine and fry in the olive oil. Add the tomatoes cut into small pieces, the garlic, saffron, salt and pepper, and the water or fish stock. Place the fish, cut as usual, in the mixture, and allow to boil fast for 15 to 20 minutes. Keep the kettle covered tightly. Remove the fish and place on some slices of French bread that have been browned in the oven. Boil the liquid down a few minutes so that it will not be watery, correct the seasoning, and pour over the fish.

The Many Uses of Sharkskin

In the age of sail, mariners caught sharks, skinned them, and dried their skins to use for holystoning the wooden decks. Pieces of sharkskin were wrapped around oars to cut down wear on the wood in the oarlock. Eventually, sharkskin came to be called *shagreen*, a word apparently derived from the Persian *saghari* and the Turkish *sagri*, leather made from

Products made from sharks: fin soup, boots, perfume, medicine, jewelry.

the tough skin of the rump of a horse. *Sagri* was made granular by imbedding hard seeds into the softened skin, then drying it. The seeds fell out, leaving permanent indentations in the skin. Sharkskin, with its pattern of denticles, resembled *saghari* or *sagri,* though in sharkskin the denticles were permanent fixtures.

By the eighteenth century, the art of working sharkskin had become so developed that a guild of *segrnywerkers* (shagreen workers) sprang up in Holland. In France Jean-Claude Galluchat and his son Denis-Claude became so famed as shagreen artists that their exquisite products were called *galuchat,* a term still used in France for polished shark and ray skin.

Inkstands, portrait frames, cases for silverware, spectacles, and watches were made of *galuchat.* Fine editions of books were bound with shagreen, and instruments, such as microscopes and telescopes, were covered with it. In the nineteenth century and in the early years of this century, when pince-nez were popular, shagreen was used to hold them in place on the nose, often with disfiguring results.

Possibly because they simply cannot believe that a shark or ray could yield such an exquisite leather, or because they are not aware of what they are handling, antique dealers today often describe shagreen-covered objects as being covered with snake, lizard, or seal skin.

The Persian *saghari,* with its rough, granular surface, was found to be ideal for sword hilts, for it gave swordsmen a good purchase on their weapons. The Japanese used sharkskin and ray skin for this same purpose. The favorite sword hilt of the Japanese came from what they call the pearl ray (*Dasyatis sephen*). (In Sumatra, where this is called the cow-tail ray, the skin is used for making drums and tambourines.)

The pearl ray produced a beautiful sword hilt, for the Japanese used the skin from the center of the ray's upper side, which bears three large, distinctive denticles that give the appearance of a row of inlaid pearls. The sword hilt had a grim utilitarian purpose, too: Even when blood-smeared, the rough-textured skin provided a dependable grip.

A cross-weave of strong fibers runs through the thick epidermis of sharkskin, forming a sinewy network that resists great strain, yet remains pliable. Tests have shown that shark leather has a tensile strength of about 7,000 pounds per square inch. Cowhide's tensile strength is about 5,000 pounds per square inch.

Denticles in sharkskin are usually polished down by hand to remove the sharp points or ground down on carborundum wheels. Shark leather workers made a "pickpocket-proof" wallet, one side of which was covered with shagreen. The denticles prevented its removal by acting as so many tiny thorns that snagged against the pocket. It could be removed only by slipping the hand between the wallet and the pocket.

CHAPTER 8

The Shark Endangered

L ike the dying canary that warns miners of danger in the mines, the sandbar shark (*Carcharhinus plumbeus*) signaled scientists that shark populations were shrinking along the U.S. Atlantic coast. Studies in 1991 showed that the abundance of sandbar sharks had declined about 20 percent compared to populations in the late 1970s. The National Oceanic Atmospheric Administration (NOAA) found that between the early 1970s and late 1980s the abundance of many shark species along the U.S. southeast coast had plummeted as much as 80 percent.

Little reliable data on shark fisheries exists in most places. But what is known reveals that throughout the world there has been a phenomenal increase in shark captures. A study by the United Nations Food and Agriculture Organization estimated that the catching of sharks, skates, and rays increased from about 220,000 tons in 1947 to more than 800,000 tons in 1994. Other estimates, based on assumptions of chronic under-reporting of shark catches, double the 1994 figure. Fishermen all over the world know, sometimes from experience, that concentrating year after year on one shark population will all but wipe out that population. And many fishermen, knowing that basic fact of biology, decide to increase the fishing pressure so they can get whatever they can before the supply runs out.

People have been catching and eating sharks since men first sought them with wooden or bone hooks. In the United States, commercial fishermen in the Atlantic, Pacific, and Gulf coasts sought the shark in the 1930s and 1940s because of the demand for shark livers, with their high vitamin A content, and sharkskin, used in high-priced leather goods. Vitamin A was used mostly to bolster poultry feed. Fishing for soupfin sharks (*Galeorhinus galeus*) on the Pacific coast was so intense that the species was almost wiped out.

Most shark fisheries went out of business after the synthesizing of vitamin A in the late 1940s. After the boom ended, commercial fishermen usually discarded sharks as trash fish caught in nets meant for shad and bluefish or on long-lines baited for tuna and swordfish. Sharks were notorious for rotting rapidly and stinking up a fishing boat.

In the 1960s, the U.S. government and state governments began encouraging fishermen to revive shark fishing as a way to reduce damage by sharks to the fishing gear of boats going after other fish. Again, shark fisheries flared up and died out in the familiar cycle. Then in the 1980s, government nutritionists urged the catching of sharks to bring an "underutilized" source of protein to the American diet. Fishermen were typically getting 25 cents a pound off the boat for shark. By the 1990s, many fishermen were getting $1 a pound. White steaks of mako, thresher, sandbar, and blacktip tasted like swordfish, at half the price. Restaurant patrons and at-home diners started developing a taste for shark.

Demands from foreign markets for shark fins also prompted many fishermen to resume shark fishing, again with governmental encouragement. The National Marine Fisheries Service (NMFS), trying to relieve pressure on other fish species, cheered on the shark fisheries and even gave fishermen the names of Chinese dealers in fins.

The essential ingredient for shark fin soup, the fins were worth as much as $20 a pound to fishermen who dealt with oriental merchants. Those merchants traditionally had got their fins from fishermen in the Caribbean, in Arabian waters, and others who fished waters off Nigeria and Mexico. By the 1980s, those areas had been fished out; the sharks had been wiped out. Australia was a possible site, but that country put new restrictions on its fisheries in 1986, effectively closing down what had been a source for Taiwanese fishermen in search of fins.

Coincidentally, in 1987, China, which had made shark fin soup a forbidden luxury, suddenly relaxed the ban. And the shark fin brokers of the world had a new, immense market. The preferred sharks for shark fin soup are sandbar, bull, hammerhead, blacktip, porbeagle, mako, thresher, and blue. (Only the lower caudal lobe from mako and thresher is considered acceptable.) But, as those sharks declined, species once ignored as sources—even dogfish—were butchered for fins.

Fishermen stripped sharks of their fins and dumped them back into the ocean to die. The practice was called "finning." (There were many reports of dying, finless sharks drifting into shallow waters and menacing swimmers.) U.S. commercial catches of shark increased in the 1980s from less than 550 to 8,250 tons a year.

Then in 1993 the NMFS suddenly shifted its concern from fishermen to sharks and clamped restrictions on catches.

North American waters contain one of the world's last great reserves of sharks. Of the 390 recognized species of sharks in the world, seventy-two are found in the U.S. Atlantic, the Gulf of Mexico, Puerto Rico, and the U.S. Virgin Islands. That American shark reserve is threatened, not only because there are few shark supporters (and relatively few shark eaters) in America but also because U.S. fishermen are filling a void created by the downfall of the traditional fisheries that supplied sharks to people who do eat them. With shark populations all but wiped out in those traditional places—the Arabian Sea, and Nigerian and Mexican waters—dealers have turned to the U.S. market. Much of the commerce is just for the fins, which can bring a fisherman $100 or more a pound. Trendy restaurants and boutique fish stores also provide a lucrative market for the shortfin mako, whose meat is widely considered to be the world's finest; it can fetch prices on a par with swordfish. Mako is also used for sashimi in Asia.

In 1994 and 1995, the NMFS put observers aboard long-line fishing boats in the Atlantic. They reported that in ninety-six fishing trips fishermen caught nearly 11,000 sharks of twenty-six different species. Sandbar sharks and blacktip sharks (*Carcharhinus limbatus*) accounted for 60 to 75 percent of the catch, and about half of them were immature. Approximately 70 percent of the sandbar sharks taken in the North Carolina area were female. During one year, about 20 to 30 percent of the mature female sandbar sharks were pregnant, but about half of the adult female blacktip sharks were pregnant. Such findings led the NMFS to extend the strict new rules governing shark catching by commercial and sports fishermen.

In 1997 the NMFS declared that "Atlantic shark populations are in a precarious state" and reduced the annual commercial quota for large coastal sharks by 50 percent—from 2,570 metric tons (mt) to 1,285 mt. The commercial quota on small coastal sharks was set at 1,760 mt; the quota for pelagic sharks was kept at 580 mt. Sports fishing was also curtailed. The prior limit had been four large coastal and pelagic sharks per vessel per trip and five small coastal sharks per person per day. The regulation combined all sharks into a limit of two sharks per vessel per trip, with the exception of Atlantic sharpnose sharks (*Rhizoprionodon terraenovae*). Fishing for five species—whale, basking, white, sand tiger, and bigeye sand tiger—was banned.

As conservationists began to worry about sharks in general, specific concern was aimed at the white shark (*Carcharodon carcharias*). A creature long despised as a "man killer," the white shark is in danger—and is being protected. In 1991 South Africa made history by declaring the white shark an endangered species and placing it at the top of the marine critical list.

"Managed" Sharks

The U.S. National Marine Fisheries Service (NMFS) in 1993 established a management plan to protect thirty-nine species of shark in Atlantic and Gulf waters within the Exclusive Economic Zone, the area that begins 200 miles offshore and continues inward to state waters. The NMFS plan aimed at stabilizing shark populations by reducing commercial and recreational fishing through licensing and quotas. The plan, which affected about 150 commercial fishermen, reduced the overall annual large coastal shark catch by 50 percent. The NMFS also limited the catch of thousands of recreational fishermen. Fishermen were also prohibited from "directed fishing" for five species considered extremely vulnerable to overfishing (whale, basking, sand tiger, bigeye sand tiger, and white sharks). The plan also banned stripping the fins from sharks and dumping the sharks back into the ocean.

The plan was revised in 1997 and 1998 to further reduce shark captures.

These are the sharks covered by the plan:

Large Coastal Sharks

sandbar (Carcharhinus plumbeus)
blacktip (Carcharhinus limbatus)
dusky (Carcharhinus obscurus)
spinner (Carcharhinus brevipinna)
silky (Carcharhinus falciformis)
bull (Carcharhinus leucas)
bignose (Carcharhinus altimus)
narrowtooth (Carcharhinus brachyurus)
Galapagos (Carcharhinus galapagensis)
night (Carcharhinus signatus)
Caribbean reef (Carcharhinus perezi)

tiger (Galeocerdo cuvieri)
lemon (Negaprion brevirostris)
sand tiger (Odontaspis taurus)
bigeye sand tiger (Odontaspis noronhai)
nurse (Ginglymostoma cirratum)
scalloped hammerhead (Sphyrna lewini)
great hammerhead (Sphyrna mokarran)
smooth hammerhead (Sphyrna zygaena)
whale (Rhincodon typus)
basking (Cetorhinus maximus)
white (Carcharodon carcharias)

Small Coastal Sharks

Atlantic sharpnose (Rhizoprionodon terraenovae)
Caribbean sharpnose (Rhizoprionodon porosus)
finetooth (Carcharhinus isodon)

blacknose (Carcharhinus acronotus)
smalltail (Carcharhinus porosus)
bonnethead (Sphyrna tiburo)
Atlantic angel (Squatina dumeril)

Pelagic Sharks

shortfin mako (Isurus oxyrinchus)
longfin mako (Isurus paucus)

porbeagle (Lamna nasus)
thresher (Alopias vulpinus)

PELAGIC SHARKS (*continued*)

bigeye thresher (*Alopias superciliosus*)
blue (*Prionace glauca*)
oceanic whitetip (*Carcharhinus longimanus*)

sevengill (*Heptranchias perlo*)
sixgill (*Hexanchus griseus*)
bigeye sixgill (*Hexanchus vitulus*)

Sharks not in the management unit but included for data reporting:

CAT SHARKS, FAMILY SCYLIORHINIDAE

Iceland cat shark (*Apristurus laurussoni*)
smallfin cat shark (*Apristurus parvipinnis*)
deepwater cat shark (*Apristurus profundorum*)
broadgill cat shark (*Apristurus riveri*)

marbled cat shark (*Galeus arae*)
blotched cat shark (*Scyliorhinus meadi*)
chain dogfish (*Scyliorhinus retifer*)
dwarf cat shark (*Scyliorhinus torrei*)

DOGFISH SHARKS, FAMILY SQUALIDAE

Japanese gulper shark (*Centrophorus acus*)
gulper shark (*Centrophorus granulosus*)
little gulper shark (*Centrophorus uyato*)
kitefin shark (*Dalatias licha*)
flatnose gulper shark (*Deania profundorum*)
Portuguese shark (*Cetroscymnus coelolepis*)
Greenland shark (*Somniosus microcephalus*)
lined lanternshark (*Etmopterus bullisi*)
broadband dogfish (*Etmopterus gracilispinis*)
Caribbean lanternshark (*Etmopterus hillianus*)
great lanternshark (*Etmopterus princeps*)
smooth lanternshark (*Etmopterus pusillus*)

fringefin lanternshark (*Etmopterus schultzi*)
green lanternshark (*Etmopterus virens*)
cookiecutter shark (*Isistius brasiliensis*)
bigtooth cookiecutter (*Isistius plutodus*)
smallmouth velvet dogfish (*Scymnodon obscurus*)
pygmy shark (*Squaliolus laticaudus*)
roughskin spiny dogfish (*Squalus asper*)
Blainville's dogfish (*Squalus blainvillei*)
spiny dogfish (*Squalus acanthias*)
Cuban dogfish (*Squalus cubensis*)
bramble shark (*Echinorhinus brucus*)

SAWSHARKS, FAMILY PRISTIOPHORIDAE

American saw shark (*Pristiophorus schroederi*)

SMOOTHHOUND SHARKS, FAMILY TRIAKIIDAE

Florida smooth hound (*Mustelus norrisi*)

smooth dogfish (*Mustelus canis*)

After researchers reported a precipitous decline of the white shark along the California coast, in 1994 California made the white shark a protected species. Protection of the white shark has also been decreed in Australian waters off Tasmania, New South Wales, and Queensland. In legislation aimed at protecting white sharks, the South Australia Fisheries Department prohibited the capture, holding, or killing of the species. To discourage chumming for sharks, the law also prohibited the use of blood, bone, meat, offal, or skin of an animal (other than in the rock lobster pot or fish trap) within two nautical miles of the state's mainland or around islands and reefs off the state coast.

Public attitude obviously has drastically changed since 1975, when the movie *Jaws* (based on the novel of the same title) first appeared on movie screens. In the antishark atmosphere produced by *Jaws*, more than a dozen white sharks were vengefully harpooned along the California coast and Sea World put the sharks on exhibition. Less than twenty years later, Sea World, like other aquariums, was sending out educational packets praising the shark. And Peter Benchley, the author of *Jaws*, had joined conservation organizations in a campaign to save the white shark and other threatened species. The campaign was launched in 1997 by a coalition of aquariums and such environmental organizations as the National Audubon Society, the Natural Resources Defense Council, and the World Wildlife Fund. The group urged an international treaty to protect sharks from being "caught and killed faster than they can reproduce." The conservationists also called for a worldwide ban on finning

The shark is an apex predator in numerous ecosystems. Without the shark to keep prey populations under control, marine food chains would shatter. Octopus, for example, is a favorite shark food in some places. If sharks are few, octopuses become many—and then decimate their food choice, the lobster. Sharks, playing the role that the great cats play on land, single out the slow, weak, or sick as prey, contributing to the genetic rule of survival of the fittest.

The fear of shark attack in the 1970s has evolved into fears about human attacks on sharks. Some environmentalists warn that makos, lemon sharks, hammerheads, and white sharks are on the path to extinction. Yet, as the Center for Marine Conservation points out, "Little effort has been made to collect even the most basic kinds of information, such as numbers of sharks caught and discarded, necessary for meeting even minimal standards of management of fisheries affecting sharks." Such information is vital for the future of the shark, whose own reproductive behavior makes it particularly vulnerable to overfishing.

Commercial fisheries are based on the reproductive strategy of bony fishes, which typically produce millions of eggs. Although relatively few hatch and produce young that live to adulthood, there are so many to begin with—and maturity comes so quickly—that fishermen view bony fish populations as perpetually self-replicating. This is not true for sharks. Most sharks take twelve to fifteen years to reach sexual maturity. The white shark matures at about fifteen years. The dusky shark (*Carcharhinus obscurus*) matures at seventeen years of age, the sandbar at fifteen to sixteen years, the seemingly prolific spiny dogfish (*Squalus acanthias*) lives ten to thirteen years before reaching maturity and has one of the longest known gestation periods of any animal: twenty-four months.

The Center for Marine Conservation in 1996 issued an "action alert" about the dogfish—historically, an incredibly prolific shark. "Fishing pressure on dogfish in the Northeast is rising dramatically, with no limits on catch in sight," the center alert said. "Despite signs of decline, aggressive marketing campaigns continue to promote dogfish as an alternative to depleted cod, haddock, and flounder, and fishery managers have delayed development of a much-needed dogfish management plan." The amount of dogfish had risen from 6,000 mt in 1989 to more than 22,000 mt in 1993. Dogfish discarded at sea probably equals the reported catch. Besides the increase in dogfish fishing for food, the demand for cartilage (see chapter 7) is also wiping out dogfish populations.

Most species carry their young, and gestation periods can be a year or more. A shark population depleted by overfishing at best can take decades to replace itself and at worst may die out. Countless commercial shark fisheries in the U.S. and abroad have abruptly failed after causing a population crash of the species of shark being pursued.

Fishermen who are *not* seeking shark also contribute to the decline in shark populations. Looking for tuna or other commercial fish, the fishermen capture—and often throw away—sharks. The number of sharks caught annually between 1989 and 1991 has been estimated at 11.6 to 12.7 million. Japanese, Korean, and Taiwanese long-line fisheries for tunas account for most of these shark by-catches. By some estimates, more than 210,000 metric tons of sharks, skates, and ray are discarded annually by numerous high-seas commercial fisheries.

Three sharks not usually believed to be endangered were singled out in 1998 by the American Elasmobranch Society, which passed resolutions at its convention calling upon the National Marine Fisheries Service Office of Highly Migratory Species to add dusky sharks, smalltooth sawfish, and largetooth sawfish to the list of endangered species that fishermen are forbidden to catch.

The dusky shark, the society resolution said, has the slowest growth rate, the latest age of maturity, and one of the lowest fecundity rates among all large coastal sharks. As for the sawfishes, they are "rare or absent from their former range ... extremely vulnerable to excess mortality because they are slow growing, late maturing, and have low fecundity rates, and ... occupy estuarine habitats that have undergone extensive destruction along the southeastern United States."

Conservationists single out the following as grave threats to the future of many shark species.

Gill nets

Used mainly to catch tuna, gill nets also catch sharks. The Taiwanese Gillnet Fishery reports that in 1986–87 the by-catch of sharks was 295.7 ton; in 1987–88 it was 20.7. This tremendous drop in less than two years shows that sharks cannot stand intense fishing pressure, especially by gill net fishermen.

Antishark nets

These nets, placed along the KwaZulu/Natal coast of South Africa to protect bathing beaches, trap sharks. Prevented from moving, the snarled sharks cannot pass fresh, oxygen-rich water through their gills, and they die. For several years, counts were kept on the number of sharks enmeshed in the South African nets. From December 1, 1939 to December 1, 1940, the nets caught 751. In the next year, 705 were caught. Netting ceased during most of World War II, but by 1948 the annual number of sharks caught was down to 260. Since then, the number of sharks caught each year has continued to decrease, indicating a general decrease in the shark population. By the 1960s, the nets were often empty day after day, while barely a mile off the beaches, sports fishermen were still regularly catch sharks twelve to fifteen feet long.

A study in 1988 showed that of the 1,400 sharks that died in the nets in an average year, 35 percent are inside the netted area and heading seaward. Of the trapped sharks, 87 percent were sandbar sharks, blacktips, and spinner sharks (*Carcharhinus brevipinna*), all rated as harmless to bathers. The nets also ensnared rare and endangered species, such as hawksbill, loggerhead, and leatherback turtles, the humpback dolphin, and the bottlenose dolphin. Dolphin populations had been dropping at the rate of 4 to 5 percent a year.

For many years, trapped sharks were killed. Now sharks that are alive—about 250 of the annual 1,400 average—are tagged and released as part of a behavioral study.

South Africa followed up its action to protect the white shark by investigating alternatives to shark nets: electrical shark barriers and a device that creates a protective electrical field around swimmers and divers.

The Fin Trade

"Live-finning"—cutting fins off live sharks and throwing them back into the sea—has had such an impact on U.S. shark populations that some conservationists have urged a return of federal Prohibition laws, this time not for liquor, but for the consumption of shark fin soup. Undoubtedly, this would be perceived as cultural discrimination, for Americans of Asiatic descent cherish the soup. Their culinary preference for shark fins has made the United States a major consumer of shark fins.

The fins' cartilaginous tissues are used like noodles to thicken and flavor soup. Long strands are prized. Demand for shark's fins has sky-rocketed in China. In Hong Kong alone, people buy an estimated 3 million kilograms of shark fins a year.

Australian officials estimate that Japanese long-line fishermen finned 34,000 blacktip sharks in just two months of fishing inside Australia's exclusive economic zone. The Basking Shark Project, which watches over the giant sharks, says that as many as 5,000 basking sharks are being taken each year for their fins. Project officials say that the basking shark is gradually disappearing from areas where they were previously common. Basking sharks are hunted in California, Scotland, Norway, the Lofoten Islands, and Portugal. In British waters, basking sharks are protected within a three-mile zone off the Isle of Man. In 1998, conservation officials were considering regulations that would provide total protection for up to twelve miles offshore. Also in 1998, the Philippines outlawed the catch, sell, purchase, possession, transport, or export of whale sharks or manta rays, both of which are considered delicacies. Fisheries officials said that about 200 whale sharks and 200 manta rays were caught in Philippine seas in 1997, but there was no official estimate of the remaining populations.

Demand for Cartilage

Like shark fins, shark cartilage has produced an industry. Promoting cartilage as a medicine and a cancer cure (see chapter 7), the cartilage industry has given fishermen another reason to hunt sharks. Prices for the shark-made panacea have not soared as high as those for shark fins, however. And so, luckily for sharks, cartilage mostly is a by-product of a by-catch.

Shark Fisheries

Although the NMFS curbs on U.S. commercial shark fishing may be slowing down the decline of shark populations, elsewhere in the world the damage already has been done. Shark fisheries are collapsing or have already collapsed off many coasts. One biologist estimated that if the bodies of sharks killed each year were placed nose to tail, they would circle the Earth five times.

Sports Fishing

Sports anglers should tag and release unwanted sharks, rather than killing them. Nonlethal means of determining their size for record keeping should be researched and introduced. Some tournaments are judged simply on the basis of the weight of fish caught, and as a result many sharks are being killed, weighed, and discarded. So-called catch-and-return tournaments are not an answer. Although touted as humanitarian, the practice—hooking, hauling in, unhooking, and throwing back—puts some sharks under such stress that they do not long survive their return to the sea.

Environmental Destruction

Pollution of the oceans by oil, pesticides, plastics, and the refuse of civilization hurts all creatures in the sea, including sharks. Because offshore waters are the least affected by pollution, adult sharks escape most of the damage. But estuarine nurseries, where many species of sharks are born, are rapidly deteriorating, putting future generations of shark at hazard.

Coastal wetlands are disappearing at an average rate of about 25 square miles a year. In some areas, this rate may be even higher—Louisiana, for example, loses nearly twice that much a year. This prime habitat for shark nurseries is also a prime region for environmental degradation. Here is where navigation channels are built and maintained, where levees and marinas are developed, where sewers and factories discharge their wastes, where pesticides and fertilizers run off.

The NMFS estimated in 1994 that many shark species may have declined by as much as 75 percent from the early 1970s to the mid-1980s. One proposed treatment was a closure of nursery grounds to fishing during pupping season. But conservationists and NMFS officials lack adequate information on shark reproduction.

Efforts to learn about shark biology have been enhanced by the Cooperative Tagging Program begun by the NMFS in 1963. Thousands of volunteers—biologists, anglers, commercial fishermen—tag 7,000 to 9,000 sharks a year. The tagging, which extends from U.S. waters to Portugal, has dramatically increased knowledge of seasonal movement by many species. Eight sharks tagged off Portugal, for example, showed movements up to 1,232 nautical miles. One sandbar shark was recaptured twenty-eight years after it was tagged. Sandbar sharks tagged and recaptured in 1996 had been at liberty from two days to fifteen and a half years. Distances traveled ranged from less than one nautical mile to 1,677 nautical miles. This shark was originally tagged off Long Island, New York, by a sport fisherman and recaptured west of Progreso, Mexico, by a gill net fisherman after nearly 5.8 years at liberty. It was the forty-fifth sandbar shark tagged

Tagged Sharks

Taggings in 1996 by members of the Cooperative Shark Tagging Program set records for numbers of fish tagged and fish recaptured (602). The increase was primarily due to a surge in the number of blue sharks tagged. Researchers suggested that unseasonably cool water temperatures drew the blue sharks to the surface—bottom temperatures were the lowest since data records began in 1978.

Species	Number Tagged	Species	Number Tagged
Blue shark	6078	Galapagos shark	21
Sandbar shark	1407	Bull shark	19
Tiger shark	459	Silky shark	17
Blacktip shark	244	Scalloped hammerhead	16
Dusky shark	204	Hammerhead, unspecified	11
Shortfin mako	122	Brown/Dusky, unspecified	8
Atlantic sharpnose shark	85	Thresher shark	8
Nurse shark	64	Smooth hammerhead	6
Porbeagle	63	Longfin mako	6
Spinner shark	52	Finetooth shark	5
Blacknose shark	49	Bigeye thresher	5
Dogfish	42	Oceanic whitetip shark	3
Bonnethead	39	Great hammerhead	3
Reef shark	36	Bignose shark	1
Lemon shark	28	Atlantic angel shark	1
Night shark	28	Miscellaneous sharks	26
Sand tiger	27	Miscellaneous rays	20
		Total Sharks	**9203**

in U.S. waters that was recaptured off Mexico. (The record holder was a blue shark that traveled 3,740 miles.)

In studies of nurseries in Delaware Bay, newborn and juvenile sandbar sharks were tagged. From these studies has come new knowledge of nursery populations and the ranging of young sharks in their first years. Preliminary analysis of the results showed that sandbar distribution in the bay may be related to salinity and distribution of fishes that the sandbar sharks feed on. Juveniles, for example, seem to move in groups with the tides.

"As we become more familiar with sharks, the move to protect them may spread," writes Dr. Eugenie Clark, who has long studied and admired sharks. "...We may come to appreciate and understand sharks, as we are coming to know other animals above and beneath the sea. With further research we may one day be able to predict sharks' behavior with great accuracy. When that day comes, I feel certain we will recognize that sharks present no threat to mankind..."

Sharks' Popular and Scientific Names

Atlantic angel shark: *Squatina dumeril*
Atlantic sharpnose shark: *Rhizoprionodon terraenovae*
Bahamas sawshark: *Pristiophorus schroederi*
Basking shark: *Cetorhinus maximus*
Bigeye thresher: *Alopias superciliosus*
Bigeye sand tiger: *Odontaspis noronhai*
Bigeyed sixgill shark: *Hexanchus vitulus*
Bignose shark: *Carcharhinus altimus*
Black dogfish: *Centroscyllium fabricii*
Blacknose shark: *Carcharhinus acronotus*
Blacktip reef shark: *Carcharhinus melanopterus*
Blacktip shark: *Carcharhinus limbatus*
Blue shark: *Prionace glauca*
Bonnethead: *Sphyrna tiburo*
Bramble shark: *Echinorhinus brucus*
Broadband dogfish: *Etmopterus gracilispinis*
Brown cat shark: *Apristurus brunneus*
Brown smoothhound: *Mustelus henlei*
Bull shark: *Carcharhinus leucas*
Bullhead sharks: members of the family
    Heterodontidae
Caribbean sharpnose shark: *Rhizoprionodon porosus*
Carpet sharks: members of the order
    Orectolobiformes
Chain dogfish: *Scyliorhinus retifer*
Cigar shark (also Spined Pygmy shark): *Squaliolus
    laticaudus*
Cookie-cutter shark: *Isistius brasiliensis*
Crocodile shark: *Pseudocarcharias kamoharai*
Cuban dogfish: *Squalus cubensis*

Dusky shark: *Carcharhinus obscurus*
Dwarf dogfish: *Etmopterus perryi*
False cat shark: *Pseudotriakis microdon*
Filetail catshark: *Parmaturus xaniurus*
Finetooth shark: *Carcharhinus isodon*
Frilled shark: *Chlamydoselachus anguineus*
Galapagos bullhead: *Heterodontus quoyi*
Galapagos shark: *Carcharhinus galapagensis*
Ganges shark: *Glyphis gangericus*
Goblin shark: *Mitsukurina owstoni*
Gray nurse shark: *Odontaspis arenarius*
Gray reef shark: *Carcharhinus amblyrhynchos*
Gray smoothhound: *Mustelus californicus*
Great white shark: *Carcharodon carcharias* (also
    white shark)
Green lanternshark: *Etmopterus virens*
Greenland shark: *Somniosus microcephalus*
Hammerheads: family Sphyrnidae
    Great hammerhead: *Sphyrna mokarran*
    Scalloped hammerhead: *Sphyrna lewini*
    Smooth hammerhead: *Sphyrna zygaena*
Horn shark: *Heterodontus francisci*
Houndsharks: members of the family Triakidae or
    the genus *Mustelus*
Japanese sawshark: *Pristiophorus japonicus*
Kitefin shark: *Dalatias licha*
Largetooth cookie-cutter: *Isistius plutodus*
Lemon shark: *Negaprion brevirostris*
Leopard shark: *Triakis semifasciata*
Longfin mako: *Isurus paucus*

Mackerel sharks: members of the family Lamnidae
Mako: see longfin mako, shortfin mako
Megamouth: *Megachasma pelagios*
Mexican horn shark: *Heterodontus mexicanus*
Narrowtooth shark: *Carcharhinus brachyurus*
Night shark: *Carcharhinus signatus*
Nurse shark: *Ginglymostoma cirratum*
Oceanic whitetip shark: *Carcharhinus longimanus*
Pacific angel shark: *Squatina californica*
Pacific sharpnose shark: *Rhizoprionodon longurio*
Pacific sleeper shark: *Somniosus pacificus*
Pelagic thresher: *Alopias pelagicus*
Porbeagle: *Lamna nasus*
Port Jackson shark: *Heterodontus portusjacksoni*
Portuguese shark: *Centroscymnus coelolepis*
Prickly shark: *Echinorhinus cookei*
Pygmy ribbontail cat shark: *Eridacnis radcliffei*
Ragged-tooth shark: *Odontaspis ferox*
Reef shark: *Carcharhinus perezi* (also Caribbean
    reef shark)
Requiem sharks: members of the family
    Carcharhinidae
Salmon shark: *Lamna ditropis*
Sand tiger: *Eugomphodus taurus*
Sandbar shark: *Carcharhinus plumbeus*
Sawsharks: sharks of the family Pristiophoridae
School shark: *Galeorhinus galeus* (also soupfin shark)
Sevengill shark: *Notorynchus cepedianus*

Sharpnose sevengill shark: *Heptranchias perlo*
Shortfin mako: *Isurus oxyrynchus*
Sicklefin lemon shark: *Negaprion acutidens*
Sicklefin smoothhound: *Mustelus lunulatus*
Silky shark: *Carcharhinus falciformis*
Silvertip shark: *Carcharhinus albimarginatus*
Sixgill shark: *Hexanchus griseus*
Smalltail shark: *Carcharhinus porosus*
Smooth dogfish: *Mustelus canis*
Soupfin shark: *Galeorhinus galeus* (also school shark)
Spadenose shark: *Scoliodon laticaudus*
Spinner shark: *Carcharhinus brevipinna*
Spiny dogfish: *Squalus acanthias*
Spitting shark: *Nebrius ferrugineus*
Spotted wobbegong: *Orectolobus maculatus*
Swell shark: *Cephaloscyllium ventriosum*
Thresher shark: *Alopias vulpinus*
Tiger shark: *Galeocerdo cuvieri*
Whale shark: *Rhincodon typus*
Whaler sharks: members of the genus *Carcharhinus*
White shark: *Carcharodon carcharias* (also great
    white shark)
Whitetip shark: see oceanic whitetip shark
Whitetip reef shark: *Triaenodon obesus*
Winghead shark: *Eusphyra blochii*
Wobbegongs: members of the family Orectolobidae
Zebra shark: *Stegostoma fasciatum*

252

Official Shark Catch Records
of the
International Game Fish
Association

SPECIES	LINE CLASS	WEIGHT	PLACE	DATE	ANGLER
Shark, blue	M-01 kg (2 lb)	53.97 kg 119 lb	Shinnecock, Long Island, New York, USA	July 1, 1983	Stephen Sloan
Shark, blue	M-02 kg (4 lb)	83.46 kg 184 lb	Montauk, Long Island, New York, USA	Oct. 7, 1984	Stephen Sloan
Shark, blue	M-03 kg (6 lb)	113.85 kg 251 lb	Montauk, Long Island, New York, USA	Oct. 5, 1981	Stephen Sloan
Shark, blue	M-04 kg (8 lb)	115.50 kg 254 lb 10 oz	East Port Hacking, N.S.W., Australia	Nov. 20, 1983	Denis Pearce
Shark, blue	M-06 kg (12 lb)	179.50 kg 395 lb 11 oz	Port Hacking, N.S.W., Australia	Nov. 3, 1991	Robert Egan
Shark, blue	M-08kg (16 lb)	189.00 kg 416 lb 10 oz	Botany Bay, Sydney, Australia	Nov. 3, 1985	Jayson Heyward
Shark, blue	M-10 kg (20 lb)	166.00 kg 365 lb 15 oz	Wollogong, Australia	Oct. 3, 1993	Brad Major
Shark, blue	M-15 kg (30lb)	198.22 kg 437 lb	Catherine Bay, N.S.W., Australia	Oct. 2, 1976	Peter Hyde
Shark, blue	M-24 kg (50 lb)	198.10 kg 436 lb 11 oz	Mayor Island, Bay of Plenty, New Zealand	Feb. 8, 1993	Graeme Smith
Shark, blue	M-37 kg (80 lb)	205.93 kg 454 lb	Martha's Vineyard, Massachusetts, USA	July 19, 1996	Pete Bergin
Shark, blue	M-60 kg (130 lb)	181.43 kg 400 lb	Le Morne, Mauritius	Oct. 17, 1976	Philip Fleming
Shark, blue	Tippet 01 kg (2 lb)	2.33 kg 5 lb 2 oz	Taits Beach, Hawkes Bay, New Zealand	Feb. 27, 1993	Dennis Graham Niethe
Shark, blue	Tippet 02 kg (4 lb)	41.27 kg 91 lb	Montauk, Long Island, New York, USA	Sept. 14, 1989	Stephen Sloan
Shark, blue	Tippet 03 kg (6 lb)	52.05 kg 114 lb 12 oz	Shinnecock, Long Island, New York, USA	June 28, 1980	Stephen Sloan

SPECIES	LINE CLASS	WEIGHT	PLACE	DATE	ANGLER
Shark, blue	Tippet 04 kg (8 lb)	34.00 kg 74 lb 15 oz	Kaikoura, New Zealand	Feb. 16, 1997	Howard Lewis
Shark, blue	Tippet 06 kg (12 lb)	83.46 kg 184 lb	Montauk, Long Island, New York, USA	Sept. 28, 1989	Stephen Sloan
Shark, blue	Tippet 08kg (16 lb)	63.50 kg 140 lb	Anacapa Island, California, USA	July 1, 1988	Steve Abel
Shark, blue	Tippet 10 kg (20 lb)	67.58 kg 149 lb	Martha's Vineyard, Massachusetts, USA	July 9, 1994	Barry Bordner
Shark, blue	W-0 1 kg (2 lb)	39.46 kg 87 lb	Snug Harbor, Rhode Island, USA	July 18, 1997	Shawna M. Oliver
Shark, blue	W-02 kg (4 lb)	70.00 kg 154 lb 5 oz	Whakatane, New Zealand	March 26, 1989	Cynthia Dreifuss
Shark, blue	W-03 kg (6 lb)	87.54 kg 193 lb	Botany, N.S.W., Australia	Dec. 15, 1974	Mrs. Dulcie Chee
Shark, blue	W-04 kg (8 lb)	118.00 kg 260 lb 2 oz	Port Hacking, N.S.W., Australia	Aug. 26, 1995	Kylie P. Daly
Shark, blue	W-06 kg (12 lb)	140.00 kg 308 lb 10 oz	Swansea, N.S.W., Australia	Sept. 29, 1990	Michelle Jones
Shark, blue	W-08 kg (16 lb)	143.50 kg 316 lb 5 oz	East Port Hacking, N.S.W., Australia	Oct. 5, 1996	Danielle Williams
Shark, blue	W-10 kg (20 lb)	167.00 kg 368 lb 2 oz	Swansea, Australia	Nov. 3, 1984	Narelle Wanless
Shark, blue	W-15 kg (30 lb)	191.80 kg 422 lb 13 oz	Te Kaha, New Zealand	Feb. 23, 1994	Martha Walker
Shark, blue	W-24 kg (50 lb)	170.60 kg 376 lb 1 oz	Tutukaka, New Zealand	March 19, 1984	Bernadette Brown
Shark, blue	W-37 kg (80 lb)	185.97 kg 410 lb	Rockport, Massachusetts, USA	Aug. 17, 1967	Martha C. Webster
Shark, blue	W-60 kg (130 lb)	151.50 kg 334 lb	Rockport, Massachusetts, USA	Sept. 4, 1964	Cassandra Webster
Shark, hammerhead	M-01 kg (2 lb)	4.53 kg 10 lb	Biscayne Bay, Miami, Florida, USA	Sept. 10, 1983	Max L. Kamerman
Shark, hammerhead	M-02 kg (4 lb)	12.36 kg 27 lb 4 oz	Port Canaveral, Florida, USA	July 12, 1984	Troy Perez
Shark, hammerhead	M-03 kg (6 lb)	46.20 kg 101 lb 13 oz	Luanda, Angola	Dec. 29, 1974	M. Quintela Maia de Loureiro
Shark, hammerhead	M-04 kg (8 lb)	88.11 kg 194 lb 4 oz	Key West, Florida, USA	Feb. 22, 1991	Herbert G. Ratner, Jr.
Shark, hammerhead	M-06 kg (12 lb)	151.95 kg 335 lb	Miami, Florida, USA	March 19, 1977	Bill Peacock
Shark, hammerhead	M-08 kg (16 lb)	153.80 kg 339 lb I oz	Takau Bay, Bay of Islands, New Zealand	April 7, 1992	Geoff Stone
Shark, hammerhead	M-10 kg (20 lb)	184.00 kg 405 lb 10 oz	East Botany Bay, Sydney, Australia	Jan. 29, 1984	Barry Yates
Shark, hammerhead	M-15 kg (30 lb)	258.00 kg 568 lb 12 oz	Port Stephens, N.S.W., Australia	Feb. 27, 1994	Denis Castronini
Shark, hammerhead	M-24 kg (50 lb)	246.98 kg 544 lb 8 oz	Boca Grande, Florida, USA	May 20, 1981	Clark Balsinger
Shark, hammerhead	M-37 kg (80 lb)	281.23 kg 620 lb	Freeport, Texas, USA	Aug. 15, 1976	Dan Wright
Shark, hammerhead	Tippet 01 kg (2 lb)	Vacant			
Shark, hammerhead	Tippet 02 kg (4 lb)	Vacant			

SPECIES	LINE CLASS	WEIGHT	PLACE	DATE	ANGLER
Shark, hammerhead	Tippet 03 kg (6 lb)	Vacant			
Shark, hammerhead	Tippet 04 kg (8 lb)	2.83 kg 6 lb 4 oz	Key West, Florida, USA	March 25, 1996	Bennet M. Stern
Shark, hammerhead	Tippet 06 kg (12 lb)	3.62 kg 8 lb	Islamorada, Florida, USA	April 8, 1992	Capt. Ben Taylor
Shark, hammerhead	Tippet 08 kg (16 lb)	48.30 kg 106 lb 8 oz	Key West, Florida, USA	Feb. 11, 1987	Mike Stidham
Shark, hammerhead	Tippet 10 kg (20 lb)	69.85 kg 154 lb	Key West, Florida, USA	March 7, 1993	Rick Gunion
Shark, hammerhead	W-01 kg (2 lb)	3.17 kg 7 lb	Sugarloaf Key, Florida, USA	Sept. 17, 1983	Jacqueline Leader
Shark, hammerhead	W-02 kg (4 lb)	17.00 kg 37 lb 7 oz	Whitsundays, N. Qsld., Australia	Feb. 16, 1986	Teena Draper
Shark, hammerhead	W-03 kg (6 lb)	Vacant			
Shark, hammerhead	W-04 kg (8 lb)	15.08 kg 33 lb 4 oz	Pinas Bay, Panama	Jan. 24, 1994	Deborah Maddux Dunaway
Shark, hammerhead	W-06 kg (12 lb)	139.00 kg 306 lb 7 oz	Auckland, New Zealand	Dec. 29, 1986	Raewyn Curin
Shark, hammerhead	W-08 kg (16 lb)	111.00 kg 244 lb 11 oz	Cape Brett, New Zealand	Feb. 1, 1985	Viki Johnson
Shark, hammerhead	W-10 kg (20 lb)	189.00 kg 416 lb 10 oz	Port Stephens, N.S.W., Australia	Feb. 26, 1984	Monique Eady
Shark, hammerhead	W-15 kg (30 lb)	185.00 kg 407 lb 13 oz	Bermagui, N.S.W., Australia	Jan. 21, 1984	Stephenie Newman
Shark, hammerhead	W-24 kg (50 lb)	340.19 kg 750 lb	Boca Grande, Florida, USA	June 8, 1986	Connie L. Cora
Shark, hammerhead	W-37 kg (80 lb)	210.01 kg 463 lb	Key Largo, Florida, USA	April 30, 1993	Heidi Mason
Shark, hammerhead	W-60 kg (130 lb)	184.16 kg 406 lb	Lottin Point, New Zealand	Feb. 26, 1974	Mrs. H. M. Wood
Shark, mako	M-01 kg (2 lb)	37.00 kg 81 lb 9oz	Cape San Lucas, Baja Calif., Mexico	May 5, 1992	George E. Hogan, Jr.
Shark, mako	M-02 kg (4 lb)	75.00 kq 165 lb 5 oz	Port Hacking, N.S.W., Australia	Sept. 30, 1989	Edward Paul Caughlan
Shark, mako	M-03 kg (6 lb)	155.13 kg 342 lb	Port Hacking, N.S.W., Australia	Sept. 22, 1974	Norman Richard Smith
Shark, mako	M-04 kg (8 lb)	72.50 kg 159 lb 13 oz	New Plymouth, New Zealand	March 28, 1997	Philip George Knight Collins
Shark, mako	M-06 kg (12 lb)	296.00 kg 652 lb 8 oz	Port Hacking, N.S.W., Australia	July 10, 1997	Jason Andrew Caughlan
Shark, mako	M-08 kg (16 lb)	317.50 kg 699 lb 15 oz	Botany Bay, Sydney, Australia	Oct. 30, 1993	Mark Johnston
Shark, mako	M-10 kg (20 lb)	329.00 kg 725 lb 5 oz	Swansea, N.S.W., Australia	Nov. 25, 1979	Neil Williamson
Shark, mako	M-15 kg (30 lb)	443.50 kg 977 lb 11 oz	Botany Bay, Sydney, Australia	Nov. 4, 1995	Andrew Nasr
Shark, mako	M-24 kg (50 lb)	489.88 kg 1080 lb	Montauk, Long Island, New York, USA	Aug. 26, 1979	James L. Melanson
Shark, mako	M-60 kg (130 lb)	505.76 kg 1115 lb	Black River, Mauritius	Nov. 16, 1988	Patrick Guillanton

SPECIES	LINE CLASS	WEIGHT	PLACE	DATE	ANGLER
Shark, mako	M-37 kg (80 lb)	463.80 kg 1022 lb 7 oz	Hawke's Bay, Napier, New Zealand	Feb. 17, 1990	Martin Shanaghan
Shark, mako	Tippet 01 kg (2 lb)	Vacant			
Shark, mako	Tippet 02 kg (4 lb)	12.45 kg 27 lb 8 oz	Bellambi, Australia	Sept. 16, 1995	Gregory Phillip Clarke
Shark, mako	Tippet 03 kg (6 lb)	17.00 kg 7 lb 11 oz	Tekaha, Bay of Plenty, New Zealand	Jan. 1, 1997	Andrew A. Macgrath
Shark, mako	Tippet 04 kg (8 lb)	18.60 kg 41 lb	Hawke's Bay, New Zealand	Jan. 25, 1995	Carl Angus
Shark, mako	Tippet 06 kg (12 lb)	29.80 kg 65 lb 11 oz	Hawke's Bay, New Zealand	March 11, 1990	Sam Mossman
Shark, mako	Tippet 08 kg (16 lb)	32.88 kg 72 lb 8 oz	Anacapa Island, California, USA	July 21, 1991	Steve Abel
Shark, mako	Tippet 10 kg (20 lb)	31.00 kg 68 lb 5 oz	Whakatane, New Zealand	Feb. 23, 1993	Keith Alding
Shark, mako	W-01 kg (2 lb)	19.00 kg 41 lb 14 oz	Tutukaka, New Zealand	March 26, 1995	Kelly Pou
Shark, mako	W-02 kg (4 lb)	7.80 kg 17 lb 3 oz	Tutukaka, New Zealand	March 8, 1995	Kelly Pou
Shark, mako	W-03 kg (6 lb)	52.16 kg 115 lb	Botany Bay, N.S.W., Australia	Oct. 27, 1974	Mrs. Dulcie Chee
Shark, mako	W-04 kg (8 lb)	48.90 kg 107 lb 12 oz	Blackhead, Hawke's Bay, New Zealand	Feb. 18, 1997	Tobi Jayne Henderson
Shark, mako	W-06 kg (12 lb)	131.20 kg 289 lb 3 oz	Port Hacking, N.S.W., Australia	Sept. 30, 1995	Kylie Daly
Shark, mako	W-08 kg (16 lb)	150.50 kg 331 lb 12 oz	Sydney, Australia	May 4, 1986	Connie Rolley
Shark, mako	W-10 kg (20 lb)	181.00 kg 399 lb	Port Stephens, N.S.W., Australia	March 3, 1990	Cheryl Adams
Shark, mako	W-15 kg (30 lb)	288.00 kg 634 lb 14 oz	Port Stephens, N.S.W., Australia	Feb. 29, 1992	Cheryl Adams
Shark, mako	W-24 kg (50 lb)	316.20 kg 697 lb 1oz	Tutukaka, New Zealand	Feb. 2, 1986	Joy Clements
Shark, mako	W-24 kg (50 lb) Tie	317.00 kg 698 lb 13 oz	Redhead, N.S.W., Australia	Oct. 11, 1987	Lesley Martin
Shark, mako	W-37 kg (80 lb)	399.16 kg 880 lb	Bimini, Bahamas	Aug. 3, 1964	Florence Lotierzo
Shark, mako	W-60 kg (130 lb)	413.56 kg 911 lb 12 oz	Palm Beach, Florida, USA	April 9, 1962	Audrey Cohen
Shark, porbeagle	M-01 kg (2 lb)	Vacant			
Shark, porbeagle	M-02 kg (4 lb)	48.75 kg 107 lb 7 oz	Gosport, England	Aug. 8, 1984	Denis J. Froud
Shark, porbeagle	M-03 kg (6 lb)	37.19 kg 82 lb	Padstow, Cornwall, England	July 31, 1980	Ian Bunney
Shark, porbeagle	M-04 kg (8 lb)	98.43 kg 217 lb	Padstow, Cornwall, England	July 11, 1984	Ian Bunney
Shark, porbeagle	M-06 kg (12 lb)	111.58 kg 246 lb	Padstow, Cornwall, England	Sept. 7, 1983	Ian Bunney
Shark, porbeagle	M-08kg (16 lb)	173.27 kg 382 lb	Hartland Pt., Devon, Cornwall, England	July 28, 1982	Brian Stewart Taylor
Shark, porbeagle	M-10 kg (20 lb)	152.40 kg 336 lb	Padstow, Cornwall, England	June 20, 1982	Ian Bunney

SPECIES	LINE CLASS	WEIGHT	PLACE	DATE	ANGLER
Shark, porbeagle	M-15 kg (30 lb)	188.69 kg 416 lb	Padstow, Cornwall, England	May 26, 1986	Ian Bunney
Shark, porbeagle	M-24 kg (50 lb)	188.00 kg 414 lb 7 oz	Pentland Firth, Scotland	March 9, 1992	Robert Richardson
Shark, porbeagle	M-37 kg (80 lb)	230.00 kg 507 lb	Pentland Firth, Scotland	March 9, 1993	Christopher Bennett
Shark, porbeagle	M-60 kg (130 lb)	210.92 kg 465 lb	Padstow, Cornwall, England	July 23, 1976	Jorge Potier
Shark, porbeagle	Tippet 01 kg (2 lb)	Vacant			
Shark, porbeagle	Tippet 02 kg (4 lb)	Vacant			
Shark, porbeagle	Tippet 03 kg (6 lb)	Vacant			
Shark, porbeagle	Tippet 04 kg (8 lb)	Vacant			
Shark, porbeagle	Tippet 06 kg (12 lb)	Vacant			
Shark, porbeagle	Tippet 08 kg (16 lb)	Vacant			
Shark, porbeagle	Tippet 10 kg (20 lb)	Vacant			
Shark, porbeagle	W-01 kg (2 lb)	Vacant			
Shark, porbeagle	W-02 kg (4 lb)	Vacant			
Shark, porbeagle	W-03 kg (6 lb)	Vacant			
Shark, porbeagle	W-04 kg (8 lb)	Vacant			
Shark, porbeagle	W-06kg (12 lb)	39.68 kg 87 lb 8 oz	Padstow, Cornwall, England	June 16, 1984	Pamela Jane Bunney
Shark, porbeagle	W-08 kg (16 lb)	Vacant			
Shark, porbeagle	W-10 kg (20 lb)	Vacant			
Shark, porbeagle	W-15 kg (30 lb)	100.92 kg 222 lb 8 oz	Isle of Wight, England	Aug. 14, 1969	Mrs. Paula Everington
Shark, porbeagle	W-24kg (50 lb)	108.18 kg 238 lb 8 oz	Montauk, Long Island, New York, USA	May 17, 1966	Bea Harry
Shark, porbeagle	W-37 kg (80 lb)	107.04 kg 236 lb	Padstow, Cornwall, England	Aug. 1, 1981	Mrs. Marie Potier
Shark, porbeagle	W-60 kg (130 lb)	167.37 kg 369 lb	Looe, Cornwall, England	July 20, 1970	Mrs. Patricia Winifred Smith
Shark, thresher	M-01 kg (2 lb)	Vacant			
Shark, thresher	M-02 kg (4 lb)	16.32 kg 36 lb	Santa Monica Bay, California, USA	April 12, 1989	Robert I. Levy
Shark, thresher	M-03 kg (6 lb)	41.50 kg 91 lb 8 oz	Santa Monica Bay, California, USA	May 14, 1977	James D. Olson
Shark, thresher	M-04 kg (8 lb)	26.85 kg 59 lb 3 oz	False Bay, South Africa	Feb. 22, 1997	Mike Casserley
Shark, thresher	M-06kg (12 lb)	72.34 kg 159 lb 8 oz	Santa Monica Bay, California, USA	Oct. 11, 1987	Donald McPherson, Jr.
Shark, thresher	M-08 kg (16 lb)	104.32 kg 230 lb	Newport Beach, California, USA	May 5, 1994	Dave Elm
Shark, thresher	M-10 kg (20 lb)	119.00 kg 262 lb 5 oz	Mdumbi, Transkei	Dec. 16, 1991	Gregory Tew
Shark, thresher	M-15 kg (30 lb)	220.00 kg 485 lb	Albarella, Adriatic Sea	Aug. 14, 1996	Vittadello Massimo
Shark, thresher	M-24 kg (50 lb)	348.00 kg 767 lb 3 oz	Bay of Islands, New Zealand	Feb. 26, 1983	D.L. Hannah
Shark, thresher	M-37 kg (80 lb)	335.20 kg 739 lb	Tutukaka, New Zealand	Feb. 17, 1975	Brian Galvin

SPECIES	LINE CLASS	WEIGHT	PLACE	DATE	ANGLER
Shark, thresher	M-60 kg (130 lb)	306.62 kg 676 lb	Mayor Island, New Zealand	Feb. 23, 1978	Robert Charles Faulkner
Shark, thresher	Tippet 01 kg (2 lb)	Vacant			
Shark, thresher	Tippet 02 kg (4 lb)	Vacant			
Shark, thresher	Tippet 03 kg (6 lb)	Vacant			
Shark, thresher	Tippet 04 kg (8 lb)	Vacant			
Shark, thresher	Tippet 06 kg (12 lb)	Vacant			
Shark, thresher	Tippet 08 kg (16 lb)	Vacant			
Shark, thresher	Tippet 10 kg (20 lb)	Vacant			
Shark, thresher	W-01 kg (2 lb)	Vacant			
Shark, thresher	W-02 kg (4 lb)	Vacant			
Shark, thresher	W-03 kg (6 lb)	15.42 kg 34 lb	Santa Monica Bay, California, USA	June 8, 1977	Ruth Kameon
Shark, thresher	W-04 kg (8 lb)	Vacant			
Shark, thresher	W-06 kg (12 lb)	62.59 kg 138 lb	Santa Monica Bay, California, USA	May 15, 1977	Sylvia A. Naibert
Shark, thresher	W-08 kg (16 lb)	63.95 kg 141 lb	Santa Monica Bay, California, USA	Oct. 20, 1987	Lisa Zipser Derr
Shark, thresher	W-10 kg (20 lb)	79.15 kg 174 lb 8 oz	Santa Monica Bay, California, USA	May 28, 1977	Sylvia A. Naibert
Shark, thresher	W-15 kg (30 lb)	136.90 kg 302 lb	Kona Coast, Hawaii, USA	May 28, 1994	Jocelyn J. Everette
Shark, thresher	W-24 kg (50 lb)	203.21 kg 448 lb	Montauk, Long Island, New York, USA	July 8, 1984	Lynnette M. Pintauro
Shark, thresher	W-37 kg (80 lb)	363.80 kg 802 lb	Tutukaka, New Zealand	Feb. 8, 1981	Dianne North
Shark, thresher	W-60 kg (130 lb)	330.67 kg 729 lb	Mayor Island, New Zealand	June 3, 1959	Mrs. V. Brown
Shark, tiger	M-01 kg (2 lb)	1.64 kg 3 lb 10 oz	Boca Raton, Florida, USA	June 19, 1991	Jim Ingalls
Shark, tiger	M-02 kg (4 lb)	72.12 kg 159 lb	Key West, Florida, USA	March 17, 1991	Herbert G. Ratner, Jr.
Shark, tiger	M-03 kg (6 lb)	115.89 kg 255 lb 8 oz	Key West, Florida, USA	Feb. 20, 1990	Herbert G. Ratner, Jr.
Shark, tiger	M-04 kg (8 lb)	Vacant			
Shark, tiger	M-06 kg (12 lb)	164.42 kg 362 lb 8 oz	Islamorada, Florida, USA	April 1, 1983	Andrew A. MacGrath
Shark, tiger	M-08 kg (16 lb)	344.50 kg 759 lb 7 oz	East Swansea, N.S.W., Australia	May 22, 1993	Peter David Noakes
Shark, tiger	M-10 kg (20 lb)	411.50 kg 907 lb 3 oz	Swansea, N.S.W., Australia	Nov. 22, 1981	Gary Hoff
Shark, tiger	M-10 kg (20 lb) Tie	412.00 kg 908 lb 4 oz	Broughton Island, Australia	June 7, 1986	Mick Volkens
Shark, tiger	M-15 kg (30 lb)	619.00 kg 1364 lb 10 oz	Swansea, N.S.W., Australia	Sept. 29, 1990	Glen Kirkwood
Shark, tiger	M-24 kg (50 lb)	579.50 kg 1277 lb 9 oz	Swansea, N.S.W., Australia	June 1, 1996	Trent Visscher
Shark, tiger	M-37 kg (80 lb)	591.94 kg 1305 lb	Sydney, N.S.W., Australia	May 17, 1959	Samuel Jamieson
Shark, tiger	M-60 kg (130 lb)	807.40 kg 1780 lb	Cherry Grove, South Carolina, USA	June 14, 1964	Walter Maxwell

SPECIES	LINE CLASS	WEIGHT	PLACE	DATE	ANGLER
Shark, tiger	Tippet 01 kg (2 lb)	Vacant			
Shark, tiger	Tippet 02 kg (4 lb)	Vacant			
Shark, tiger	Tippet 03 kg (6 lb)	Vacant			
Shark, tiger	Tippet 04 kg (8 lb)	46.26 kg 102 lb	Key West, Florida, USA	March 15, 1996	Rick Gunion
Shark, tiger	Tippet 06 kg (12 lb)	33.56 kg 74 lb	Key West, Florida, USA	Feb. 24, 1996	Rick Gunion
Shark, tiger	Tippet 08 kg (16 lb)	28.00 kg 61 lb 12 oz	Key West, Florida, USA	Feb. 23, 1992	Rick Gunion
Shark, tiger	Tippet 10 kg (20 lb)	99.79 kg 220 lb	Key West, Florida, USA	Jan. 23, 1995	Gary Spence
Shark, tiger	W-01 kg (2 lb)	Vacant			
Shark, tiger	W-02 kg (4 lb)	7.70 kg 16 lb 15 oz	Shute Harbour, Qld., Australia	April 11, 1987	Tracy Hallam
Shark, tiger	W-03 kg (6 lb)	Vacant			
Shark, tiger	W-04 kg (8 lb)	49.24 kg 108 lb 9 oz	Key West, Florida, USA	Feb. 13, 1991	Dixie Lee Burns
Shark, tiger	W-06 kg (12 lb)	97.97 kg 216 lb	Key West, Florida, USA	Feb. 5, 1991	Barbara A. Martin
Shark, tiger	W-08 kg (16 lb)	163.29 kg 360 lb	Gulf of Mexico, Boca Grande, Florida, USA	May 30, 1988	Connie L. Cora
Shark, tiger	W-10 kg (20 lb)	194.00 kg 427 lb 11 oz	Broken Bay, Sydney, Australia	March 15, 1997	Sharon Hegner
Shark, tiger	W-15 kg (30 lb)	548.00 kg 1208 lb I oz	N.S.W., Australia	April 16, 1989	Leanne Grieves
Shark, tiger	W-24 kg (50 lb)	497.00 kg 1095 lb 10 oz	Swansea, N.S.W., Australia	March 17, 1985	Bronwyn L. Norris
Shark, tiger	W-37 kg (80 lb)	532.06 kg 1173 lb	Cronulla, N.S.W., Australia	March 24, 1963	June Irene Turnbull
Shark, tiger	W-60 kg (130 lb)	596.02 kg 1314 lb	Cape Moreton, Qld., Australia	July 27, 1953	Mrs. Robert Dyer
Shark, white	M-01 kg (2 lb)	Vacant			
Shark, white	M-03 kg (6 lb)	Vacant			
Shark, white	M-04 kg (8 lb)	Vacant			
Shark, white	M-02 kg (4 lb)	Vacant			
Shark, white	M-06 kg (12 lb)	81.00 kg 178 lb 9oz	Dudley, N.S.W., Australia	May 5, 1991	David Ashman
Shark, white	M-08 kg (16 lb)	95.50 kg 210 lb 8 oz	Swansea, N.S.W., Australia	Oct. 29, 1983	Gary Kenneth Hoff
Shark, white	M-10 kg (20 lb)	484.44 kg 1068 lb	Cape Moreton, Qld., Australia	June 18, 1957	Robert Dyer
Shark, white	M-15 kg (30 lb)	477.63 kg 1053 lb	Cape Moreton, Qld., Australia	June 13, 1957	Robert Dyer
Shark, white	M-24 kg (50 lb)	850.94 kg 1876 lb	Cape Moreton, Qld., Australia	Aug. 6, 1955	Robert Dyer
Shark, white	M-37 kg (80 lb)	1063.23 kg 2344 lb	Streaky Bay, South Australia	Nov. 6, 1960	Alfred Dean
Shark, white	M-60 kg (130 lb)	1208.38 kg 2664 lb	Ceduna, South Australia	April 21, 1959	Alfred Dean
Shark, white	Tippet 01 kg (2 lb)	Vacant			
Shark, white	Tippet 02 kg (4 lb)	Vacant			

SPECIES	LINE CLASS	WEIGHT	PLACE	DATE	ANGLER
Shark, white	Tippet 03 kg (6 lb)	Vacant			
Shark, white	Tippet 04 kg (8 lb)	Vacant			
Shark, white	Tippet 06 kg (12 lb)	Vacant			
Shark, white	Tippet 08 kg (16 lb)	Vacant			
Shark, white	Tippet 10 kg (20 lb)	Vacant			
Shark, white	W-01 kg (2 lb)	Vacant			
Shark, white	W-02 kg (4 lb)	Vacant			
Shark, white	W-03 kg (6 lb)	Vacant			
Shark, white	W-04 kg (8 lb)	Vacant			
Shark, white	W-06 kg (12 lb)	Vacant			
Shark, white	W-08 kg (16 lb)	Vacant			
Shark, white	W-10 kg (20 lb)	167.37 kg 369 lb	Cape Moreton, Qld., Australia	July 6, 1957	Mrs. Robert Dyer
Shark, white	W-15 kg (30 lb)	364.23 kg 803 lb	Cape Moreton, Qld., Australia	July 5, 1957	Mrs. Robert Dyer
Shark, white	W-24 kg (50 lb)	363.33 kg 801 lb	Cape Moreton, Qld., Australia	June 11, 1957	Mrs. Robert Dyer
Shark, white	W-37 kg (80 lb)	413.68 kg 912 lb	Cape Moreton, Qld., Australia	Aug. 29, 1954	Mrs. Robert Dyer
Shark, white	W-60 kg (130 lb)	528.00 kg 1164 lb	The Pages, South Australia	March 11, 1994	Janet Forster
Shark, Atlantic sharpnose	All-tackle	7.25 kg 16 lb	Port Mansfield, Texas, USA	Oct. 12, 1994	R. Bruce Shields
Shark, Caribbean reef	All-tackle	69.85 kg 154 lb	Mollasses Reef, Florida, USA	Dec. 29, 1996	Rene G. De Dios
Shark, Greenland	All-tackle	775.00 kg 1708 lb 9oz	Trondheimsfjord, Norway	Oct. 18, 1987	Terje Nordtvedt
Shark, bigeye thresher	All-tackle	363.80 kg 802 lb	Tutukaka, New Zealand	Feb. 8, 1981	Dianne North
Shark, bignose	All-tackle	167.80 kg 369 lb 14 oz	Markham River, LAE, Papua New Guinea	Oct. 23, 1993	Lester J. Rohrlach
Shark, black-mouth cat	All-tackle	1.37 kg 3 lb	Mausundvar, Trondheim, Norway	Sept. 17, 1994	Per Arne Hagen
Shark, blacknose	All-tackle	18.86 kg 41 lb 9 oz	Little River, South Carolina, USA	July 30, 1992	Jon-Paul Hoffman
Shark, blacktail	All-tackle	33.70 kg 74 lb 4 oz	Kosi Bay, Zululand, Rep. of South Africa	May 25, 1987	Trevor Ashington
Shark, blacktip	All-tackle	122.75 kg 270 lb 9 oz	Malindi Bay, Kenya	Sept. 21, 1984	Jurgen Oeder
Shark, blacktip reef	All-tackle	13.55 kg 29 lb 13 oz	Coco Island, Indian Ocean	Oct. 22, 1995	Dr. Joachim Kleidon
Shark, blue	All-tackle	205.93 kg 454 lb	Martha's Vineyard, Massachusetts, USA	July 19, 1996	Pete Bergin
Shark, bonnethead	All-tackle	10.76 kg 23 lb 11 oz	Cumberland Sound, Georgia, USA	Aug. 5, 1994	Chad Wood
Shark, bull	All-tackle	222.26 kg 490 lb	Dauphin Island, Alabama, USA	Aug. 30, 1986	Phillip Wilson
Shark, dusky	All-tackle	346.54 kg 764 lb	Longboat Key, Florida, USA	May 28, 1982	Warren Girle
Shark, great hammerhead	All-tackle	449.50 kg 991 lb	Sarasota, Florida, USA	May 30, 1982	Allen Ogle

SPECIES	LINE CLASS	WEIGHT	PLACE	DATE	ANGLER
Shark, gulper	All-tackle	7.34 kg 16 lb 3oz	Bimini, Bahamas	July 15, 1997	Doug Olander
Shark, gummy	All-tackle	30.80 kg 67 lb 14 oz	Mcloughins Beach, Victoria, Australia	Nov. 15, 1992	Neale Blunden
Shark, lemon	All-tackle	183.70 kg 405 lb	Buxton, North Carolina, USA	Nov. 23, 1988	Colleen D. Harlow
Shark, leopard	All-tackle	18.42 kg 40 lb 10 oz	Oceanside, California, USA	May 13, 1994	Fred Oakley
Shark, narrowtooth	All-tackle	242.00 kg 533 lb 8 oz	Cape Karikari, New Zealand	Jan. 9, 1993	Gaye Harrison- Armstrong
Shark, night	All-tackle	76.65 kg 169 lb	Bimini, Bahamas	July 13, 1997	Capt. Ron Schatman
Shark, nurse	All-tackle	95.25 kg 210 lb	Bahia Honda Bridge, Florida Keys, USA	April 6, 1997	Rene De Dios
Shark, oceanic whitetip	All-tackle	66.45 kg 146 lb 8 oz	Kona, Hawaii, USA	Nov. 11, 1992	Pamela S. Basco
Shark, porbeagle	All-tackle	230.00 kg 507 lb	Pentland Firth, Caithness, Scotland	March 9, 1993	Christopher Bennet
Shark, reef	All-tackle	34.47 kg 76 lb	Walker's Cay, Bahamas	July 15, 1994	Gary Spence
Shark, sand tiger	All-tackle	158.81 kg 350 lb 2 oz	Charleston Jetty, Charleston, South Carolina, USA	April 29, 1993	Mark Thawley
Shark, sandbar	All-tackle	117.93 kg 260 lb	Gambia Coast, Gambia	Jan. 2, 1989	Paul Delsignore
Shark, scalloped hammerhead	All-tackle	152.40 kg 335 lb 15 oz	Latham Island, Tanzania	Dec. 3, 1995	Capt. Jack Reece, Q.P.M.
Shark, sevengill	All-tackle	32.80 kg 72 lb 4 oz	Weymouth Channel, Manukou Harbour, New Zealand	Oct. 23, 1995	Shane Sowerby
Shark, shortfin mako	All-tackle	505.76 kg 1115 lb	Black River, Mauritius	Nov. 16, 1988	Patrick Guillanton
Shark, silky	All-tackle	346.00 kg 762 lb 12 oz	Port Stephen's, N.S.W., Australia	Feb. 26, 1994	Bryce Robert Henderson
Shark, silvertip	All-tackle	150.00 kg 330 lb 11 oz	Watamu, Kenya	Oct. 22, 1991	Christopher Wood
Shark, sixgilled	All-tackle	485.00 kg 1069 lb 3 oz	Faial, Azores	Oct. 18, 1990	Capt. Jack Reece
Shark, smallfin gulper	All-tackle	2.40 kg 5 lb 4 oz	Lae, Huon Gulf, Papua New Guinea	Feb. 13, 1993	Justin Mallett
Shark, smooth hammerhead	All-tackle	148.10 kg 326 lb 7 oz	Lachlan Ridge, Hawke Bay, New Zealand	Feb. 24, 1994	Tony Hill
Shark, spinner	All-tackle	86.18 kg 190 lb	Flagler Beach, Florida, USA	April 3, 1986	Mrs. Gladys Prior
Shark, thresher	All-tackle	363.80 kg 802 lb	Tutukaka, New Zealand	Feb. 8, 1981	Dianne North
Shark, tiger	All-tackle	807.40 kg 1780 lb	Cherry Grove, South Carolina, USA	June 14, 1964	Walter Maxwell
Shark, white	All-tackle	1208.38 kg 2664 lb	Ceduna, South Australia	April 21, 1959	Alfred Dean
Shark, whitetip reef	All-tackle	18.25 kg 40 lb 4 oz	Isla Coiba, Panama	Aug. 8, 1979	Jack Kamerman

SPECIES	LINE CLASS	WEIGHT	PLACE	DATE	ANGLER
Tope	M-01 kg (2 lb)	22.30 kg 49 lb 2 oz	Parengarenga Harbor, New Zealand	Jan. 14, 1990	Mark Feldman
Tope	M-02 kg (4 lb)	25.10 kg 55 lb 5 oz	Parengarenga Harbor, New Zealand	Jan. 14, 1990	Mark Feldman
Tope	M-03 kg (6 lb)	Vacant			
Tope	M-04 kg (8 lb)	26.70 kg 58 lb 13 oz	Parengarenga Harbor, New Zealand	Dec. 16, 1986	Mark L. Feldman
Tope	M-06 kg (12 lb)	29.00 kg 63 lb 14 oz	Parengarenga Harbor, New Zealand	Dec. 16, 1986	Mark L. Feldman
Tope	M-08 kg (16 lb)	32.50 kg 71 lb 10 oz	Parengarenga Harbor, New Zealand	Jan. 4, 1991	Toby Martens
Tope	M-10 kg (20 lb)	26.36 kg 58 lb 2 oz	Baggy Pt., North Devon, England	Oct. 22, 1982	Raymond John White
Tope	M-15 kg (30 lb)	44.67 kg 98 lb 8 oz	Santa Monica, Califomia, USA	Oct. 20, 1994	Fred Oakley
Tope	M-24 kg (50 lb)	32.50 kg 71 lb 10 oz	Knysna, Rep. of South Africa	July 10, 1982	William F. De Wet
Tope	M-37 kg (80 lb)	30.25 kg 66 lb 11 oz	Parengarenga Harbor, New Zealand	Jan. 1, 1987	Wes Martens
Tope	Tippet 01 kg (2 lb)	Vacant			
Tope	Tippet 02 kg (4 lb)	Vacant			
Tope	Tippet 03 kg (6 lb)	Vacant			
Tope	Tippet 04 kg (8 lb)	Vacant			
Tope	Tippet 06 kg (12 lb)	Vacant			
Tope	Tippet 08 kg (16 lb)	Vacant			
Tope	Tippet 10 kg (20 lb)	Vacant			
Tope	W-01 kg (2 lb)	16.50 kg 36 lb 6 oz	Parengarenga Harbor, New Zealand	Jan. 29, 1987	Elizabeth M. Feldman
Tope	W-02 kg (4 lb)	17.50 kg 38 lb 9 oz	Parengarenga Harbor, New Zealand	Jan. 30, 1987	Melanie Feldman
Tope	W-03 kg (6 lb)	Vacant			
Tope	W-06 kg (12 lb)	31.00 kg 68 lb 5 oz	Parengarenga Harbor, New Zealand	Dec. 20, 1987	Heather M. Morton
Tope	W-04 kg (8 lb)	24.40 kg 53 lb 12 oz	Parengarenga Harbor, New Zealand	Dec. 3, 1987	Laurel Martens
Tope	W-08 kg (16 lb)	28.40 kg 62 lb 9 oz	Parengarenga Harbor, New Zealand	Nov. 29, 1987	Jennifer Sutton
Tope	W-10 kg (20 lb)	27.50kg 60 lb 10 oz	Parengarenga Harbor, New Zealand	Dec. 12, 1987	Jenepher Cummins
Tope	W-15 kg (30 lb)	24.00 kg 52 lb 14 oz	Parengarenga Harbor, New Zealand	Dec. 3, 1985	Melanie Feldman
Tope	W-24 kg (50 lb)	33.00 kg 72 lb 12 oz	Parengarenga Harbor, New Zealand	Dec. 19, 1986	Melanie B. Feldman
Tope	W-37 kg (80 lb)	30.50 kg 67 lb 3 oz	Parengarenga Harbor, New Zealand	Nov. 28, 1987	Jessica Lighiband
Tope	All-tackle	44.67 kg 98 lb 8 oz	Santa Monica, California, USA	Oct. 20, 1994	Fred Oakley

BIBLIOGRAPHY

This bibliography is drawn from several sources, including the author's bibliography from *Shadows in the Sea*, and from publications recommended by the Smithsonian Institution. (The bibliography of the earlier edition of *Shadows in the Sea* includes older works that may be of interest.)

Allen, Thomas B. *Shadows in the Sea.* New York: Lyons & Burford, 1996. New edition of book originally published with same title by H. W. McCormick, T. Allen, and Capt. Wm. Young, a shark fisherman who provided observations of shark behavior. (See Young, W. E., and H. S. Mazet. *Shark! Shark!* New York: Gotham House, 1933.)

Baldridge, H. D. *Shark Attack.* New York: Berkley, 1974. (Baldridge has compiled a database from early case histories in The International Shark Attack File. This and other publications are available through The International Shark Attack File, American Elasmobranch Society, Florida Museum of Natural History, University of Florida, Gainesville, FL 32611, USA).

———. "Shark aggression against man: beginnings of an understanding." *California Fish and Game*, 74 (4):208–17 (1988).

———. "Shark repellent: not yet, maybe never." *Military Medicine*, 155 (8):358–61 (August 1990).

Bigelow, H. B., and W. C. Schroeder *Fishes of the Western Northern Atlantic, Memoir No. 1; Part One, Lancelets, Cyclostomes, Sharks; Part Two, Sawfishes, Guitarfishes, Skates, Rays and Chimaeroids.* Memoir of the Sears Foundation for Marine Research, New Haven, CT: Yale University Press, 1948.

———. *Sawfishes, Guitarfishes, Skates and Rays, Fishes of the Western North Atlantic,* Memoir of the Sears Foundation for Marine Research. New Haven, CT: Yale University Press, 1953.

————. *Guide to Commercial Shark Fishing in the Caribbean Area.* U.S. Dept. of Interior, Fish and Wildlife Service, Fishery Leaflet No. 135, 1945.

————, and S. Springer. "New and Little Known Sharks from the Atlantic and from the Gulf of Mexico." *Bull. Mus. Comp. Zool.* (Harvard Univ.), 109 (3):213–76 (July 1953).

Branstetter, S. (ed.). "Conservation biology of elasmobranchs." U.S. National Marine Fisheries Service, NOAA Technical Report NMFS 115 (1993).

Budker, P. *The Life of Sharks.* New York: Columbia University Press, 1971.

Bushnell, Dennis M., and Jerry N. Hefner. (eds.). *Viscous Drag Reduction in Boundary Layers.* NASA Langley Research Center, Vol. 123, Progress in Astronautics and Aeronautics.

Carroll, R. L. *Vertebrate Paleontology and Evolution.* New York: W.H. Freeman, 1988.

Castro, J. I. *The Sharks of North American Waters.* College Station, Texas: Texas A&M University Press, 1983.

Cech, Joseph J., Jr., and Peter B. Moyle. *Fishes: An Introduction to Ichthyology.* Englewood Cliffs, NJ: Prentice Hall, 1982.

Clark, Eugenie. "Into the lairs of sleeping sharks." *National Geographic,* 47, (4):570–84 (April 1975).

————. "Whale sharks." *National Geographic,* 182 (6):123–39 (December 1992).

————. "Sharks: Magnificent and Misunderstood. *National Geographic,* 160 (2):138–86 (1981).

————. *The Lady and the Sharks.* New York: Harper & Row, 1969.

Cliff, Geremy. "Shark Attack!" *Conserva,* November 1990: 10–13

————. "Keeping Sharks at Bay" and "Sharks: Are They a Threat?" *The Naturalist* 32 (3):4–17 (Nov. 1988).

Colbert, Edwin H. *Evolution of the Vertebrates.* New York: Wiley, 1955.

Compagno, L.J.V. *Sharks of the World.* Rome: FAO Species Catalogue. FAO Fisheries Synopsis No. 125, Vol. 4, Part 1 and Part 2. United Nations Development Programme, Food and Agriculture Organization of the United Nations, 1984.

————, D. A. Ebert, and M. J. Smale. *Guide to the Sharks and Rays of Southern Africa.* Cape Town: Struik Publishers, 1989.

Coppleson, V. M. *Shark Attack.* London: Angus & Robertson, 1959.

Davis, C. "The awesome basking shark." *Sea Frontiers,* 29 (2):78–85 (1983).

Dayton, L. "Save the sharks." *New Scientist,* 130 (1773):34–38, (1991).

Ellis, Richard. *The Book of Sharks.* New York: Grosset and Dunlap, 1967.

———— and J. McCosker. *Great White Shark.* New York: HarperCollins, in collaboration with Stanford University Press, 1991.

Fussman, C. "Hunting the hunter." *Time* 14 (10):22–28, 30 (1991).

Gilbert, P. W. (ed.). *Sharks and Survival*. Boston: D.C. Heath and Company, 1963.

———, L. P. Schultz, and S. Springer, "Shark Attacks During 1959." *Science*, 132 (3423):323–26 (1960).

———, R. F. Mathewson, and D.P. Rall (eds.). *Sharks, Skates, and Rays*. Baltimore: Johns Hopkins Press, 1967.

———, and C. Gilbert. "The baffling basking shark." *Animal Kingdom*, 89 (3):35–37 (1986).

Gruber, S. H. (ed.). *Discovering Sharks*. Highlands, New Jersey: American Littoral Society, 1991.

———. "Sharks of the shallows." *Natural History,* 97 (3):50–59 (March 1988).

———. "Why Do Sharks Attack Humans?" *Naval Research Review* No. 1, 1988: 2–13.

Hodgson, E. S., and R. F. Mathewson (eds.). *Sensory Biology of Sharks, Skates, and Rays*. Arlington, Virginia: Office of Naval Research Dept. of the Navy, 1978.

Hutchins, B. "Megamouth: gentle giant of the deep." *Australian Natural History*, 23 (12):910–17 (1992).

Ketchen, K. S. *The Spiny Dogfish* (Squalus acanthias) *in the Northeast Pacific and a History of its Utilization*. Canadian Special Publication of Fisheries and Aquatic Sciences 88, 1986.

Klimley, A. Peter. "The predatory behavior of the white shark." *American Scientist*, Vol. 82, March–April 1994, pp. 122–33.

Lavenberg, R. J. "Megamania. The continuing saga of megamouth sharks." *Terra*, 30 (1):30–39 (Fall 1991).

Lea, R. N., and D. J. Miller. "Shark Attacks off the California and Oregon Coasts: An Update, 1980-84." *Memoirs of the Southern California Academy of Science*, 9:136–49 (1985).

Lineaweaver, T. H. and R. H. Backus. *The Natural History of Sharks*. New York: Lyons & Burford, 1984.

MacLeish, W. H. (ed.). "Sharks." *Oceanus* 24 (4):1–79 (1981).

McCosker, J. E. "White Shark Attack Behavior: Observations of and Speculations about Predator and Prey Strategies." *Memoirs of the Southern California Academy of Science* 9:123–35 (1985).

Maxwell, G. *Harpoon Venture*. New York: Viking, 1952.

Michael, S. W. *Reef Sharks and Rays of the World: A Guide to their Identification, Behavior, and Ecology*. Monterey, California: Sea Challengers, 1993.

Miller, D. I. and R. S. Collier. "Shark attacks in California and Oregon 1926-1979." *California Fish and Game*, 67:76–104 (1980).

Morrissey, J. F. and H. Butcher. "The natural history of tiger sharks." *Sea Frontiers*, 34 (5):264–71 (Sept.-Oct. 1988).

Moss, S. A. *Sharks. An Introduction for the Amateur Naturalist*. Englewood Cliffs, New Jersey: Prentice-Hall, 1984.

Nammack, M. F., J. A. Musick, and J. A. Colvocoresses. "Life history of the spiny dogfish off the northeastern United States." *Transactions of the American Fisheries Society,* 114:367–76 (1985).

National Marine Fisheries Service, National Oceanic and Atmospheric Administration, U.S. Department of Commerce. *Fishery Management Plan for Sharks of the Atlantic Ocean*, 1993.

Nelson, D. R. and R. H. Johnson. "Behavior of the reef sharks of Rangiroa, French Polynesia." *National Geographic Society Research Reports*, 12:479–99 (1980).

———, J. N. McKibben, and G. G. Pittenger. "Agonistic attacks on divers and submersibles by gray reef sharks, *Carcharhinus amblyrhynchos:* anti-predatory or competitive?" *Bulletin of Marine Science*, 38, (1):68–88 (1986).

Northcutt, R. G. (ed.) "Recent advances in the biology of sharks." *American Zoologist*, 17 (2):287–515 (1977).

Otwell, W. S. et al. *Manual on Shark Fishing*. Sea Grant Report No. 73. Florida Sea Grant College, Gainesville, Florida, 1985.

Pepperell, J. G. (ed.). *Sharks: Biology and Fisheries*. CSIRO, Australia, 1992. Also issued as: *Australian Journal of Marine and Freshwater Research*, 43(1):1–343.

Perrine, D. "Reef shark attack! New clues raise new questions about why sharks bite people." *Sea Frontiers*, 35 (1):31–41 (Jan.–Feb. 1989).

Pratt, H. L. Jr., S. H. Gruber, and T. Taniuchi (eds.). "Elasmobranchs as Living Resources: Advances in the Biology, Ecology, Systematics, and the Status of the Fisheries." *Proceedings of the Second United States-Japan Workshop, East-West Center, Honolulu, Hawaii, 9–14 December 1987. NOAA Technical Report NMFS* 90. U.S. Department of Commerce. Seattle, Washington, 1990.

Randall, J. E. *Sharks of Arabia*. London: Immel Publishing, 1986.

Reader's Digest (eds.) *Sharks, Silent Hunters of the Deep*. Sydney, London, New York, Montreal, Capetown: Reader's Digest Services, 1986.

Romer, A. S. *Paleontology*, 3rd ed. Chicago: University of Chicago Press, 1966.

Russo, R. "Whitetip—the cave shark." *Sea Frontiers*, 30 (1):30–36 (Jan.-Feb. 1984).

Schwartz, F. J. *Sharks, Sawfish, Skates, and Rays of the Carolinas*. Moorehead City, North Carolina: Institute of Marine Sciences, 1984.

Sibley, G., J. A. Seigel, and C. C. Swift, (eds.) "Biology of the white shark." *Memoirs of the Southern California Academy of Sciences*, 9:1–150 (1985).

Springer, V. G., and J. P. Gold. *Sharks in Question*. Washington, DC.: Smithsonian Institution Press, 1989.

Steel, R. *Sharks of the World*. New York: Blandford Press, 1985.

Stevens, J. D. (ed.). *Sharks*. New York: Facts on File, 1987.

Taylor, L. *Sharks of Hawaii. Their Biology and Cultural Significance*. Honolulu: University of Hawaii Press, 1993.

Thorson, T. B., (ed.). *Investigations of the Ichthyofauna of Nicaraguan Lakes*. Lincoln, Neb.: School of Life Sciences, University of Nebraska, 1976.

Welton, B. J., and R. F. Farish. *The Collector's Guide to Fossil Sharks and Rays from the Cretaceous of Texas*. Lewisville, Texas: Before Time, 1993.

Whitley, G. P. *Australian Sharks : A Guide to Sharks in Australian Waters.* Melbourne: Lloyd O'Neil, 1983.

Woods Hole Oceanographic Institution. "Sharks." *Oceanus*, 24 (4) Winter 1981/82.

Wourms, J. and L. Demski, (eds.). "Reproduction and Development of Sharks, Skates, Rays and Ratfishes." *Environmental Biology of Fishes*, 38 (1–3) 1993.

Yano, Kazunari, John F. Morrissey, Nakaya Yabumoto, and Yoshitaka Kazyhiro (eds.). *Biology of the Megamouth Shark*. Tokyo: Tokai University Press, 1997.

Zahuranec, B. J. *Shark Repellents from the Sea—New Perspectives*. American Association for the Advancement of Science, Washington, DC, AAAS Selected Symposium 83, 1983.

INDEX